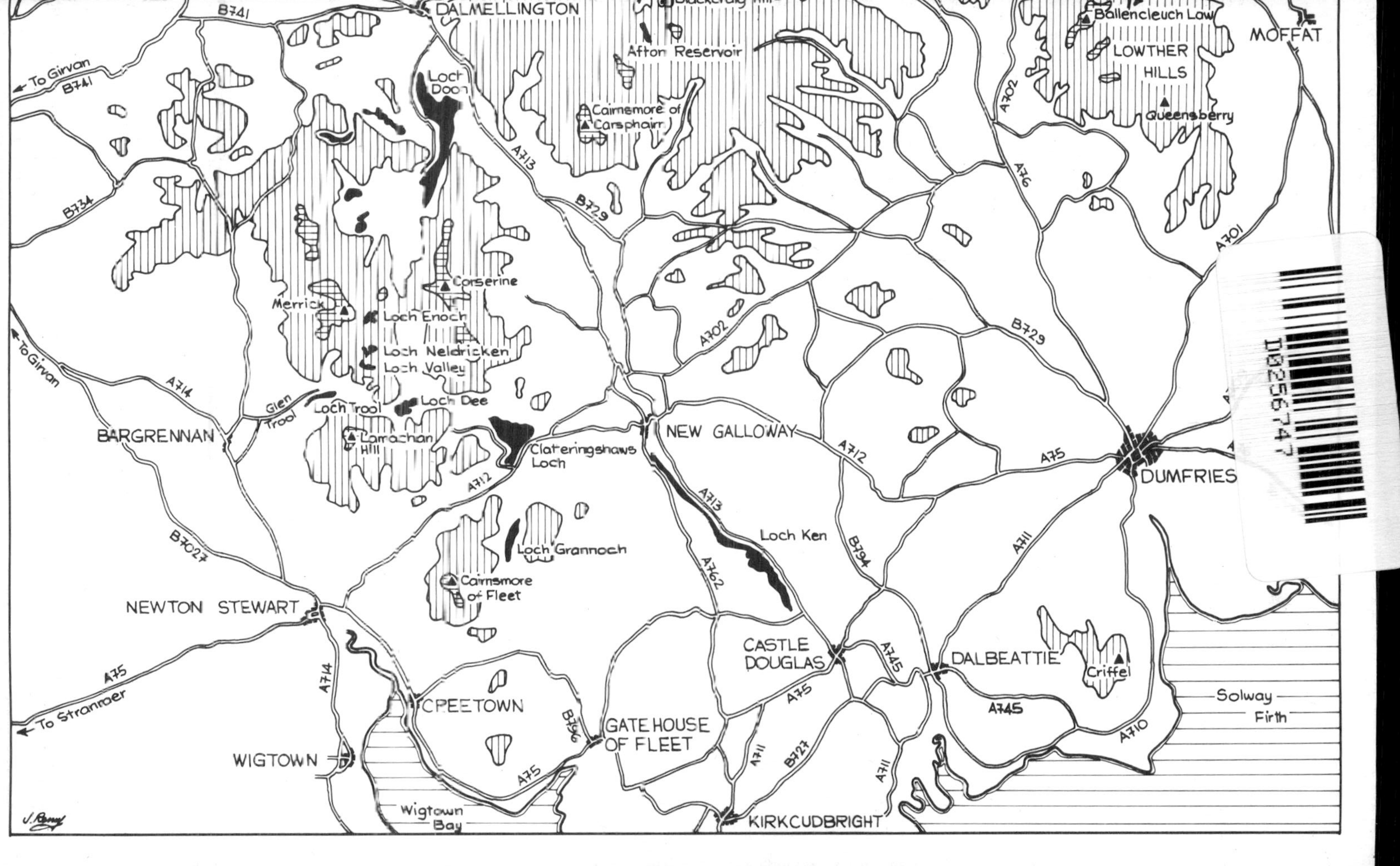
DALMELLINGTON
Afton Reservoir
Ballencleuch Law
LOWTHER
HILLS
Queensberry
MOFFAT
To Girvan
B741
Loch
Doon
Cairnsmore of
Carsphairn
A713
A702
A76
B734
B729
A701
Corserine
Merrick
Loch Enoch
Loch Neldricken
Loch Valley
Loch Dee
Loch Trool
Glen
Trool
A714
BARGRENNAN
Lamachan
Hill
Clatteringshaws
Loch
NEW GALLOWAY
A712
A75
DUMFRIES
Loch Ken
B794
A711
Loch Grannoch
B7027
Cairnsmore
of Fleet
A762
NEWTON STEWART
CASTLE
DOUGLAS
A745
DALBEATTIE
Criffel
Solway
Firth
To Stranraer
CREETOWN
B796
GATEHOUSE
OF FLEET
A710
WIGTOWN
B727
Wigtown
Bay
KIRKCUDBRIGHT
J. Renny

Scottish Mountaineering Club
District Guide Books

THE SOUTHERN UPLANDS

General Editor: MALCOLM SLESSER

DISTRICT GUIDE BOOKS

Southern Highlands
Central Highlands
Western Highlands
Northern Highlands
Islands of Scotland
Island of Skye
The Cairngorms
Southern Uplands

Munro's Tables

SCOTTISH MOUNTAINEERING CLUB

DISTRICT GUIDE BOOKS

THE Southern Uplands

by K. M. Andrew and A. A. Thrippleton

THE SCOTTISH MOUNTAINEERING TRUST

EDINBURGH

First published in Great Britain in 1972 by
THE SCOTTISH MOUNTAINEERING TRUST

First Edition 1972
Reprinted with Amendment 1976
2nd Reprint 1983

SBN 901516 57 0

Printed by
BROWN, SON & FERGUSON, LTD., (The Nautical Press) GLASGOW

Bound by
HUNTER & FOULIS LTD., EDINBURGH

CONTENTS

ILLUSTRATIONS

all photographs by the authors

FOREWORD

This is the first Scottish Mountaineering Club guide to the Southern Uplands of Scotland. The long neglect, when all other areas had been served with first and subsequent editions, may imply an area of little interest to hill-men. This is far from the case. Though the hills lack, for the most part, the more dramatic features of the Highlands, they offer all the other rewards, and in these crowded days one may find more peace and quiet in the Southern Uplands than in the over-burdened North.

Most Scottish climbers living in the midland belt penetrate southwards from time to time, if only for variety and because of the astonishing accessibility of the hills. Such explorations need not be confined to the ageing hillwalker or the salvationist, as a perusal of this guide will show. Those from further afield hurtling on their way north to fabled peaks may be tempted to stop-by.

The area is so large that it proved impossible to find any one person to undertake the whole task, and so it was shared. The two authors, Ken Andrew and Alan Thrippleton between them know it all, and a good deal of each other's territory forebye. The S.M.C. gladly records its gratitude to these two who gave up so much of their time over the last year to produce this guide. The result is a new look at the Southern Uplands, and the key to many a fascinating hill area.

Malcolm Slesser, *Glasgow*, January, 1972.

PREFACE

THIS guide has been prepared to help walkers and climbers find exercise, stimulation and enjoyment from the hills of the Southern Uplands. The novice will find helpful information to guide him over unfamiliar territory, while those who have been over the hills before may find background information, or a hill here and there, that they have missed. Rock climbers are also catered for in a section devoted to the crags.

The authors have been glad to share the work of preparation to make their tasks more manageable. With one of us living in Ayrshire and the other in Lanarkshire the arrangement was made to split the district into two sections – on either side of the A74 Glasgow to Gretna road. We have worked independently, apart from occasional consultations, on our allotted halves, and our sympathies are due to Dr Malcolm Slesser the guide-book editor, for the troubles we have caused him in welding the pieces together. Any mistakes or shortcomings in these pages are not his, but belong to Andrew for the western half, or Thrippleton for the eastern side.

The authors welcome any additional information from readers so that future guide-books may be more complete.

ACKNOWLEDGEMENTS

THE authors wish to thank all those who have helped them in the preparation of this guide.

Considerable assistance has been given by the office of the South Conservancy of the Forestry Commission in Dumfries, which has supplied large scale maps of many of the forests and other information. Individual foresters have also rendered help locally.

The Ordnance Survey's department in Ayr has been very patient with requests to consult their store of maps, and has given much valuable help. Their headquarters at Southampton has also dealt speedily and obligingly with requests for information.

Officials of various county councils have provided information on high-level Rights of Way. Ayr and Berwick C.C.s also sent several large scale maps.

We are grateful to Mr K. D. Collins for his article on the physical geography of the Southern Uplands, and to Mr C. E. Palmar, Curator of Natural History at the Kelvingrove Museum in Glasgow, who has been most helpful in providing information on the wild life in the area, and in checking the notes on it in the introduction.

Both Mr L. G. Martin and Dr K. S. Leong have rendered great assistance by the very generous loan of photographic equipment and Mr Martin's continued support during the whole project is most gratefully recorded. Mr Anderson of the Meteorological Office in Edinburgh offered very welcome assistance in the provision of Meteorological data.

The assistance of Messrs Oliver and Boyd for permission to reproduce a short extract from 'Arthur's Seat' is also acknowledged, while the details of rock climbing on Cheviot are reproduced from the National Park Guide No. 7 by permission of the Controller of Her Majesty's Stationery Office. Graham Tiso of Edinburgh has been kind enough to permit free reference to his guide *Creag Dubh and the Eastern Outcrops*, and similar and most generous assistance has been given by Gordon Davison of Newcastle on Fast Castle

Head. We are grateful to the present committee of the Edinburgh University Mountaineering Club for permission to reproduce an early guide to Arthur's Seat.

Many members of the Scottish Mountaineering Club have helped generously in many ways. That Kilmarnock triumvirate of Messrs Wallace, Stirling and Simpson are due special praise for information on rock climbing in the area, and for examining some of the crags that we unearthed.

The staffs of numerous libraries went on wild goose chases at our behest. Ayr Burgh Library chased up everything we asked for on Galloway, allowing us to quote the most useful in a selected bibliography of the many books on this large area.

Our thanks are also due to the dozens of companions who have explored these hills with us, provided transport, or posed for our photographs; and to the farmers, herds and locals who have shown us our routes, pointed out features of interest, or passed on items of information that we would otherwise have missed.

We are also indebted to those writers listed in the bibliographies who have provided material to build on in the preparation of this guide.

ACCURACY

While the authors, on behalf of the Scottish Mountaineering Club, have sought to maintain the highest accuracy in the preparation of this guide book, they cannot be held responsible for any consequences arising out of errors or misinterpretations. A note of any inaccuracies will be welcomed for inclusion in future editions.

PROPRIETARY AND SPORTING RIGHTS

The Scottish Mountaineering Trust desire to impress upon all those who avail themselves of the information given in their Guide Books that it is essential to consider and respect proprietary and sporting rights.

During the shooting season, from about the beginning of August to the middle of October, harm can be done in deer forests and on grouse moors by people tramping through them. During this period walkers and climbers should obtain the consent of the local stalkers and gamekeepers before walking over shooting lands. At times it is not easy to recognise what constitutes shooting lands. In cases of doubt it is always wise to ask some local resident.

It should also be noted that many of the roads in the upper glens were made and are maintained by the proprietors, who do not acknowledge a public right to motor over them, though they may follow the lines of established rights-of-way. It is, however, frequently possible to obtain permission to motor over some of them, but, as the situation is liable to change, local enquiries should be made in advance.

WARNING TO HILL WALKERS

The Guide Books issued by The Scottish Mountaineering Trust describe routes which range from difficult climbs to what are in fine weather mere walks. It cannot be stressed too strongly that an expedition, which in fine weather is simple, may cease to be so if the weather becomes bad or mist descends. The conditions especially arising in the Cairngorms are set out in the Introduction.

Equipment. All parties should carry simple first aid equipment, torch, whistle, watch, one-inch Ordnance Survey map, and compass, and know how to use them. Except for a few spots in Skye where the rocks are magnetic, the compass direction is certain to be correct even if it differs from one's sense of direction. Ice-axes should be carried if there is any chance of snow or ice, and a rope unless it is certain not to be required.

Clothing. At all times reserve clothing should be carried. Temperatures change rapidly, especially at high levels. Clothing should be warm; in winter a Balaclava helmet and thick woollen gloves should be carried. Well shod boots should always be worn.

Food. Each member of a party should carry his own food. Climbers will find from experience what kind of food suits their individual need. Normally jams and sugar are better than meat as more rapidly converted into energy. Alcohol should not be carried; it increases the loss of body heat and thus will worsen any case of exposure. Light meals at frequent intervals are better than heavy meals at long intervals. In winter it may be advisable to make an early stop for food in a sheltered spot.

INTRODUCTION

General

Scotland is often described as a country of three regions – the Highlands, Central Lowlands, and Southern Uplands – with the boundary between the last two being the fault line between Girvan and Dunbar. This is a simple and normally convenient description, but also somewhat inaccurate.

The Central Lowlands are by no means all low-lying, nor are the Southern Uplands all upland. Geography is rarely so simple, and Scotland is no exception. Considerable areas of upland country lie within the Central Lowlands zone while Wigtownshire in the Southern Uplands only just reaches 1000 ft. (300m.). Accordingly, the uplands described in this book include all the main areas of high ground on the mainland between the Clyde–Forth Canal and the English border. The restrictions imposed by the border have not been allowed to exclude Cheviot, lying as it does so close to the line, but the comments on that group have been largely confined to access from the Scottish side.

While these upland hills cannot compare in grandeur with many of the Highland hills, most of them can be reached more easily by the bulk of the population of Scottish climbers and walkers. Most Scots tend to go northwards to the hills, leaving the Uplands to a few stay-at-homes and invading Englishmen temporarily jaded with the Lake District. The Southern Uplands can prove valuable to Scots though, in acting as a contrast to the Highland hills. Missing out Glencoe for an occasional day spent in the Uplands could add breadth to many a climber's outlook, even if it only helps to show Glencoe in a new light on the next visit. But the Uplands have their character also; in their towns and villages, people and animals, farms and buildings, history and traditions, as well as in their hills, glens, and rivers.

Each area has its differences, just as Torridon differs from Skye, or Lochaber from the Cairngorms. The differences are generally more subtle, but they are there all the same. Those who decry the Southern

Uplands do not know them. They cannot be assessed in half a dozen visits.

Layout of guide

The boundaries of the regions described in this book are not always obvious, due to the problem of sorting out uplands from lowlands in such a complex part of the country. On the whole, definite hill ranges form the basis of individual chapters, e.g. the Pentlands, or the Lowthers. The latter group of hills is extensive and is split by the Dalveen Pass, so this division is maintained in the guide by splitting the chapter into two sections.

The region of Galloway cannot be split successfully into different chapters, so it is included in one large chapter having six sections, each with a short introduction, all prefaced by a larger general introduction.

In some cases the upland hills do not lie in definite ranges. In these circumstances they are grouped in chapters within boundaries formed by convenient roads. Some of the isolated hills have been grouped into one chapter for convenience, while all the rock climbing in the area has been grouped together in an appendix at the back of the book. A list of hills and heights, access, paths and accommodation is given in each chapter as affecting that group.

The index should be used in the first instance to find a hill, and the contents list to find a range or district. The index also acts as a link between the hills and the rock climbing areas listed in the appendix.

Maps, scales and tables

The best overall picture of the area is given in Bartholomew's 6 miles to the inch coloured sheet, No. 6. The most generally useful maps are the 1-inch O.S. now in the seventh series. The appropriate sheets are listed in each chapter. These maps are contoured at 50 ft. (15m.) intervals and embody colour identification for water, woods and roads. The national 1km. square grid appears on these sheets and forms the basis of the map reference system. In the Moffat–Peebles area it will be found that the hills to some degree overlap the borders of sheets 68 and 69 and it may be found advantageous to make one sheet by joining these two, using the flat paper edition and trimming the vertical edges to suit. An accurate join on the north-south line, with suitable adjustments to restore to a usable size, will be found a worthwhile modification.

The whole area is now covered by the Provisional Edition of the 1:25,000 O.S. maps (ap. 2½ inches to 1 mile). Each sheet covers an area of 10kms. by 10kms. with variations on the coastal sheets. Parts of Midlothian, Selkirk and Peebles are covered by the Second Series O.S. maps in the 1:25,000 scale, these sheets covering 20kms. by 10kms. There are, finally, the O.S. maps in the 6 inches to 1 mile scale (1:10,560).

A gradual move towards metrication is taking place in this country. The metric system is now being taught in our schools, and the next generation of climbers will be more used to measuring heights and distances in metres than in feet.

The Ordnance Survey are in an unenviable position as map-makers attempting to cater for both systems during the transition period. Their policy at present is to maintain the one-inch map in the present style until 1976 for those sheets covering Scotland. After these dates only an interim metric series will be available, to be replaced later by a new series. No decision has yet been taken on the scale of the new series pending the results of market research into map users' requirements, but whatever the outcome of this, the replacement of existing maps will take many years.

To minimise the problems, it is proposed, that the interim metric series will be on the same scale, format and sheet lines as the new series, but will be based on the detail of the existing one-inch maps.

Work has already started on replacing the 1:10,560 (6 inches to 1 mile) series with 1:10,000. The 1:25,000 (2½ inches to 1 mile) series is likely to be dropped.

To cover the transition period this guide shows heights, distances and areas in both imperial and metric units. Imperial units are shown first followed by metric units in brackets.

Bartholomew's half-inch maps are also handy as they often show regions complete which cannot be contained within one of the one-inch maps. They also are listed chapter by chapter. They are colour shaded for contours at 250 ft. (76m.) intervals and may be found to convey the height of the land more readily to some readers. The half-inch maps have the disadvantage that they cannot show nearly as accurately as the one-inch, the undulating nature of the hills.

Only the numbers of the one-inch maps required are shown in the appendix of rock climbing areas, as the half-inch scale is too small to show the crags, and National Grid references cannot be used with half-inch maps.

It will be found in some instances that there is a discrepancy between the height of a hill as shown in the guide and as quoted on the 1-inch O.S. map. The heights used are based on the 6-inch O.S. maps and the reader is referred to Section 3 of 'Munro's Tables' (i.e. Donald's Tables of the hills in the Scottish Lowlands 2000 ft. in height and above) for further details. Heights of hills below 2000 ft. are taken from the 1-inch O.S. map, Seventh Series 1963–65. There have been reprints at other dates of the seventh series of this map and in some cases heights have been altered slightly which is another reason for variations between map and guide.

Time and distance

The most useful formula for estimating the time required for a cross-country walk is that evolved by W. W. Naismith many years ago. The formula is well tried and allows for normal stops: For each 3 miles (4·8kms.) of linear distance allow 1 hour and to this total add 30 minutes for each 1000 ft. (305m.) of ascent.

Navigation in mist

On many of these hills, navigation is facilitated in mist by following fences or dykes. These often follow the ridges along county or parish boundaries. Many are mentioned in the guide and other information can be found in Donald's Tables, where also are listed details by which the summits and tops may be recognised. Hill-walkers should take care not to damage fences and dykes, as gaps will allow sheep to stray causing great inconvenience to shepherds.

Transport

Public transport facilities have been contracting steadily in the Southern Uplands for some time. Transport costs have risen sharply while passenger traffic has fallen away as more and more people become car-owners. There are no signs that this situation will improve and even further curtailment of services should be expected. The information provided at the start of each chapter on the transport available is correct at the time of writing, but should be checked.

Abbreviations

O.S. — Ordnance Survey		mls. — miles
ap. — approximate		m. — metres
ft. — feet		kms. — kilometres
M.R. — Map Reference		

Weather

Sunshine. The reduction in the number of hours of sunshine to be expected on high ground as compared with more-favoured valleys may be assessed by comparing the 900 hours per year recorded for Lowther Hill (2377 ft. (725m.)) with at least 1300 hours for the Ayrshire plain and 1438 for Berwick-on-Tweed.

Wind. The main factor is the approach and passage of depressions from the North Atlantic, since the area falls within the main circulation route. The presence of high pressure over northern latitudes frequently introduces an opposing synoptic pattern particularly during the early part of the year. The highest wind speeds recorded at Lowther Hill over a four year period were 120 m.p.h. (193 k.p.h.) (February 1962), 117 m.p.h. (188 k.p.h.) (December 1962) and 115 m.p.h. (185 k.p.h.) (January 1963). Gusts of 92 m.p.h. (148 k.p.h.) or more have occurred over this period in all months except April, July and August.

Rainfall. The pattern of rainfall in the South of Scotland differs slightly from that which is evident in the part of the country lying to the north of the Clyde Valley. There, the prevailing south-west winds cause a high precipitation on the mountains of the western seaboard with an almost dramatic fall to much drier conditions as one travels east. This tendency may be demonstrated, perhaps, by comparing the mountain groups lying between Ben Nevis and the head of Loch Long with the Cairngorm group some sixty miles to the north-east. The mountains of the west have quite large areas of ground where the annual rainfall is 125 inches (318cms.) with peaks of 150 inches (381cms.) whereas the Cairngorms show a uniform average of only 60 inches (152cms.).

In the South of Scotland the wettest area, as might be expected, is the district containing the Galloway hills. Here the average fall is 90 inches (229cms.) a year, with local increases to 100 inches (254cms.); yet fifty-five miles (89kms.) to the north-east we still find an average fall of 80 inches (203cms.) over the Hart Fell and Broad Law groups.

It can be seen therefore that the general tendency of a high rainfall in the west, diminishing rapidly to much drier areas in the east, is not followed in the area under discussion, the rainfall being distributed more evenly over the high ground and largely irrespective of the distance from the west coast.

The south bank of the Clyde estuary, from Erskine to Gourock, shows a progressive rise in rainfall as the journey is made westwards, an annual fall of 37 inches (94cms.) in Glasgow, rising to 60 inches (153cms.) in Gourock. The high moorland to the south of Gourock shows a further rise to 90 inches (228cms.) and this is repeated on the Galloway Hills where one or two small areas, notably Merrick and Corserine, have a fall of 100 inches (254cms.).

The district round Queensberry, to the west of Moffat, also has a rainfall of 80 inches (203cms.) and this is repeated over the Hart Fell–White Coomb area and again over Broad Law. There is a continuous belt of country between Liddel Water and Tweedsmuir with a minimum fall of 60 inches (152cms.) and only in the Cheviot area do we find high ground with a significantly lower rainfall. The summit of Cheviot and the moors for almost twenty miles to the south-west have a relatively low fall of 45 inches (114cms.).

The Pentlands and the Moorfoot hills reach a peak of 45 inches (114cms.) with the Lammermuirs, some way east of Edinburgh, ranging from 30 to 40 inches (76–102cms.).

Nature Reserves. The environmental contrast between the Cheviot plateau and the meadows and woods of Lower Tweeddale is repeated in the character of the sea coast, where the cliffs of the Mull of Galloway or the Bass Rock support a wealth of bird life quite distinct from that found on the tidal sands of the Solway or Loch Ken. The area is rich in nature reserves and other places of special interest to the naturalist and a list, with brief details, has been added below. The areas have been listed county by county.

Animals and birds

The area covered by the guide does not, generally speaking, contain any very large tracts of almost uninhabited country, such as occur in the mountainous areas north of the Highland Line. It is hardly to be expected, therefore, that large herds of red deer will be found, but these do occur in the south-west where the Galloway hills offer suitable ground. Even so the red deer is restricted, though possibly increasing. The roe deer, on the other hand, is common in wooded country and may be found within three miles (5kms.) from the centre of Glasgow. The fox is common, as might be expected and may also be found within the Glasgow city limits. The hedgehog, on the other hand, although equally common, seems unable to cope with motor traffic and its habit of rolling into a defensive ball if disturbed when crossing a road at night leads to quite a high mortality rate. Both the badger and the otter are to be found, although neither is common. Neither the wild cat, pine marten nor polecat occur, although there are reports from time to time that wild cats have been seen in the Galloway area. It seems more likely that these have been 'tabby' domestic animals, which have avoided human contact for some time and acquired some of the shyness of the wild animal.

Feral goats in small numbers have existed for some time in the more remote parts of the south-west and mention might also be made of the herd of white cattle in the High Parks at Hamilton, one of the few remaining herds in the kingdom.

Three of the four larger reptiles are relatively common, being the adder, the common lizard and the slow-worm, which is a legless lizard and completely harmless. The grass snake does not occur at all in the area nor, indeed, anywhere else in Scotland but the observant walker over heather-covered ground will be aware how often the common lizard may be seen and this applies also to the small field voles. The adder is an extremely shy creature and it is depressing to find so many people prepared to kill it on sight, when its only instinct is to escape. There are only one or two recorded instances of adult fatalities from adder bites in the British Isles, though deaths of children number slightly more.

Both the brown hare and the blue mountain hare are common and the hill walker will be very familiar with the mountain variety, not only because of its change to a white coloration during the winter months, but also through its habit of running for a short distance when disturbed and then stopping to re-assess the danger. The fox, stoat and weasel all have this characteristic of deliberately assessing the intruding human when disturbed, sometimes apparently dismissing the risk as unimportant and continuing along their original course.

As regards the birds, both the golden eagle and the common buzzard occur in the area and both are known to breed, but only on a restricted scale, the eagles in particular rarely forming a breeding pair. It is sometimes supposed that the two birds may be distinguished one from the other by noting the separation of the individual feathers of the wingtips in flight, but both species exhibit this characteristic and the surest identification is the apparently very short head of the buzzard as compared with the longer head and longer tail of the eagle. Both birds will soar in flight for long periods. Of the other predatory birds, both the peregrine falcon and the merlin are to be found in the higher hills with the peregrine in the crags and the merlin hunting over heather-covered ground. At somewhat lower altitudes the sparrowhawk, kestrel and hen harrier are all present and all these species are recorded as breeding birds in the area, although only the kestrel may be accounted as common, the others being much more restricted.

On the higher hills the raven may be found, again restricted as regards breeding, while the carrion crow, with its much wider range, is relatively common. The hooded crow, so common north of the Highland line does not normally appear to be found at all within the area of the Southern Uplands and the same comment applies to the ptarmigan.

Five species of owls complete the list of raptorial birds. The tawny owl is fairly common in wooded country, with the short-eared being found in plantations of younger trees. The long-eared owl also occurs in mature conifers, with the barn owl more likely to be found in the vicinity of farm buildings or in cliffs or crags. The little owl breeds in Berwickshire on a very restricted scale, though it is possibly on the increase.

The bird whose call, perhaps more than any other sound, is so evocative of the moors and high ground beloved of the hill walker is the curlew and this is a common bird in the area. The green plover is also common, with the golden plover somewhat more restricted.

The continued growth in forestry planting will almost certainly tend to increase both the deer population and the numbers of the smaller birds, since open unplanted hillsides support a fairly low bird population. It may be expected, therefore, that such birds as the song and missel thrushes, willow warblers, blackbirds, wrens, robins and hedgesparrows will tend to increase in numbers and the same comment will apply to the woodpigeon, the chaffinch, bullfinch, crossbill, lesser redpoll, goldcrest and sparrowhawk.

Special mention must be made of the wildfowl, which winter on and near the Solway shores and inland lochs. Feral greylag geese breed locally and both white-fronted and pink-footed geese are common as visitors during the winter. Barnacle geese in particular may be seen in the Caerlaverock reserve. There is equal variety and profusion in the duck population for mallard, teal, tufted duck and shovellers all breed on the lowland and hill lochs in the south-west.

There is, finally, ample scope for the bird watcher on the coast where conditions vary from high cliffs at St Abb's Head and the Mull of Galloway to the tidal flats and sands of the Solway and the Ayrshire coast. There are terneries on Horse Island and Lady Isle (Ayrshire), while the largest breeding colony of cormorants in Scotland is found on Mochrum Loch (Wigtownshire). The black guillemot nests on the cliffs of the Mull of Galloway and the more widely distributed gulls include the common and herring gulls, the black-headed and both lesser and greater black-backed. Both kittiwake and fulmar are to be found and there are important gannet colonies on Ailsa Craig, the Bass Rock (p. 199), and Scaur Rocks in Luce Bay.

The counties of Lanark, Ayr, Dumfries, Kirkcudbright and East Lothian all possess notable heronries and these birds, in particular, should not be disturbed. The foregoing does not claim to be an exhaustive account.

Areas of Special Interest to the Naturalist

AYRSHIRE

Horse Island

1-inch O.S. map, sheet 59.

A Nature Reserve of the Royal Society for the Protection of Birds. Access by permit only – 21 Regent Terrace, Edinburgh.

Lady Isle

1-inch O.S. map, sheet 67.

A Nature Reserve of the Scottish Society for the Protection of Wild Birds.

AYRSHIRE–KIRKCUDBRIGHT

Glen Trool National Forest Park

1-inch O.S. map, sheets 67 and 73.

Contains the State Forests of Glen Trool, Carrick, Garraries, Kirroughtree, and parts of Bennan, Clatteringshaws and Dundeugh. Area of 230 square miles (600 sq. kms.). The Merrick hills lie within the Park.

BERWICKSHIRE

St Abb's Head
1-inch O.S. map, sheet 64.
Interesting sea-bird cliffs; fulmar colony.

DUMFRIES

Forest of Ae
1-inch O.S. map, sheets 68 and 74 or 75.
A State Forest of the Forestry Commission.

Tynron Juniper Wood
1-inch O.S. map, sheet 74.
A National Nature Reserve.

Castle Loch and Hightae Loch
1-inch O.S. map, sheet 75.
A Nature Reserve of Dumfries County Council and the Nature Conservancy. Notable for wildfowl.

Caerlaverock
1-inch O.S. map, sheet 75.
A National Nature Reserve on the Solway. Large flocks of geese and other wildfowl. Limited access.

DUMFRIES–ROXBURGH

Border Forests and Border National Forest Park
1-inch O.S. map, sheet 70.
This area, stretching over the border into Cumberland and Northumberland, forms the largest planted forest in the British Isles, covering almost 300 sq. miles (1296 sq. kms.). On the Scottish side the forests are Newcastleton in Roxburgh and Dumfries and Wauchope in Roxburgh.

KIRKCUDBRIGHT

Silver Flowe
1-inch O.S. map, sheet 73.
A small National Nature Reserve of specialist interest, lying in the Glen Trool National Forest Park near the Merrick.

Loch Ken
1-inch O.S. map, sheet 73.
A wildfowl refuge, notably geese and swans.

Kirkconnel Flow
1-inch O.S. map, sheets 74 or 75.
A National Nature Reserve, mainly of specialist botanical interest. Access by permit only.

LANARKSHIRE
Possil Marsh
1-inch O.S. map, sheet 60.
A Nature Reserve of the Scottish Society for the Protection of Wild Birds.

EAST LOTHIAN
Eyebroughty, Fidra, Lamb Island
1-inch O.S. map, sheet 56.
Nature Reserve of the Royal Society for the Protection of Birds. Breeding sea-birds. Access by permit only – 21 Regent Terrace, Edinburgh.

Aberlady Bay
1-inch O.S. map, sheet 62.
A local Nature Reserve of East Lothian County Council and the Nature Conservancy.
A wildfowl refuge and migration point.

Bass Rock
1-inch O.S. map, sheet 56.
See p. 199.

MID LOTHIAN
Inchmickery
1-inch O.S. map, sheet 62.
Island in the Firth of Forth. Nature Reserve of the Royal Society for the Protection of Birds. Breeding sea-birds. Access by permit only.

Duddingston Loch
1-inch O.S. map, sheet 62.
A Nature Reserve, Royal Park Sanctuary and Regional Wildfowl Refuge.

PEEBLES
Glentress Forest
1-inch O.S. map, sheet 62.
A State Forest owned by the Forestry Commission.

RENFREW
Castle Semple Loch, Lochwinnoch
1-inch O.S. map, sheet 60.
A Nature Reserve of Renfrew County Council. Wildfowl.

WIGTOWNSHIRE
Mochrum Loch and Castle Loch
1-inch O.S. map, sheet 79.
Unofficial wildfowl refuges; notable for geese and cormorants.

Great Scaur
1-inch O.S. map, sheet 79.
An inaccessible stack in Luce Bay. Gannets and other sea-birds.

Mull of Galloway
1-inch O.S. map, sheet 79.
The cliffs near the lighthouse are of interest for the sea-birds.

Bibliography (General)

Other works are listed at the ends of the chapters.

The Scenery of Scotland, A. Geikie – 1865.
The Drove Roads of Scotland, A. R. B. Haldane – Edinburgh, 1952.
Forestry in the Landscape, Forestry Commission Booklet No. 18 – H.M.S.O., 1966.
Forests of Central and Southern Scotland, Herbert L. Edlin, Forestry Commission Booklet No. 25 – H.M.S.O., 1969.
The Evolution of Scotland's Scenery, J. B. Sissons – Oliver & Boyd, 1967.
Tweeddale, Will Grant – Edinburgh, 1948.
The Lothians, Ian Finlay – London, 1960.
Across Watersheds, A. S. Alexander, Robert Maclehose – Glasgow, 1939.
The Highway Man, David E. T. Bell – *Ayrshire Post*, 1970.
Dumfries and Galloway Highways and Byways Guide to 200 Walks and Climbs, R. D. Walton (based on H. Truckell) – Dinwiddie, Dumfries.
The Hill Paths, Drove Roads and 'Cross Country' Routes in Scotland from the Cheviots to Sutherland, Walter A. Smith.
Scottish Mountains on Ski, Vol. I, Malcolm Slesser – West Col Productions, 1970.

British Regional Geology: The South of Scotland, J. Pringle, 2nd ed., revised – H.M.S.O., 1948.

— The Midland Valley of Scotland, M. & A. G. MacGregor, 2nd ed., revised – H.M.S.O., 1948.

Munro's Tables and Other Tables of Lesser Heights – Scottish Mountaineering Trust, 1969.

Early Fortifications in Scotland, David Christison – Edinburgh, 1898.

The Ancient Stones of Scotland, W. Douglas Simpson – London, 1965.

Roman Roads in Britain, Vol. II, Ivan D. Margary – London, 1957.

Roman and Native in North Britain, I. A. Richmond – London, 1961.

The North Britons. Prehistory of a Border People, Richard Feachem – London, 1965.

Prehistoric Scotland, Richard Feachem – London, 1963.

Arthur's Seat, a History of Edinburgh's Volcano, G. P. Black – Edinburgh, 1966.

Scottish Mountaineering Club Journal:

Vol. II Lanarkshire Hills, Hugh Boyd Watt.

Vol. VIII A Bit of the Berwickshire Coast and its Birds, W. Douglas.

Vol. IX The Southern Uplands.

Vol. XII The Bird Cliffs of St. Abb's, W. Douglas.

Vol. XIV Some Hill Roads in Scotland, Walter A. Smith.

Vol. XV Saturday Hill Walks Near Glasgow, W. W. Naismith and Gilbert Thomson.

Vol. XX The Two-Thousand Feet Tops of the Scottish Lowland Uplands, Percy Donald.

Vol. XXV The Meteorology of the Scottish Mountains, K. K. Hunter.

Lowlands of Scotland, G. Scott Moncrieff – London, 1948.

Stories of the Border Marches, John and Jean Lang – London, 1947.

Edinburgh Geology. An Excursion Guide, Mitchell, Walton, Grant – Edinburgh.

Mountain Flowers, Raven and Walters – London, 1956.

Britain's Nature Reserves, E. M. Nicholson – London, 1957.

Shell Nature Lovers' Atlas, James Fisher – London, 1966.

Ancient Border Highways, Proc. Socy. Antiquaries of Scotland, Vol. 58 – 1924.

The Roman Wall in Scotland, Sir Geo. Macdonald – London, 1934.

Prehistoric Man in Ayrshire, John Smith – Elliot Stock, London, 1895.

The Geographical Setting of Southern Scotland

Kenneth D. Collins, B.Sc.

Southern Scotland is usually considered to be the region which is bounded to the south by the Solway Firth and the Cheviot Hills and to the north by the line of the Southern Uplands Fault which strikes from Dunbar in the north-east to the area just south of Ballantrae in the south-west. It is for the most part a region of upland but it is really only in the north-east along the northern edge of the Moorfoot and Lammermuir Hills where less resistant rocks lie on the Central Lowlands side of the fault that the latter is a clear topographic boundary. For the rest of its length, the rocks on either side are almost equally as tough and there is little difference in relief and so topographically, the region extends tongues of upland on either side of the Clyde Valley well into the 'Midland Trough'. For the most part these extensions consist of low rounded hills of around 400–600m. which gradually die out towards the north but in the Tinto Hills of South Lanarkshire a felsitic intrusion has resulted in a summit of about 800m. on the 'wrong' side of the fault line.

It is usually agreed by writers on the region that there are within it two quite distinct sub-regions and that the boundary between them is the valley of the Nith. To the north-east there lies the Border country in whose smooth, grassy slopes is reflected centuries of sheep-rearing and domination by man whose settlements are to be found mainly in the valleys and in the lower ground of the Tweed basin. The hills are higher and more difficult to traverse in the north and at the head-waters of the Tweed and its tributaries than in the south and east where the narrow, steep-sided valleys open out into the undulating, cultivated Merse of Berwick which continues without interruption to the eastern coast and thence south into Northumberland. In the south west, however, in Galloway, granitic intrusions have caused the scenery to be much more craggy and rugged and indeed although its maximum height is only the 842m. of the Merrick, south of Loch Doon, it has often been compared with parts of the West Highlands.

The landscape in Southern Scotland has been moulded by a number of influences some of which are still active in the region and of which geological structure, lithology, erosional processes, present and past climate, vegetation and settlement history are a few of the most important. The Southern Uplands are really a dissected plateau of Ordovician and Silurian rocks, the former occurring in a broad band almost from coast to coast in the north and the latter having a similar distribution in the south. Both consist of tightly folded beds of mudstones, slates, greywackes, grits and conglomerates, none of them of any great thickness and it is only seldom that any of them appear at the surface for they are mostly masked by a covering of frost-shattered debris. Alan Ogilvie wrote in 1928 that the region had been 'modelled out of the southern limb of a great anticlinorium . . .' and this theory, sometimes in modified form has had wide acceptance until more recent geological research has shown the structure to be less clear. Monoclinal interpretations are favoured by some writers but the true situation is still open to some argument. What certainly seems to be true is that the scenery over much of the region is a product of the thin, narrow outcrops and the nature of the rocks themselves and that the smooth rounded forms have been produced by the weathering of these outcrops into small stones and other fine material. By and large, there are few massive structures and so the formation of a wild, rugged, angular, boulder-strewn landscape is precluded.

In Galloway, however, granitic intrusions in Lower Old Red Sandstone times into the sedimentary country rock have produced a landscape which is rougher and more fragmented. The most important of these intrusions which are so distinctive as to be identifiable on an ordinary topographic map, are the Criffel, Cairnsmore of Fleet and Loch Doon masses. The latter is easily the most extensive and it occupies an area stretching from Loch Doon itself to Loch Dee, a distance of some 18km. while at its widest point it is about 10km. from east to west. It is this area in particular with its harsh, rough-walled valleys strewn with lochs that has invited comparison with the West Highlands. In the words of Tivy (1962) '. . . the granite "cauldron" of Loch Doon is comparable to, though more difficult of access than, the Moor of Rannoch and must have acted as one of the main centres of ice-accumulation in southern Scotland.' The relationship between rocks and scenery is certainly very strong and the highest land corresponds to a girdle of metamorphic rocks which encircle the intrusion itself and form the Merrick and the Kells Range which rises to 813m. in the Rhinns of Kells. Criffel and Cairnsmore of Fleet the other two intrusions mentioned are neither so extensive nor so scenically dramatic having maximum heights of 569m. and 710m. respectively while the smaller intrusions such as Cairnsmore of Carsphairn are simple 'corrie-sided masses with no obvious rim of metamorphic rocks.'

Also in Lower Old Red Sandstone times there occurred great outpourings of lava and these find topographic expression in Roxburghshire as part of the Cheviot Volcanic Series which, together with thick Carboniferous strata, form much of the hill country in the south east of that county. Igneous rocks in the eastern part of Southern Scotland, however, are mainly of Carboniferous age and their importance in terms of scenery is that they introduce rougher and more craggy forms into an otherwise placid and smooth landscape. The Eildon Hills (369, 420 and 404m.) whose appearance gives an impression of stratification and which overlook the Tweed valley at Melrose are really a composite trachytic intrusion while in Berwickshire, the hills of the Dirrington Laws (397 and 362m.) west of Duns have been formed from felsitic intrusions in Upper Old Red Sandstone conglomerates and sandstones. Elsewhere in the intermediate plateau which surrounds the Merse there is a number of volcanic rocks and sills which form hills which rise up to 100m. above the general level.

Thus the upland areas of Southern Scotland are composed mainly of resistant Ordovician and Silurian structures intruded and sometimes overlain by Old Red Sandstone and Carboniferous igneous and metamorphic material. It is, however, to the lower ground around the coast of Galloway and the basins of the rivers which flow into the Solway Firth on the one hand, and to the valleys of the eastward-flowing Tweed and its tributaries on the other, that one must go to find sedimentaries of Old Red and more recent deposition. These younger rocks have been stripped from off the rest of the region thus resulting in the exhumation of the ancient surfaces that compose the contemporary landscape. They have, in fact, been preserved only in the areas of low altitude where they have been protected from the devastating effects of Tertiary erosion. At this time it is held that the land was submerged by a high sea level and that as a consequence of this submergence a series of horizontal surfaces known as erosion surfaces were formed. It is certainly true that there is an accordance of peaks over most of the region readily observable from any high point and that these peaks often rise up quite sharply from a lower, flat plateau. It is this kind of evidence that has led many writers including Geikie (1901), Ogilvie (1930) and George (1955, 1965, 1966) to measure and speculate upon the origin of the erosion surfaces. George has shown the existence of horizontal surfaces at levels of approximately 800, 700, 500, 325 and 180 metres and has argued in favour of the marine origin mentioned above. But if the scale of the landscape has been decided by major elements of structure, the occurrence of igneous and metamorphic material and successive submergences and emergences, for an explanation of the forms and the nature of the surface, it is necessary to turn to the processes by which the ancient landscape has been modified. The drainage system has been one major influence whose explanation has taxed many geographers and geologists. It can easily be observed by studying any map of the region that many of the rivers and streams of Southern Scotland do not flow in a direction that is in accordance with the north-east, south-west 'grain' of the country as established by the severe differential erosion of Tertiary times which produced a multitude of strike valleys and depressions along belts of weak rock. The drainage system must therefore have originated on a surface which was at least as high as the present summits and whose rocks have long since been stripped except in the sedimentary low ground. The date of origin is not really established although one idea which has gained considerable support is that the streams started flowing in Cretaceous times on a layer of chalk (Linton 1933, 1951) which sloped from west to east in the Southern Uplands from a height of about 1060m. around the headwaters of the Tweed to around 825m. at the Cheviot.

However, Sissons (1967) has shown that this set of circumstances should have given rise to more eastward-flowing streams and that 'the discordant streams show far more relation to the present distribution of high ground than to an eastward-tilted surface.' Instead, he has pointed out that there is a watershed dividing eastward-flowing streams from westward and that this divide corresponds more or less to the areas of highest ground. That is to say it passes through the Broad Law (839m.), Hart Fell (808m.) area and thence by way of the hilly country between Dumfriesshire and Roxburghshire into the Cheviots and the Pennine system of Northern England. It is suggested that this be interpreted as the axis of an up-warp and that when the land began to emerge from the sea at the end of the Tertiary submergence then this was the area to emerge first. The streams, so this account suggests, began to flow east and west from that time. It is further pointed out that minor axes running east-west through Galloway just south of the Southern Uplands Fault, and on the east, south of the Teviot, would explain the direction of flow of streams into the Solway Firth and the Firth of Clyde respectively on the one hand and into the Tweed and the North of England system on the other. The explanation has an elegance and a simplicity which recommend it in favour of earlier more elaborate suggestions.

The picture, however, is still far from complete for although the landscape of South Scotland is one whose main elements of relief were established by late Tertiary times, the several stages of the Ice Age were of momentous importance to the region. During this time, the land surface was covered, sometimes only in part but sometimes completely by great thicknesses of ice, and the features which had been produced by marine and subaerial erosion were further modified. The ice moved out from the Loch Doon area for this was its main gathering ground owing to the high precipitation, but because of the presence of Highland ice to the north, it was compelled to move east and south, scouring and abrading, gouging and denuding as it went. Glacial features abound throughout the region. On the low ground of the coastal fringe of Galloway and in the Lower Tweed as well as in the valleys proper there have been deposited quite considerable thicknesses of till or glacial debris of an unsorted nature. These are in the form of moraines of various kinds or drumlins, swarms of which occur especially in the area around Castle Douglas and Newton Stewart in Galloway. Sand and gravel deposits also occur in the form mainly of kames, eskers and outwash fans, having been produced by the sorting action of the meltwaters from the decaying ice on the unsorted material mentioned above. The finer, clay particles were washed away and the material re-deposited consisted only of the coarser sands and gravels.

In the upland areas, however, the features are mainly erosional. For example, around Loch Doon itself the land was scraped and denuded by the ice and there are now great areas of exposed rock pitted with many lochs and breached by wide, steep-sided glaciated valleys. Such glacial breaches can be seen in the channel connecting Loch

Dee and Loch Trool, and the Mennock Pass between Thornhill and Sanquhar is also the product of breaching and indeed, from the constricted nature of the Nith Valley at this point, it seems possible that the Upper Nith once flowed into Ayrshire. In the region of the Upper Tweed, the pass connecting what is now the Talla reservoir and the Megget Water (a tributary of the Yarrow) is thought to be a glacial breach while another connects the head of the Moffat Water to the steep-sided valley of the Yarrow itself. Even the through valley of the Biggar Gap is possibly, at least in part, due to breaching. Other common effects of glacial erosion in upland areas in Britain of course include the formation of corries. However, these are not well developed in Southern Scotland being found in only a few instances in the Tweedsmuir Hills and with a greater frequency in the granitic areas of upland Galloway but in the former case especially they tend towards a smoothness and simplicity of form not usually associated with such features. The concentration of corries in Galloway is partly explained by higher altitudes and levels of precipitation in that area and partly by the fact that this was the centre of much of the ice in Southern Scotland. That this was so can be ascertained by observing the alignments of both erosional and depositional features in the areas around Loch Doon. Thus, for example, striations on rock surfaces indicate radial movement from this area and confirm the limited extent of this movement to the north while erratic boulders originating around Dalmellington have been found in the Upper Nith at Sanquhar. Similarly the 'grained' pattern produced by deposited material supports the eastward and southward movement of the ice and indeed the alignments of drumlins and ground moraines has had an effect on the pattern of minor roads in the Lower Tweed. There is a strong tendency for them to follow the system of low swells and shallow depressions trending at first north-east and then to swing round into an east-west alignment towards the coast.

Implicit in the foregoing descriptions has been yet another point of contrast between Galloway on the one hand, the Border country on the other. In the west, erosional features continue as far as the coast whereas in the east the low ground is a fertile, agricultural area for long settled by man and farmed in big, regular, efficient units. Galloway, however, has considerable areas of bare rock both on the intermediate upland surfaces and even on the coastal fringe of Wigtownshire. There are also extensive areas of impeded drainage where cultivation is impossible and even near the coast it is often only on the slopes of the myriads of drumlins that farming becomes an economic proposition. The kind of agriculture that is carried on in the west is, in part, at least a function of the kind of landscape that has evolved there for instead of concentrating on the growing of crops of cereals and so on as they do in the Merse of Berwick, the farmers of Galloway are more concerned with the rearing of cattle and particularly with the production of milk on the low ground. The dominant crop is grass and its growth is encouraged by the mild, damp climate which is the other half of the explanation of the kind of farming in the area.

It is difficult to make any kind of generalisations about the climatic conditions in Southern Scotland for these are differences not only between east and west but between low ground and the hills. It is true that Galloway has a mild, soft, but damp climate around its coastal fringe of lowland with temperatures only occasionally dropping much below zero even in winter while in summer the indented Solway coast with its extensive beaches backed by low cliffs has the reputation of being one of the sunniest and warmest areas in Scotland. (It should be pointed out that, as yet, perhaps because of its comparative inaccessibility, this reputation has not led to any great holiday industry.) The annual precipitation on the low ground decreases from some 125cm. in the west to something under 80cm. in the Merse of Berwick where the climate is more 'extreme' with a much greater frequency of sub-zero temperatures in winter. However, in the upland areas, climatic conditions are quite different and over much of the hill country the precipitation is in the region of 175cm. per annum with a fairly high proportion of this falling as snow. Temperatures are lower, wind speed is higher and the whole environment is much harsher.

This is substantiated by Sissons (1967) when he points out that on the summit of Broad Law '... the soil is often frozen from late December until early April apart from the diurnal thawing of a thin surface layer.' Thus, periglacial conditions are known to prevail in these upland areas and it is not unusual to find evidence in the form of stone stripes and polygons and wave-like terraces showing the instability of the soil cover and its tendency to move downhill under the constant expansion and contraction effect of freezing and thawing. In other words, there is abundant evidence that owing to the climatic conditions obtaining in these upland areas, the surface forms of the contemporary landscape are still being modified.

The extent of the harsh, hill conditions is shown by the failure of improved land to penetrate much above about 400m. in the Border country and about 200m. in the wetter Galloway area. Above this level, Southern Scotland is a region of moorland, sheep farming and, in the west, forestry. The vegetation of the region is a further confirmation of the dichotomy between Galloway and the Border country for while the associations of plants in the moorland of the former are of the wet type, those in the east are dry. Thus in Galloway, there are extensive areas of ill-drained land covered in considerable thicknesses of peat and the moorland is dominated by purple moor-grass (Molinia caerulea) which is tolerant of acid, wet soils, cotton grass (Eriophorum vaginatum) in the more waterlogged areas, and bog myrtle (Myrica gale). On the higher surfaces heather is more common and is often found together with both the purple moor-grass and deer sedge (Scirpus caespitosum). In the east, however, where it is drier and the soils better drained the associations are quite different. There is no bog myrtle and the purple moor-grass is replaced by moor mat grass (Nardus stricta) and heath rush (Juncus squarrosus) while the deposits of peat are eroded and now dominated by heather.

Throughout the region, however, the moorland is used as sheep pasture although the number of sheep per acre is higher in the east and Galloway with its emphasis on cattle does not have such strong historic associations with the animal that is true of the Border country. The great Cistercian abbeys of Dundrennan, Glenluce and Sweetheart in the west and of Melrose, Dryburgh, Kelso and Jedburgh in the east established the tradition of sheep farming in the region and in the Tweedsmuir hills it has flourished almost exclusively ever since. The influence of the Cistercians has been described as 'the most potent factor in the biological history of the highland zone (of Britain)' and certainly in Southern Scotland it is one that is easily recognised. Centuries of sheepgrazing and of moorburning designed to encourage the growth of new, fresh shoots has served to destroy much of the heather and it has been replaced by the species of grass listed above which give the eastern uplands their smooth, rather uninteresting appearance. The sheep tend to graze very selectively and destroy plants other than grass while their close trampling has the effect of '. . . puddling the surface so that the beneficial effect of frost-heaving on soil aeration are quickly lost' (Pearsall, 1950). Many of the lower slopes have been invaded by the common bracken (Pteridium aquilinum), again because of the selective grazing of the sheep – by contrast, cattle eat bracken – and this has the long term effect of destroying these slopes as pastures while on some of the steeper hillsides soil erosion is in a fairly advanced stage.

Southern Scotland, then, is a region dominated by hills where forms have been produced by the action of a multitude of geological and biological influences. It is a region containing much diversity of scenery, from the wet, dark, craggy hills of the west to the drier, green grassy slopes of the east and from moorland trodden only by sheep and shepherd to the rich farmlands of the Merse, domesticated and cultivated for generations. Its urban population is comparatively small and has changed little since last century although, like the Highlands, emigration from the region to the Central Lowlands, to England or even farther afield is a disturbing feature of everyday life. The comparison with the Highlands can be carried further for there too is a landscape whose main elements have been decided by geological structure which has been modified by the action of ice and water and which is a region of difficulty for man, not least because of his own mismanagement. Southern Scotland also bears the scars of overgrazing by sheep and here too is a landscape ready for 'discovery' by those whose love of such environments leads them not only to exploration but also to understanding.

BIBLIOGRAPHY

Charlesworth, J. K., The glacial geology of the Southern Uplands west of Annandale and Upper Clydesdale, Trans. Roy. Soc. Edin. 55, 1926, pp. 1–23.

Geikie, A., *The Scenery of Scotland*, London, 1901.

George, T. N., Drainage in the Southern Uplands: Clyde Nith and Annan, Trans. Geol. Soc. Glas. 22, 1955, pp. 1–34.

— The Geological Growth of Scotland in the geology of Scotland, ed. G. Y. Craig, Edinburgh, 1965, pp. 1–48.

Gregory, J. W., The Tweed Valley and its Relation to the Clyde and Solway, Scot. Geog. Mag., 31, 1915, pp. 478–86.

Linton, D. L., The Origin of the Tweed Drainage System, Scot. Geog. Mag. 49, 1933, pp. 162–74.

— Problems of Scottish Scenery, Scot. Geog. Mag. 67, 1951, pp. 65–68.

— *Morphological Contrasts between Eastern and Western Scotland.*
— *In Geographical Essays in Memory of Alan S. Ogilvie*, ed. by R. Miller and J. W. Watson, Edinburgh, 1959, pp. 16–45.
MacKinder, H. J., *Britain and the British Seas*, London, 1902.
McVean, D. N., *Ecology and Land Use in Upland Scotland*, Edinburgh, 1969.
Ogilvie, A. G., *Great Britain:* Essays in regional geography, Cambridge, 1930.
Pearsall, W. H., *Mountains and Moorlands*, London, 1950.
Pringle, J., *The South of Scotland*, British Regional Geology (2nd ed.), Department of Scientific and Industrial Research London, H.M.S.O., 1948.
Sissons, J. B., Erosion surfaces, cyclic slopes and drainage systems in southern Scotland and northern England, Trans. Inst. Brit. Geog. 28, 1960, pp. 23–38.
— *The Evolution of Scotland's Scenery*, Edinburgh, 1967.
Tansley, A. G., *The British Isles and Their Vegetation*, Cambridge, 1953.
Tivy, J., *The South of Scotland: In Great Britain:* Geographical essays, ed. J. Mitchell, Cambridge, 1962.
— *The Scottish Marchlands in Field Studies in the British Isles*, ed. J. A. Steer, London, 1964.

WESTERN HILLS

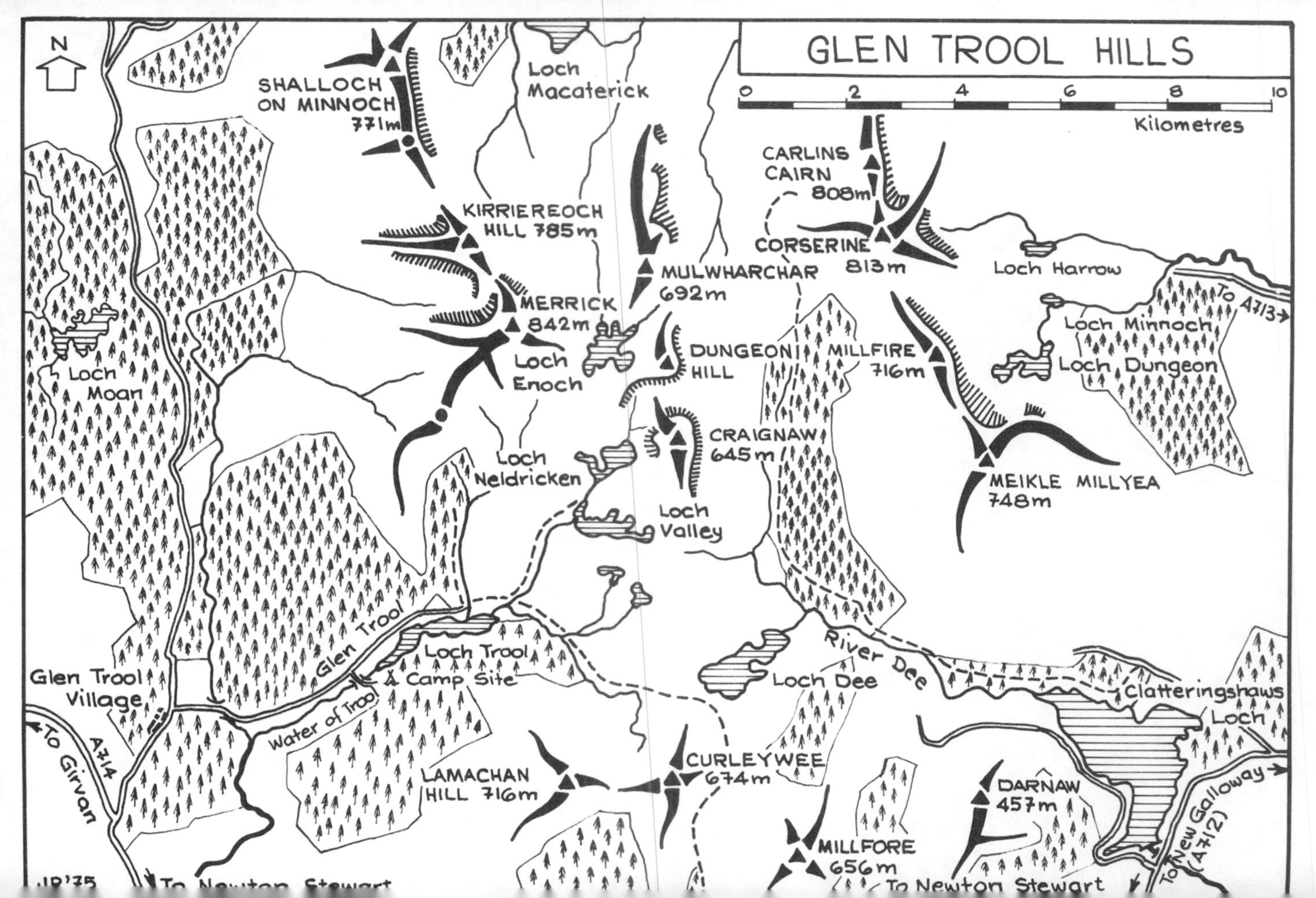
GLEN TROOL HILLS
0
2
4
6
8
10
Kilometres
N
SHALLOCH ON MINNOCH 771m
Loch Macaterick
KIRRIEREOCH HILL 785m
MERRICK 842m
Loch Enoch
Loch Neldricken
Loch Moan
MULWHARCHAR 692m
DUNGEON HILL
CRAIGNAW 645m
Loch Valley
CARLINS CAIRN 808m
CORSERINE 813m
Loch Harrow
To A713
Loch Minnoch
Loch Dungeon
MILLFIRE 716m
MEIKLE MILLYEA 748m
Glen Trool
Loch Trool
Camp Site
Glen Trool Village
Water of Trool
To Girvan
A714
River Dee
Loch Dee
Clatteringshaws Loch
LAMACHAN HILL 716m
CURLEYWEE 674m
DARNAW 457m
MILLFORE 656m
To New Galloway (A712)
To Newton Stewart
To Newton Stewart

1

West Renfrewshire and North Ayrshire

(1)	**Hill of Stake**	1713 ft. (522m.)	M.R. 273630
(2)	**Irish Law**	1587 ft. (484m.)	M.R. 260591
(3)	**Kaim Hill**	1272 ft. (388m.)	M.R. 228534

Maps: O.S. 1-inch, Seventh Series, sheet 59.
Bartholomew ½-inch, sheet 44.

The hills of this region are known by such names as the Renfrewshire Heights, the North Ayrshire Hills, the Largs Hills, the Kilbarchans, or the Kilmacolms, according to the viewpoint and prejudice of the individual. The boundary between Ayrshire and Renfrewshire runs across the highest summits in the range, while the area occupies the nose of land which the River Clyde flows around in its transition from a river at Glasgow to a mighty firth opposite Arran. The Clyde bounds the area on the north and west, while inland, a rough boundary may be taken as the roads running from Port Glasgow through Kilmacolm, Lochwinnoch, Kilbirnie and Dalry to Ardrossan. The uplands tend to merge gradually with the lowlands on the east but are much steeper above the Clyde.

In general, the area is one of volcanic rocks and is a tableland rather than a hill range. Streams flow in all directions from its heart. Many of these have bitten deeply into the rock to produce scenic valleys which give a welcome contrast to the featureless moorland on the higher ground.

The region is well provided with roads, and apart from those on its perimeter, there are useful cross-country roads from Largs to Greenock, Largs to Kilbirnie, Inverkip to Loch Thom, Loch Thom to Kilmacolm, West Kilbride to Dalry, and Dalry to Hunterston. In addition there is a road into Glen Calder, and a series of minor roads behind Kilbirnie which bring the hills nearer.

The region is surrounded intermittently with holiday, residential and industrial towns and villages, while farmlands make inroads into the hill country. Much of the rainfall on these hills is captured in reservoirs which meet the needs of the large populations residing and working nearby, thus access to certain parts is restricted. The largest reservoirs are Loch Thom and the Gryfe Reservoir for the Greenock area and the Muirhead and Camphill Reservoirs which supply Paisley.

The nearness of these hills to the Clyde Valley and the Ayrshire Plain makes the area a useful recreational ground. Thousands take to the area at week-ends and holidays and the roads can become very busy. Walkers taking to the hills are soon on their own though.

Some of the views from this region are among the best in Scotland. The Clyde coast, Arran, Bute, the Cumbraes and Cowal are magnificent in many prospects, while farther off, Galloway, the Pentlands, Ben Lomond, the Arrochar Hills, the Trossachs, and the Paps of Jura are frequently visible. While the high moorland core of the region may offer walkers little more than training for better hills farther away, it should be understood that the area has a unique character.

A Renfrewshire Regional Park covering 47 sq. mls. (120 sq. kms.) is being set up, extending from Inverkip and Gourock to the Lochwinnoch area. Only a tiny part of this in Glen Calder has been opened officially to the public but other areas are promised including cross-country walks and pony-trekking routes.

Transport

There are regular daily bus services on all the main roads. These connect Ardrossan and Greenock; Gourock, Port Glasgow and Johnstone; Johnstone, Lochwinnoch, Kilbirnie and Largs; Kilbirnie, Dalry and West Kilbride; and Dalry, Kilwinning and Ardrossan.

Western S.M.T. Co. Ltd.

Clyde Coast Services Ltd., Saltcoats.

Rail services are operated from Glasgow through Paisley to – Bridge of Weir and Kilmacolm; Port Glasgow, Greenock and Gourock; Inverkip and Wemyss Bay; and Glengarnock, Dalry, Ardrossan, West Kilbride, Fairlie and Largs. There are no Sunday services at Kilmacolm, Bridge of Weir or Glengarnock.

Ardrossan, Fairlie, Largs, Wemyss Bay and Gourock are also served by steamers or car ferry. The region can therefore be visited in conjunction with a tour of Arran or Argyll.

Caledonian Steam Packet Co. Ltd., Gourock.

Hill of Stake 1713 ft. (522m.) lies to the north-east of Largs and is the highest point of the region forming the watershed between Ayrshire and Renfrewshire. One of the most interesting routes to the hill, but also one of the longest, is to ascend the valley of the River Garnock to its source near the summit. This route starts at a bridge over the River Garnock near the farm of Blackburn north of Kilbirnie. Follow the track past the farm to the ruins of Glengarnock Castle which sit on a promontory above the river. A path leads to the far side of the river across a weir and up to a dam which impounds most of the water for Paisley's supply. Alternatively, the walker can stay high above the east bank of the river and follow the contours of the valley. In wet periods, the east bank is probably safer, as trouble could be met on the west bank in crossing the King's Burn and the Surge Burn where they join the Garnock. These have carved out impressive little canyons which normally need only short detours upstream to pass.

Glen Garnock is very fine scenically with numerous waterfalls. The grandest of these is the Spout of Garnock beyond the junction with the Surge Burn. The Spout is a white cascade of about 40 ft. (12m.) where the Garnock breaks out from the moorland plateau. It marks a transition in the scenery. Below it the glen is steep, rocky and impressive; above it, there is another world of open moors traversed by a small gurgling burn. The upper world is a huge anticlimax – a tedious expanse of bog and heather with scarce a feature on it save for the butts of grouse-shooters. Fortunately the summit is quite near. This is a drier elevated mound on the moor and is crowned by an O.S. pillar and a cairn.

The view is rather blocked off by the surrounding high ground, although the hills north of the Clyde are well seen. The Glengarnock Steel Works are prominent at the foot of the Garnock Valley signposting the route back, but smoke from the I.C.I. Works at Ardeer should not be mistaken for this. The way back may be varied by visiting Misty Law 1662 ft. (507m.) along the county boundary. This follows the highest ground over East Girt Hill, where a plane was wrecked, but only an occasional cairn marks the route. Misty Law has more character to it than the other tops.

The Hill of Stake appears much more of a hill from Glen Calder to the east where there is a Country Park at Muirshiel Estate Policies. This area has a car park, information centre, picnic sites, lavatories, scenic walks and a nature trail and was Renfrew County Council's contribution to European Conservation Year (1970). Beyond the policies, the road (closed to cars) continues across the River Calder to a barytes mine on the north-east slope of the hill. The mine was closed in 1969.

The hill may be tackled from the west by several routes. The road up the Noddsdale Water from Largs gives a good start to those with transport, while the Gogo Water may be walked from Largs. Both valleys are worth seeing although the upper parts of these routes again are over moorland. The best starting point from the Noddsdale valley is the reservoir under Peat Hill. For the Gogo Glen, follow the road from the centre of Largs past the gasometer and the school to the farm of Flatt east of the town. Take the steep road up the hill from Bellesdale Avenue. This runs along the north side of the glen and gives fine views of Largs, the Cumbraes and the Clyde. Higher up it crosses the Greeto Water and both burns offer interesting, if rough, routes to the hill.

Irish Law 1587 ft. (484m.) is a prominent point on this generally featureless upland plateau. It lies to the north of the Muirhead Reservoir on the road between Largs and Dalry. The route leads over the Knockside Hills which are three shapely tops. The views to Arran and the Clyde are very good but those inward to the Hill of Stake are dreary. Those heading for the latter should choose their route carefully to conserve energy on the undulating moor.

Kaim Hill 1272 ft. (388m.) sits above Fairlie and may be ascended with Blaeloch Hill or the Crosbie Hills in a traverse of this area from a variety of starting points. Kaim Hill itself may be climbed from the Fairlie Glen, past the ruins of an ancient keep known as Fairlie Castle, or from the scenic moor road that climbs steeply from Hunterston past the south side of the hill. Millstones were at one time hewn from the slopes of this hill which is one of the finest viewpoints on the Clyde.

BIBLIOGRAPHY

Scots Magazine – September 1960.
Days in the Heart of the Renfrew Heights, Elizabeth Orr Boyd.

Scottish Mountaineering Club Journal –
Vol. II *Renfrewshire Hills*, Hugh Boyd Watt.
Vol. XXI *The North-West Renfrewshire Hills*, G. F. Todd

The following booklets have been produced by Renfrew County Council and are available at the Information Centre in Glen Calder:
Renfrewshire Regional Park
Muirshiel Estate Country Trail

Other publications to become available are:
The Geology of the Regional Park, Dr John Hamilton.
The Archaeology of the Regional Park, Frank Newall.
The Botany of the Regional Park, E. T. Idle.
An Ornithological Survey of the Regional Park, Barry Thurston.

2

Eaglesham to Sanquhar

(1)	**Ballageich Hill**	1084 ft. (330m.)	M.R. 531501
(2)	**Corse Hill**	1230 ft. (375m.)	M.R. 599465
(3)	**Loudoun Hill**	1036 ft. (316m.)	M.R. 609379
(4)	**Wedder Hill**	1411 ft. (430m.)	M.R. 596309
(5)	**Nutberry Hill**	1712 ft. (522m.)	M.R. 743339
(6)	**Cairn Table**	1945 ft. (593m.)	M.R. 724243
(7)	**Cairn Kinny**	1618 ft. (493m.)	M.R. 784214
(8)	**Corsencon Hill**	1559 ft. (475m.)	M.R. 671148

Maps: O.S. 1-inch, Seventh Series, sheets 60, 67 and 68.
Bartholomew ½-inch, sheets 40 and 45.

This region lies roughly between the Clyde Valley and the Ayrshire Coastal Plain. It is a region of elevated moorland rather than a range of definite hills. The boundary line between the Southern Uplands and the Central Lowlands is blunted here and the high moorlands stretch northwards to merge gradually with the lowlands. Only Cairn Table comes anywhere near the 2000 ft. (610m.) mark, but there are numerous elevations over 1000 ft. (305m.) and large tracts of the region are uninhabited and undeveloped. The region consequently has some appeal to walkers, especially those seeking to escape from the crowded lowlands nearby.

Several main roads traverse the region dividing it into four sections. These occupy the areas between Eaglesham, Darvel and Strathaven; Darvel, Sorn and Muirkirk; Strathaven, Muirkirk and Douglas; and Muirkirk, New Cumnock, Sanquhar and Crawfordjohn. Muirkirk is centrally situated for all these areas except that between Eaglesham, Strathaven and Darvel.

Transport

Buses run to Eaglesham, Strathaven, Darvel, Muirkirk, Douglas, Sorn, Cumnock, Kirkconnel and Sanquhar.

1. Glen Garnock from the Spout of Garnock.

2. The Spout of Garnock.

3. Loch Thom from the west.

4. Arran and the Cumbraes from Irish Law.

5. Loudoun Hill from the south-east.

6. Looking north-east from Cairn Table to Tinto.

7. Cairn Table from the Macadam Cairn on the Old Sanquhar Road.

8. Corsencon Hill and the River Nith.

9. The Mennock Pass.

Western S.M.T. Co. Ltd.
Central S.M.T. Co. Ltd.

Kirkconnel and East Kilbride have the only railway stations that might be of use.

Ballageich Hill 1084 ft. (330m.) lies on the north side of the Fenwick to Eaglesham road and is too near the road to offer much strenuous exercise. It can be included in a cross-country walk from the Glasgow to Kilmarnock road. The views from it are good.

Corse Hill 1230 ft. (375m.) is the highest point on the moors between Eaglesham and Darvel but is an undistinguished hill.

Loudoun Hill 1036 ft. (316m.) is the remnant of a volcanic plug. It rises east of Darvel, north of the road to Strathaven, and has great appeal for walkers and rock climbers. The former should ascend from the west on a path through the trees from the fields above Loudounhill House. The south and east faces are precipitous and should only be tackled by experienced climbers.

The summit has an O.S. pillar and gives a fine view of the Irvine Valley. The site of a Roman fort to the south of the hill has been almost completely quarried away. Proposals have also been made to quarry Loudoun Hill itself – which would complete the outrage! A Roman road is thought to have passed close to the hill heading westwards, but as yet, no substantial finds have been made on the Firth of Clyde coast to back the theory that they had a port this way. The ruins of a hamlet lie at the foot of the northern slopes and there are other ruins on the south.

In 1307 Robert the Bruce defeated the Earl of Pembroke in a battle under the hill. Another battle was fought at Drumclog nearby in 1679 when the Covenanters defeated Claverhouse's troops. The hill is thought to have been a beacon hill in conjunction with Tinto and the Hill of Stake.

Just below the summit at the top of the south face there is a plaque to a Strathaven climber who pioneered many of the climbs on the hill. It is inscribed:

'In memory of John Jackson
Killed in the Italian Alps
20 July 1968
Aged 20 years.'

Wedder Hill 1411 ft. (430m.) is a dreary summit that is relieved by having two ancient monuments nearby. The hill lies east of Sorn and to the north of the highest point on the road to Muirkirk. It may be climbed from the summit of this road or from the farm of Blacksidend on the south-west side of the hill. Both routes reach ridge-level at a large cairn on Blacksidend. The cairn is thought to date from the Bronze Age but has been much altered by visitors. About $1\frac{1}{4}$ mls. (2kms.) along the ridge to the north-east there is another large and conspicuous cairn on Glen Garr, just below the summit of Wedder Hill. This also is thought to be of Bronze Age date. Loudoun Hill is conspicuous from this end of the hill, to the right of Distinkhorn 1259 ft. (384m.). The River Avon has its source in the col between Distinkhorn and Wedder Hill and flows north-eastwards. There is an ancient fort some distance down the river that is known as Main Castle.

Nutberry Hill 1712 ft. (522m.) is the highest summit between Strathaven, Douglas and Muirkirk. It may be reached easily from a number of points including the road up the Logan Water, and that up the Birkenhead Burn to Logan Farm, although the latter is rough. There is also a good road as far as Cumberhead on its east side, or it may be tackled from Glenbuck in the south.

The hills of this region are not very high or exciting but they occupy a large expanse of moorland and offer quite hard walking from one side to the other. Two covenanting monuments in the area are worth noting, that to John Brown under Priesthill Height where he was shot, and a remote monument to the convenanters by the Back Burn on Auchingilloch above the Kype Water. The latter can be reached from a public road that runs to the Kype Reservoir.

Cairn Table 1945 ft. (593m.) lies to the south-east of Muirkirk and is easily climbed from there. It is the highest hill in the region and is a popular walk. Several paths lead on to it, but the two main routes from Muirkirk start at the disused railway station and the farm of Auldhouseburn.

The route from the station runs south-east over the Steel, which is a pleasant ridge with a well-trodden path. The slopes are of heather, which becomes more stunted at the rocky summit.

Auldhouseburn is reached from the east end of the village. The road to it crosses the River Ayr, turns right at a junction, then runs uphill to the farm. The route goes round the farm on the left and up to a small reservoir east of the Auldhouse Burn. A path runs up the east bank of this burn straight for the hill. Alternatively the route from the station can be joined as it goes over the Steel.

The summit is marked by an O.S. pillar and two large cairns on the county boundary. The more easterly cairn marks the true summit but the inhabitants of Muirkirk have done their best to capture the hill for Ayrshire, by constructing a towering cairn 13 ft. (4m.) high further west which is clearly higher. This was erected as a war memorial to the dead of the 1914–18 war. A metal pipe runs down the centre of the cairn and contains a scroll bearing the names of those from the district who died.

Cairn Kinny 1618 ft. (493m.) is a prominent little peak in the area between Muirkirk and Crawfordjohn. It shows up well from the east and is approached by a public road running up Glentaggart from Glespin. Numerous walks are possible in this area but there are few features of interest.

Corsencon Hill 1559 ft. (475m.) dominates the upper Nith valley. It sits east of New Cumnock and is a short climb from the road from New Cumnock along the north side of the Nith. It gives good views down the Nith Valley and westwards into Ayrshire and is said to have been a beacon hill.

Hill Paths

Eaglesham to Darvel 11 mls. (18kms.)
This is an old drove road and a Right of Way. It has long stretches of motorable road at either end which can cut down the walking distance. The section from Eaglesham runs southwards to the farm of Carrot M.R. 577481 where a rough road continues through young forest plantations and around Myres Hill to Myres. The path beyond here is overgrown but goes west of Crook Hill to High Overmuir where the road to Darvel is met. Motorists from the Darvel side will find the surface good as far as Low Overmuir.

One of several alternatives to the above outing is to come from Eaglesham as far as Myres, then cut westwards across the moors to Lochgoin Farm. The house here has various covenanting relics and a monument nearby. The farm road leads to the B764 and the bus back to Eaglesham.

Muirkirk to Kirkconnel 14 mls. (23kms.)
This route follows the Old Sanquhar Road from Kaimes which sits south-west of the disused railway station at Muirkirk. The road heads up the Garpel Water on the west side of Cairn Table. There is a cairn just beyond Kaimes to John Loudon Macadam the roadmaker. According to the plaque 'This cairn marks the site of his tar kilns.' This was a road-making scheme worked in conjunction with Lord Dundonald.

The road crosses the Garpel at the 'Sanquhar Brig', and just before this there is a natural mound known as 'Whiskey Knowe.' According to tradition whisky lies buried below it from smuggling days. It then climbs between Wardlaw Hill and Stony Hill and passes on the left, near the top, the 'White Horse' – a saddle-backed grey stone. Beyond this the track degenerates, until well past the summit where it bears left to contour round Pepper Hill and Drummond's Knowe above the empty house of Penbreck. The area around Penbreck has been forested and the Sanquhar track joins up with the forest road to lead out to Fingland M.R. 754177. The public road from here may be followed to Sanquhar or it may be left again at the 'long turn', where a track continues through the gap south of High Knypes to Kirkland and Kirkconnel.

Several variations to this crossing may be made such as following the Gass Water or the Glenmuir Water towards Cumnock, or taking the old drove road from Fingland to Spango Bridge on the B740. Armstrong's map of 1775 shows a road running from Cumnock to Crawfordjohn by Glenmore (glenmuir), but none between Muirkirk and Sanquhar.

Muirkirk to Glespin by Shawhead M.R. 782219 13 mls. (21kms.)
This route goes between Cairn Table and Little Cairn Table to North Bottom, Greenburn and Shawhead to join the road down Glentaggart.

Douglas to Crawfordjohn 5½ mls. (9kms.)
A direct Right of Way to the east of Auchensaugh Hill.

BIBLIOGRAPHY

Kilmarnock Standard Annual 1962. Loudoun Hill, John Woodburn.

Through the Parish of Muirkirk, James M. Hodge – Arthur Guthrie & Son, Ardrossan.

Muirkirk and its Neighbourhood, Rev. Peter Mearns – Arthur Guthrie, Ardrossan, 1883.

3

The Lowther Hills

This range is conspicuous to travellers following the main road and rail routes from the western side of the Central Lowlands to the English border. These routes follow the valleys to the east and west of the hills.

The range is contained between the A76 road (Sanquhar to Dumfries) down the Nith Valley to the west and south-west, and the A74 (Abington to Beattock) and A701 (Beattock to Dumfries) roads to the north-east, east, and south-east. The hills rise a long way north of Dumfries, so most hill-walkers will recognise the hill-road from Carronbridge past Mitchellslacks to Ae Bridgend as the southern boundary. The B740 Crawick to Crawfordjohn road marks the north-western boundary.

The range is split by two important passes – the Mennock and the Dalveen. These provide useful cross-country routes for travellers moving east-west, and also give easy access to many of the hills. The Mennock Pass rises in 7 mls. (11kms.) from the Nith valley to Wanlockhead at 1350 ft. (410m.) ap. – the highest village in Scotland. The summit of the road reaches 1537 ft. (468m.) before descending to the village of Leadhills where it splits – one branch following the Glengonnar Water to Abington and the other following the Elvan Water to Elvanfoot. The Dalveen Pass is more used and has its summit at 1140 ft. (347m.). The road from Carronbridge runs through it to Elvanfoot without passing any villages.

Leadhills was once the centre of an important mining industry. The area contains deposits of gold, silver, lead and other minerals. Lead mining has been carried on intermittently in the area for centuries but the mines are closed at present. It was thought at one time that hens could not survive in the area due to the danger of lead-poisoning from the impregnated ground, but there appears to be little truth in this.

The mines at Leadhills are mainly concentrated around the head of the Glengonnar Water, while others at Wanlockhead are mainly at the head of the Wanlock Water. Gold from the area was used to make the Crown of Scotland. The largest piece of gold found at Wanlockhead weighed nearly 5 ounces and is now in the British Museum. Individuals still try their luck panning for gold on the Shortcleuch Water and elsewhere, but deposits appear to be too small to make it worth the trouble.

A branch railway from Elvanfoot to Leadhills and Wanlockhead was opened between 1901–3 to serve the mines but closed down in the 1930s.

Large quantities of timber were needed for pit-props for the mines and charcoal for the ore smelting. The bareness of the surrounding regions today may be due to some extent to clearing of the natural woods for this purpose.

The hills are mainly rounded and grassy but heather flourishes on some slopes. The green and brown vegetation on some of the steep slopes is interrupted by conspicuous shallow gullies which end in scree fans, formed by the run-off of heavy rain.

The vast Forest of Ae, planted by the Forestry Commission, stretches across the southern and eastern slopes of Queensberry, at the south end of the range. Ae Village, built in 1947, was the first forestry village to be created in Scotland. Smaller forestry plantations lie to the east of the range, and west of the Daer Reservoir where they are conspicuous from many of the hills. The Daer Reservoir is a remarkable expanse of water in an area notable for its lack of lochs. The scheme was completed in 1956 to provide water for Lanarkshire. It has since been further developed.

Centres and accommodation

Wanlockhead is the best centre for exploring the hills north-west of the Dalveen Pass. It has a youth hostel and bed and breakfast accommodation. There is also a hotel nearby at Leadhills. The hills south-east of the Dalveen Pass are more awkward to reach for those without their own transport, but some of them are within range of Thornhill and Beattock. Those faced with a long walk-in may find useful the bothy of Burleywhag to the north-west of Queensberry (M.R. 971001).

Transport

The region is served by buses operated by:

Western S.M.T. Co. Ltd.	(W)
Eastern Scottish	(E)
Gibson's Bus Service, Dumfries	(G)
J. & J. Leith Ltd., Sanquhar	(L)

The routes covered include: through the Dalveen Pass (W and E), A74 (W and E), A76 (W), A701 (E and G), Dumfries to Ae Village (G), and Sanquhar to Wanlockhead, Leadhills and Abington (L).

SECTION I

NORTH-WEST OF DALVEEN PASS

(1)	**East Mount Lowther**	2068 ft. (630m.)	M.R. 877100
(2)	**Lowther Hill**	2377 ft. (725m.)	M.R. 890107
(3)	**Comb Head**	2060 ft. (628m.) ap.	M.R. 898094
(4)	**Green Lowther**	2403 ft. (732m.)	M.R. 900120
(5)	**Dun Law**	2216 ft. (675m.)	M.R. 917137
(6)	**Lousie Wood Law**	2028 ft. (618m.)	M.R. 932153
(7)	**Steygail**	1876 ft. (572m.)	M.R. 888084

Maps: O.S. 1-inch, Seventh Series, sheet 68.
Bartholomew ½-inch, sheet 40.

East Mount Lowther (or Auchenlone) 2068 ft. (630m.) lies to the south of the Mennock Pass from which it is a very easy climb. Despite its name, it is the most westerly of the high Lowther summits, and makes a good point for starting the traverse of the range.

The shortest route to the summit leaves the Mennock Pass just over 1 mile (1½kms.) south of Wanlockhead. The summit is flat and grassy and has a view indicator erected by the Wanlockhead Youth Club. The view is wide in all directions except to the north-east. Criffel and the Solway Firth are prominent to the south beyond Steygail, and according to the indicator, Ben More, Ben Lomond, Ben Cruachan, the Paps of Jura and Sca Fell should be visible in clear weather.

A path leaves the summit in a north-east direction and leads to the col to Lowther Hill at 1750 ft. (533m.) ap. This col is narrow and has been well trodden as it forms a cross-roads. This is the famous Enterkin Pass (described separately) and the path through here can also be used from Wanlockhead to reach the hill. The Enterkin path cuts obliquely across the col, accompanied by a line of poles carrying power cables, and descends to the south above the Enterkin Burn, with the steep slopes of Steygail almost blocking off the route. The way from East Mount Lowther to Lowther Hill bends eastwards beyond the col, and a road is joined which leads to the summit.

Lowther Hill 2377 ft. (725m.) is only a short distance south-east of Wanlockhead. Like the neighbouring Green Lowther, it is a conspicuous landmark in the district because of the man-made equipment crowning its summit. Lowther Hill carries an important radar station operated by the Board of Trade. Air routes cross over the hill, and a considerable array of masts and buildings holding tracking equipment has been assembled to aid navigation.

A road, which the public may walk but not drive over, runs from Wanlockhead right to the summit, and carries on to Green Lowther. It starts at the north-east end of the village. Like many Lanarkshire roads it is reddish-pink in colour, and it contrasts strikingly with the green slopes of the hill.

The road twists up the north-west shoulder of the hill with Green Lowther on its left above a small reservoir. The upper slopes beside the road can give good ski-ing conditions at times in winter. Some development work has been carried out and ski-tows established, but the hill is not particularly high and ski-ing here is much more of a gamble than in Glencoe or the Cairngorms.

The summit of the hill is on the east side of the radar station but is becoming increasingly hard to pin-point as the station expands around it. It was once a graveyard for suicide cases in the district. About 1 ml. (1½kms.) to the south-east there is a grassy top, shown as Cold Moss on the 1-inch O.S. map. This is named Comb Head 2060 ft. (628m.) ap. in Donald's Tables, but the 1-inch map applies this name to the end of the ridge where it drops to the Dalveen Pass. The shortest route to the summit of Lowther Hill from the Dalveen Pass is along this ridge.

Green Lowther 2403 ft. (732m.) may be ascended dryshod by simply following the road from Wanlockhead over Lowther Hill. The two hills are about 1 ml. (1½kms.) apart with a slight hump intervening.

Green Lowther is the highest summit in the range and this fact has been exploited by the G.P.O. who have established a telephone and radio repeater station on it. Television transmissions for the BBC and ITV are re-inforced here on their journey between Carlisle and Scotland. This station makes slightly less impact on the scenery than the neighbouring radar station on Lowther Hill, whose great white domes show up from here like something from another planet. Winds of 100 m.p.h. (160 k.p.h.) and more are experienced on these hills at times, and the remains of Masts and stanchions that have not stood the strain are scattered around the summits.

The summit of Green Lowther is a prominent hump standing back from the buildings, and is crowned with an O.S. pillar and a small cairn.

The ridge continues in a north-east direction from it, and runs over Dungrain Law to Dun Law and Lousie Wood Law. About $\frac{1}{3}$ ml. ($\frac{1}{2}$km.) in this direction a small rise is crossed. On its far side a fence is met coming up from the east to form an angle on the ridge. Thereafter, the fence follows the ridge to Lousie Wood Law.

Dun Law 2216 ft. (675m.) is separated from Green Lowther's north-east shoulder (Dungrain Law) by a considerable drop. Anyone returning to Wanlockhead from here faces a reascent or some awkward contouring. The hill may otherwise be climbed easily from the Elvanfoot-Leadhills or Elvanfoot-Dalveen Pass roads. The summit is marked by a few stones and lies slightly east of the fence.

Lousie Wood Law 2028 ft. (618m.) sits at the north-east end of this range. A farm road gives access to it up the Lead Burn from the Leadhills-Elvanfoot road. It may also be climbed easily from the Dalveen Pass road, crossing at the start traces of a Roman road.

Most of the walking in this range is over fairly firm ground but between this hill and Dun Law conditions are softer. The fence from Dun Law carries on over the shoulder of Lousie Wood Law cutting across the foundations of an old dyke at its highest point. The summit of the hill is about 60 yards (55m.) west of the fence. The view is extensive, with Tinto's red screes and the Daer Reservoir and its forests conspicuous.

Those making back to Wanlockhead from here, are better to contour across the hillside if the weather is reasonable, rather than descend to the road.

Steygail 1876 ft. (572m.) is a short climb from the Dalveen Pass which lies to the east. The hill is steep on all sides and gives good views of both the Dalveen and Enterkin Passes. It may be climbed on the way to Lowther Hill from Upper Dalveen. At Lower Dalveen there are remnants of an earthenwork dyke that stretched around the valley. This is popularly associated with the Deil's Dyke on the west side of the Nith Valley, which is thought to run through the Galloway Hills.

Hill Paths

Wanlockhead to Muiryhill M.R. 875035 (*the Enterkin Pass*) 7 mls. (11kms.)
A Right of Way runs south from Wanlockhead to Carronbridge and was once the main highway between Glasgow and Dumfries. The original hill-track ran from Leadhills but it is shorter to start now from Wanlockhead. The path is signposted at both ends and rises from the east side of Wanlockhead over the col between East Mount Lowther and Lowther Hill, to descend the west bank of the Enterkin Burn under the steep slopes of Steygail. At Glenvalentine it climbs over a spur and along a ridge to meet the motor road on a bend east of Inglestone. Further south at Muiryhill, where an inn once stood, the road branches three ways – west to the main Sanquhar road, and east and south-east to the road from the Dalveen Pass to Carronbridge.

A party of Dragoons was once ambushed in the Enterkin Pass by Covenanters, and their prisoners released. The Keltie Burn is said to be named after the leader of the Dragoons who was shot at the spot. Some of the Jacobites retreating from Derby in 1745 also used the pass.

Wanlockhead to Enterkinfoot M.R. 856043 7 mls. (11kms.)
This route runs west of and parallel to the Enterkin Pass. Walkers may follow one route one way and return by the other. The start of this route from Wanlockhead is the same as for the Enterkin Pass as far as the col north-east of East Mount Lowther. Then it climbs slightly up this hill and contours west of its summit to the col below Threehope Height. A descent is then made to the south, crossing the Auchenlone Burn. At this point a branch of the track goes off to the west to Glenim, where there are several short routes back to the Mennock Pass. The Enterkinfoot path continues southwards but is difficult to see. It slants uphill towards the Coshogle Rig and cuts through a gap to cross the Ha Cleuch and descend to Kirkbride.

Sanquhar to Wanlockhead 7 mls. (11 kms.)
A road past the railway station at Sanquhar leads north-east to

Dinanrig M.R. 801116. This continues as a track above Brandleys Cottage, contouring high above the Glendyne Burn, to cross the heather slopes west of Black Hill, and drop down to Wanlockhead.

A slightly longer route goes from Dinanrig to Cogshead, north-west of Willowgrain Hill. It then climbs over Glengaber Hill to join the track up the Wanlock Water to Wanlockhead.

Sanquhar to Crawfordjohn by the Snar Water 13 mls. (21kms.)
This starts off as the previous route as far as Dinanrig, Cogshead and the Wanlock Water. Instead of turning south-east to Wanlockhead, it leaves the Duntercleuch track and climbs over Reecleuch Hill to descend to Snar M.R. 863201, where the public road is taken for Crawfordjohn.

Spango Bridge to Wanlockhead 5 mls. (8 kms.)
The route starts just to the east of Spango Bridge M.R. 823179 on the B740 Crawick to Crawfordjohn road, and ascends the Wanlock Water past Clackleith and Duntercleuch to Wanlockhead.

Crawfordjohn to Leadhills by the Snar Water 8 mls. (13kms.)
This follows the B740 past Mountherrick Hill then crosses the Duneaton Water to Snar where the motor road ends. The track continues up the Snar Water to Snarhead and over a col north of Wanlock Dod to Leadhills.

SECTION II

SOUTH-EAST OF DALVEEN PASS

(1)	**Queensberry**	2285 ft. (696m.)	M.R. 989998
(2)	**Earncraig Hill**	2000 ft. (610m.)	M.R. 973013
(3)	**Gana Hill**	2190 ft. (668m.)	M.R. 953011
(4)	**Wedder Law**	2206 ft. (672m.)	M.R. 938025
(5)	**Scaw'd Law**	2180 ft. (664m.)	M.R. 923037
(6)	**Glenleith Fell**	2003 ft. (611m.)	M.R. 922024
(7)	**Ballencleuch Law**	2267 ft. (691m.)	M.R. 935050
(8)	**Rodger Law**	2257 ft. (688m.)	M.R. 945058
(9)	**Comb Law**	2120 ft. (646m.)	M.R. 944075
(10)	**Well Hill**	1987 ft. (606m.)	M.R. 913064

Maps: O.S. 1-inch, Seventh Series, sheet 68 (southern limit on sheet 74).
Bartholomew ½-inch, sheet 40.

Queensberry 2285 ft. (696m.) is the southernmost of the higher hills in the Lowthers and is centrally situated between Beattock and Thornhill, being a prominent hill in the area. It is composed of hard, massive bands of grit and is rounded in shape and rather dull in character, but it is a short, quite pleasant, and popular excursion. There are two main routes to it: one from the side road which runs westwards from Beattock; and the other from Mitchellslacks on the hill road between Carronbridge and the Village of Ae.

The first is a public road from Beattock as far as the bridge over the Kinnel Water at Kinnelhead. A rough road forks left beyond the bridge to Lochanhead, where a bee-line for the summit just misses the forests to the south. Earncraig Hill may be reached along with Queensberry from Kinnelhead, but none of the other high hills in the range are easy from here.

From Mitchellslacks, there is a track running northwards through the hills to the Daer Reservoir. This provides the best route to Queensberry. James Hogg, the Ettrick Shepherd, was herd at Mitchellslacks for a time and completed an early volume of his poems here. Other famous residents were the family of Harkness who were prominent in Covenanting days.

The track crosses two fields beyond the farm, passes through a gate on which a warning is given to 'beware bull', and heads uphill. A branch veering to the east gives a brief bit of help to those heading for the Wee Queensberry, 1679 ft. (512m.) which is knobbly and very distinctive on this side. The main track passes west of the Law by a terrace across this steep little hillock, and continues through a gate to the houses higher up the glen. There is an ancient cairn beneath The Law on the far side of the burn. Once through the gate a line can be taken for Queensberry up gentle grassy slopes above the scenic Capel Burn.

The summit is quite stony and is marked by a large cairn. There is also a smaller cairn some distance to the south. The Blue Cairn on the south-east slopes of the hill is said to mark the scene of a skirmish in which William Wallace was the victor.

Those wishing to continue round the range will find a fence to aid their navigation on the north east shoulder of the hill about 200 ft. (60m.) below the summit. This leads over Penbreck 1998 ft. (609m.), and down to the north before swinging round to the col of Earncraig Hill.

Earncraig Hill 2000 ft. (610m.) lies to the north west of Queensberry and has more character than its neighbours. The south-east face is broken up and presents a fairly formidable slope to those coming from Queensberry. The outlying top of Penbreck on Queensberry is separated from Earncraig Hill by a deep valley. It is a matter of choice whether to cross the glen directly or follow the ridge round, which, as far as the col, is leading in the opposite direction. The fence from Penbreck crosses this col and bends back to Earncraig Hill, meeting the county boundary fence from the north at the summit, and a dyke coming up from the west. Those approaching the hill directly from Mitchellslacks, can follow the path past Burleywhag to the col west of the hill and follow the dyke to the summit.

Gana Hill 2190 ft. (668m.). Navigation can be difficult on this hill, especially if the ridge between Earncraig Hill and Wedder Law is being followed in mist. Although the county boundary runs across it, the summit has neither fence nor dyke. A moderate sized cairn marks the highest point at the east end of the broad summit ridge and gives a good view of the Daer Reservoir. Those who have reached the summit should not be misled by the prominent spur of Garroch Fell 1991 ft. (607m.) to the south-west, which may appear higher.

An awkward stretch of country separates Gana Hill from Wedder Law. Walkers leaving for Wedder Law in mist should go about ½ ml. (¾km.) west, then ⅓ ml. (½km.) north-west, to reach a fence running up the Berry Grain. The fence zig-zags across the col at about 1820 ft. (555m.) and runs up to Wedder Law. A post at the col proclaims it to be the source of the River Clyde, but numerous other spots have as good a claim to the title.

Wedder Law 2206 ft. (672m.), lies to the south-west of the Daer Reservoir. The 1-inch O.S. map gives a height of 2186 ft. (666m.) for this hill slightly to the south of a 2200 foot contour. A casual glance at the map can easily give the false impression that Shiel Dod 2191 ft. (668m.), lying to the north-east on the same ridge, is higher.

Wedder Law is easily reached from the public road along the Daer Reservoir to Kirkhope. It is a straight walk over Ewe Gair and Shiel Dod to the summit, which lies by the fence on the county boundary. There are shooting butts on both sides of the fence at the summit.

The hill may also be reached by the track past Daerhead which runs over the col to the south, or from Durisdeer by Glenaggart.

Scaw'd Law 2180 ft. (664m.): 2167 ft. (660m.) on 1-inch O.S. map. This hill may be climbed from various directions. Peak-baggers will probably find it most profitable to include it in a round from the head of the Daer Reservoir. The shortest route is from Durisdeer over the Blackgrain Shoulder, and Wedder Law and Gana Hill could be included in this outing. The Durisdeer side of the range has more interest than the Daer side and contains some fine glens. The summit is the northernmost of two rises. A dyke runs across it following the county boundary, while a fence leads off to the south to a top called Glenleith Fell 2003 ft. (611m.).

Ballencleuch Law 2267 ft. (691m.) is easily reached from several directions. It sits south-east of the Dalveen Pass and is about equidistant from Durisdeer and the Daer Reservoir. The Well Path (see separate description) runs from Durisdeer to the Elvanfoot road east of the Dalveen Pass, and allows the hill to be tackled from either end. The road alongside the Daer Reservoir gives access from the east.

A fence from Comb Law runs over the summit of the hill, while its

10. Steygail above the Enterkin Pass from the col between East Mount Lowther and Lowther Hill.

11. Queensberry from the Capel Water at Mitchellslacks.

12. The Daer Reservoir and Rodger Law.

13. Lowther Hill and Green Lowther from Comb Law.

14. Looking north-west from Daer Water to the Lowther Hills. Green Lowther is on the left.

15. The slopes of the Well Hill above the Dalveen Pass from Pettylung.

16. The Fortlet by the Well Path above Durisdeer.

17. Glen Afton from Blackcraig Hill.

subsidiary north-east top of Rodger Law 2257 ft. (688m.) has an O.S. pillar.

Comb Law 2120 ft. (646m.) ap.: 2108 ft. (643m.) on 1-inch O.S. map. This hill can be climbed along with Ballencleuch Law from either the Dalveen Pass road or Kirkhope Cleuch on the west side of the Daer Reservoir. Three fences meet just to the north of its summit. One of these runs south-west and leads up on to Ballencleuch Law.

Well Hill 1987 ft. (606m.) lies to the east of the Dalveen Pass and is easily reached from it or from Durisdeer. The round of the small range that this summit commands is well worth the effort for the views of the Dalveen Pass, the Well Path, and the Lowthers beyond them. The slopes above the Dalveen Pass are remarkably steep and are probably the product of ice action and river erosion in previous ages. The Old Toll House beneath the hill receives sunlight for a short time only in midsummer, due to the surrounding heights. But its position in relation to Green Lowther at least gives it good TV reception!

The hill may be climbed anywhere from the pass by those with a head for heights, but the easiest slopes are to the north. The county fence runs north-east from its summit while a dyke starts nearby and heads south-west to the col below Penbane. A good view is obtained from just east of Penbane's summit of the 'Roman' fortlet in the valley.

Hill Paths

The Well Path 4 mls. (6½kms.) runs from Durisdeer to join the road through the Dalveen Pass at a point east of the county boundary M.R. 926085. It is a Right of Way and was once the main route between Edinburgh and the south-west, but was superseded early in the 19th century by the construction of the Dalveen Pass road on the other side of the Well Hill.

The path starts from Durisdeer as a rough road along the hillside enclosed by a dyke. This road is said to have been constructed by the Duke of Queensberry. The 1-inch O.S. map shows a Roman road running parallel to it past a Roman fortlet. The history of this fortlet known as Deer Castle is unknown but it is a well-preserved earthen-work defence. The roads join up and degenerate to a path through the heather. This leads past forest plantations on the far side of the pass to the main road.

Mitchellslacks M.R. 965962 *to Kirkhope* M.R. 963055 6½ mls. (10km.)
This route has already been mentioned for the ascents of Queensberry and Earncraig Hill. The summit of the path is at 1650 ft. (503m.) ap.

Durisdeer to Kirkhope 8 mls. (13kms.)
A rough road leaves from the lower cemetery at Durisdeer and runs south-east up Glenaggart to two empty houses on either side of the watershed. The glen is short and picturesque and leads to a level space between the hills, from which, landrover-tracks lead on to Glenleith Fell, Wedder Law and Par Hill. The path to Kirkhope and the Daer Reservoir goes up the west face of the Berry Rig, and over the col at 1820 ft. (555m.) ap.

The area above Glenaggart is a route-centre for various paths. Various alternatives to the above route are possible. Two routes from Burn in the south diverge around Bellybought Hill. Another starts further east on the Mitchellslacks road and comes up the Garroch Water under the Dod, crossing the col to the Berry Grain Burn.

BIBLIOGRAPHY

Cairngorm Club Journal, Vol. 12. A Famous Pass.
Rucksack Club Journal, Vol. 6. The Hills of Eastern Galloway.
Scottish Mountaineering Club Journal
Vol. IX *The Lowther Hills and Queensberry.*
Vol. XXII *The Lowther Hills.* J. Rooke Corbett.
Scottish Field, June 1964. *Leadhills, Village of the Gold Seekers.* Isobel Knight.
Scots Magazine, Aug. 1962, *The Lowther Passes.* L. S. Paterson.
— Aug. 1968, *The Leadhills Railway.* Robert Kinloch.

4

New Cumnock to Carsphairn

(1)	**Benbeoch**	1522 ft. (464m.)	M.R. 495083
(2)	**Hare Hill**	1950 ft. (594m.)	M.R. 659099
(3)	**Blackcraig Hill**	2298 ft. (700m.)	M.R. 648065
(4)	**Blacklorg Hill**	2231 ft. (680m.)	M.R. 655043
(5)	**Meikledodd Hill**	2100 ft. (640m.)	M.R. 661028
(6)	**Alwhat**	2063 ft. (629m.)	M.R. 647021
(7)	**Alhang**	2100 ft. (640m.)	M.R. 643011
(8)	**Windy Standard**	2288 ft. (697m.)	M.R. 620015
(9)	**Dugland**	2000 ft. (610m.)	M.R. 602009
(10)	**Moorbrock Hill**	2136 ft. (651m.)	M.R. 620984
(11)	**Cairnsmore of Carsphairn**	2612 ft. (796m.)	M.R. 595980
(12)	**Beninner**	2328 ft. (710m.)	M.R. 606972
(13)	**Colt Hill**	1963 ft. (598m.)	M.R. 698990
(14)	**Cairnkinna Hill**	1812 ft. (552m.)	M.R. 791019

Maps: O.S. 1-inch, Seventh Series, sheets 67, 68, 73 and 74.
Bartholomew ½-inch, sheets 37 and 40.

The major summits of this range follow a curved line between New Cumnock and Carsphairn across the junctions of the counties of Ayr, Kirkcudbright and Dumfries. This area is contained within the roads from Dalmellington to Carsphairn (A713), Carsphairn to Moniaive (B729), Moniaive to Thornhill (A702), Thornhill to New Cumnock (A76), and New Cumnock to Dalmellington (B741). The boundaries of this region are clearly defined by the valleys of the Muck Water, Carsphairn Lane and Water of Deugh on the south-west, and by the valley of the River Nith on the north-east. The boundaries to the north-west and south-east are less clear, as in these directions, there is a much less abrupt transition between the high and low ground. For this reason, two subsidiary tracts of wild elevated country should be dealt with briefly here as well: (1) the area between Patna, Dalmellington, New Cumnock and Cumnock; and (2) the area between High Bridge of Ken, Balmaclellan, Crocketford and Penpont. Both these areas offer scope to those in search of exercise but are of much less interest to hill-walkers than the central region. Both suffer from a shortage of definite objectives to aim for, as the countryside tends to be rolling moorland with few features of interest save for an exception like Benbeoch.

Two important valleys lead into the central region and give access to the higher hills – Glen Afton from the north and the valley of the Water of Ken from the south. The 2000 ft. (610m.) summits all lie to the north-west of the Water of Ken so that the area to its east holds less appeal to hill-walkers. This area to the east is fairly hilly nevertheless and has some quite fine glens, even if their hills tend to be too easy and lacking in interest. The valleys of the Kello, Euchan, Scaur, Shinnel and Dalwhat Waters all traverse this area, flowing away from the Water of Ken, to join the River Nith.

The course of the River Nith is remarkable. It rises on Enoch Hill to the east of Dalmellington and heads northwards at first, as though making for the Ayrshire Plain. The river's course was determined in a previous geological age though, which causes it to turn east then southwards back into the Southern Uplands, from which it had almost escaped, to emerge eventually at the Solway Firth.

The Water of Ken and the Water of Deugh, flowing towards Dalry, have been harnessed in the Galloway Water Power Scheme (see chapter 5 section III).

The Afton Reservoir is the only sheet of water of any size among these hills. The absence of lochs is unfortunate scenically as the hills tend to be rounded, grassy and featureless. Only in a few areas such as Glen Afton, mid Glen Scaur, the upper Ken Valley, and on the east faces of a few of the hills, is the rolling nature of the countryside displaced by a more rugged grandeur.

The road into Glen Afton is public to Craigdarroch, and that up the Water of Ken to just short of Lorg. From Sanquhar, cars can be taken up The Euchan Water to Glenglass. The Scaur Water Valley is motorable all the way to Polskeoch, the Shinnel Water nearly to Appin, and the Dalwhat Water to Benbuie.

Carsphairn is the best centre for this range. It has a hotel and is within walking distance of most of the hills. New Cumnock also provides accommodation but is too distant for the hills except possibly as far as Blacklorg Hill.

Bothies

Glenlee (M.R. 606047) – this lies north-west of Windy Standard. It provides shelter but is draughty and in filthy condition.

Clennoch (M.R. 603001) – lies on the south-west of Windy Standard. It was a useful bothy until recently but is now a ruin.

Transport
Dalmellington and Carsphairn are well served by the Ayr-Castle Douglas bus. Thornhill, Sanquhar, Kirkconnel, and New Cumnock have regular services from Dumfries to Cumnock and beyond. Moniaive, Tynron and Penpont have buses to Thornhill, and Moniaive to Dumfries. Buses also run between Dalmellington and New Cumnock.

Western S.M.T. Co. Ltd.

There is a railway station at Kirkconnel.

Benbeoch 1522 ft. (464m.) has considerable character although it is not very high. It is situated north-east of Dalmellington and presents a steep, rocky face to the new Cumnock-Dalmellington road, from which it is only a short walk. A rough road starts on the west side of Clawfin and runs under it to Benbain. This should be followed, and after walking for about 10 minutes, a way can be made to Benbeoch, around or through the large boulder-field under the cliffs. The cliff-line is formed of hexagonal pillars of Essexite, and an ascent can be made without trouble at either end of the face.

A large stone-built enclosure under the cliffs is a herding-point for sheep to protect them from foxes at night. The fish-shaped dyke is head high with an overlapping stone on the outside.

The firmness of the slope to Benbeoch contrasts with those of the Headmark Moss to the north. A Hawker Hurricane crashed here and now lies buried in the moss – all efforts to retrieve it being frustrated by the softness of the ground.

Hare Hill 1950 ft. (594m.) is the summit of a rather shapeless area of high ground south-east of New Cumnock which terminates the ridge running around Glen Afton. It is notable for the old antimony mine near the summit from which specimens may still be obtained. The northern end of the hill is known as the Knipe and is a popular climb from New Cumnock.

Blackcraig Hill 2298 ft. (700m.) rises in a steep, formidable slope to the east of the public road up Glen Afton. The slope is broken by outcrops of rock and deposited boulders, but may be climbed almost anywhere by all but the most inexperienced walkers.

Cars can be taken as far as Craigdarroch where a bridge crosses the Afton Water to Craig. From here a direct assault can be made on the hill or easier slopes taken on the south.

A prominent 'cave' is seen on the hill from the road down the glen. This is situated low down on the burn flowing westwards from just north of the summit. This 'cave' has very dubious historical connections. If it ever was a cave it is no longer one now, but is just a wet and overhanging gully on the burn's downward course.

Another route to the hill is by a track from Blackcraig Farm lower down the glen. This goes over the shoulder to the north and can be followed until the north ridge is gained.

The summit is an undulating stony wilderness with numerous small cairns to confuse anyone seeking the highest point. This appears to be under a well-built cairn about 40 yards (35m.) north-east of the O.S. pillar. There is a small lochan below it. A fence crosses the hill to the south of the summit and continues to Blacklorg Hill, being joined just above the col by another from the east.

Blacklorg Hill 2231 ft. (680m.), lies to the south-east of Blackcraig Hill and is best climbed along with it. The col between the two is an alarmingly soft sponge of wet moss. Crossing it beside the fence ensures that you can always pull yourself out of trouble but the going is slightly drier to the west.

The summit is at the junction of four fences. The fence to the south-east continues along the ridge to the subsidiary top of Meikledodd 2100 ft. (640m.) ap., whose highest point lies east of the fence and has no cairn. Three boundary fences meet to the north of Meikledodd separating the counties of Ayr, Kirkcudbright, and Dumfries.

A ridge from Blacklorg runs westwards to Cannock Hill 1949 ft. (594m.), then bends north-west parallel to the Afton Reservoir to Craigbraneoch Hill 1887 ft. (575m.). This is the prominent ridge that is seen blocking off Glen Afton from the road down the glen. The slope overlooking the Afton on the north-west is known as Stayamrie and is very steep in places. This is a good way off the range as the crags are easily passed. The view from Craigbraneoch Hill is the finest in the area. It looks straight along Glen Afton past Blackcraig Hill, and southwards over the whole expanse of the reservoir to Windy Standard.

Alhang 2100 ft. (640m.) ap. lies to the south of the Afton Reservoir.

The shortest route to this hill is from the road up the valley of the Water of Ken. The ascent can be made from Nether Holm of Dalquhairn by the Mid Rig or by Ewe Hill and Alwhat. The lower slopes of Ewe Hill are forested, but this route offers a view across to the Whigs Hole on Altry Hill, where the Covenanters had a large hideout in a depression. A fence runs over Ewe Hill to Alwhat 2063 ft. (629m.), which lies on the main ridge north-east of Alhang. The county fence continues between Alwhat and Alhang then down to the west.

The ascent from Glen Afton is best made over the previous hills described. A proposal is being considered at present to construct a road from the Afton Dam to the Montraw Burn area at the south end of the reservoir. This is to extract timber growing here but the road should also be of value to hill-walkers.

Windy Standard 2288 ft. (697m.) is a disappointing hill for such a notable name. It is situated south-west of the Afton Reservoir. The most direct route to it starts from Nether Holm of Dalquhairn in the Ken Valley and follows a good path climbing across the side of the Mid Hill of Glenhead. The path crosses the col south of Windy Standard and drops to Clennoch. From the col, easy slopes lead up the south ridge of the hill. There is a large stone known as the Deil's Putting Stone just off the route to the left – a natural hole in its crown would make a hand-hold for a massive limb. On either side of the ridge at this part there is evidence of old mineral workings. Just above the stone, a fence joins the ridge and runs upwards until it meets another running across its path. The summit lies a short distance north-west of here and is bare but for an O.S. pillar.

The hill may also be climbed in a round trip from Glen Afton. In this case it is better to come from Blackcraig Hill, as it is less tiring to descend over the rough grass to the Afton Dam from Windy Standard than ascend this way. It is as well to stay high on this descent as a thick belt of trees surrounds the reservoir. The fence across Windy Standard to the south of its summit is continuous to Wedder Hill above the reservoir.

Trees have also been planted to the north and west of Windy Standard, making an extensive forest around the Water of Deugh. A former path from the Deugh to Glen Afton past Glenlee is overgrown and interrupted by forestry ditches.

The Keoch Rig 2020 ft. (616m.) ap. and Trostan Hill 2035 ft.

(620m.) ap. are both listed in the appendix to Donald's Tables. The first lies 1 ml. (1½kms.) south by west of Windy Standard and the other ½ ml. (¾km.) west by north. Neither are significant enough to be true tops, but there is a top beyond Trostan Hill called Dugland 2000 ft. (610m.), lying about 1⅛ mls. (1¾kms.) west-south-west of Windy Standard. To reach these it is best to start from the farm of Moorbrock to the south, and either go or return from Dugland through the pass east of Cairnsmore of Carsphairn. Dugland has a small cairn but the other two points mentioned have none.

Moorbrock Hill 2136 ft. (651m.) lies to the north of the Ken Valley and can be climbed quickly from the farm of Moorbrock. The slope is quite steep but easy and grassy. The hill is fairly narrow with a level summit cap extending some distance along the ridge. A few stones have been placed together at the north end but the southern end seems higher though it has no cairn.

There is a steep gairy (or rocky slope) on the east side of the hill, repeating a characteristic of Cairnsmore of Carsphairn and Beninner nearby. A conspicuous feature of the view from this hill is the little lochan at the summit of Dodd Hill to the east.

Cairnsmore of Carsphairn 2612 ft. (796m.) is a very easy climb for its size. It lies north-east of Carsphairn and is also known as the Cairnsmore of Deugh. A Galloway rhyme has helped to popularise the hill –

'There's Cairnsmore of Fleet
And Cairnsmore of Dee
But Cairnsmore of Carsphairn
Is the highest of the three.'

The quickest route to it is from the Green Well of Scotland near Carsphairn. The Green Well of Scotland (or Well of Lagwine) is said to be of considerable depth and lies at the side of the Water of Deugh just off the road to Dalmellington. The waters were at one time used as a cure for scorbutic disease but the well has now been partly filled in and is overgrown with reeds. The New Statistical Account relates how a Mr Dodds was prospering by counterfeiting foreign coinage from local ore until officers of the crown appeared on the scene. Before being apprehended, he is said to have thrown his dies into the well. This tale is suspect.

This part of the Deugh is very pleasant, the burn twisting its way through a gorge alongside some fine specimens of ash, beech and sycamore. The route to the Cairnsmore is up the east bank, crossing the Benloch Burn by a bridge starting directly behind two erect and close-growing ash trees. Thereafter the climbing starts, going right of a pine wood to the open slope of Willieanna. Higher up a low dyke is met, and this runs over Willieanna and Dunool to the Black Shoulder 2258 ft. (688m.). The dyke comes to an end on this nose as the slope eases off. A faint path leads on to the summit up a gentle grassy slope studded with granite boulders. The summit has two cairns slightly apart with another one a short distance away at the top of the north ridge.

One of the summit cairns is at the end of a dyke which runs up from the Polsue Burn, which offers another direct route to the hill from the south-west, although some tree-planting has taken place here. This route passes 'the Gold Wells' a spot that one account connects with the forementioned Mr Dodds and another with its veins of mica that reflect brilliantly in the sun.

Beninner 2328 ft. (710m.) is a top to the south-east of the Cairnsmore that is often climbed along with it. The ascent of the Cairnsmore from Moorbrock Farm above the Ken Valley is made easily over Beninner. The slopes are steep and impressive on this side but easy from the south. Beninner is grassy on top and has a small cairn. The remains of an old fence cross the saddle between it and the Cairnsmore. The ground beyond it becomes gradually stonier and the grass shorter until the Cairngorm-like summit of the Cairnsmore is reached.

These hills have distinctive sweeping outlines when seen from roads to the south. The gap between Beninner and Moorbrock Hill is a very prominent feature of the landscape.

Colt Hill 1963 ft. (598m.) is the highest of the hills of this region lying to the east of the Water of Ken. It can be climbed from the bridge over the Lorg Burn near Lorg in the Ken Valley. This route goes past the Whigs Hole on Altry Hill where the Covenanters had a secret hideout in a natural depression in the hillside. The hideout gives a commanding view of the valley and could conceal a hundred people.

The northern slopes of Colt Hill have been forested but a route by the fence from Black Hill is clear of trouble. Three fences meet on Colt Hill at the summit, which has an O.S. pillar.

Cairnkinna Hill 1812 ft. (552m.) is the highest point between Sanquhar and the Scaur Water. It is quite a prominent hill from the Lowthers and other high ground to the east.

South of the road from Carsphairn to Moniaive and Thornhill
Numerous minor roads cross this large area, making any long routes seem artificial – except for those without transport. The hills are too small to offer sustained exercise, but the area has a quality of its own which makes it worth exploring on an easy day.

Glenkiln is a particularly interesting area and has sculptures by Henry Moore, Epstein and Rodin set around the landscape. Bennan Hill 1306 ft. (398m.) to the south-west has a monument at the summit to John Turner who was buried here by his own wish, after he himself had dug out the grave. Bishop Forest Hill 1286 ft. (392m.), north-west of the Glenkiln Reservoir, was the scene of an armed conventicle of the Covenanters. A monument at the Communion Stones on the south-east side of the hill commemorates these times.

Hill Paths

Rankinston M.R. 451143 *to Dalmellington* 6½ mls. (10½kms.)
This Right of Way runs up the hill from Rankinston and round the west side of Kilmein Hill at about 1175 ft. (358m.) to Benquhat. It then drops down to Craigmark and Dalmellington. It is not used much now but was formerly. The area bears the scars of former coal and iron-stone mines and ruins of the hill communities at Lethanhill and Benquhat who worked these mines. A Right of Way also exists between Lethanhill and Patna.

Lamford to New Cumnock 14 mls. (22½kms.)
The start of this walk is just off the Dalmellington-Carsphairn road on a section of older road at Lamford M.R. 521991. The route goes through a gap between Benbrack and Lamford Hill then follows the Water of Deugh north-east to the substantial house at Moor. The area beyond Craignane has been planted with trees, but a way can be made to the ruinous house of Glenlee along the burn or by firebreaks. This is the roughest part of the route, which reaches Glen Afton across the west side of Struther's Brae.

New Cumnock to Kirkconnel by Glen Afton 12 mls. (19kms.)
The road up Glen Afton is followed to Blackcraig, where the river is crossed, and the track taken across the northern shoulder of Black-

craig Hill to join the Kello Water. This is left at Corserig Hill by the road to Corserig and Kirkconnel.

Carsphairn to Sanquhar 20 mls. (32kms.)
This route runs from near Knockgray M.R. 573931 to Moorbrock and Nether Holm of Dalquhairn across the southern edges of Cairnsmore of Carsphairn, Moorbrock Hill and Dodd Hill. The road is then followed to the bridge below Lorg where a track goes through the gap to Polskeoch M.R. 687023 and the road down the Scaur Water. This road is left at Polgown for a track over Cloud Hill to Sanquhar.

5

Galloway Hills

The name Galloway is now usually applied only to that part of south-west Scotland within the counties of Wigtown and Kirkcudbright. Formerly its boundaries were wider and included parts of Dumfriesshire, and the southern part of the county of Ayr, which is known as Carrick. The uplands rising north of the Solway Firth spill over into Carrick though, so that the Galloway Hills are still taken to be the hills of Kirkcudbrightshire and those of South Ayrshire. The northern tip of Kirkcudbrightshire lying beyond Carsphairn has been omitted from this chapter, as the hills there are continuous with those of New Cumnock and have been included in chapter 4.

The area is divided into 6 sections:

(1) The Awful Hand
(2) The Dungeon Range
(3) The Kells Range
(4) The Minnigaff Hills
(5) The Solway Hills
(6) South-West Ayrshire

The ranges of sections 1–4 are all compact areas contained within the roads from Newton Stewart to New Galloway (A712), New Galloway to Dalmellington (A762 and A713), Dalmellington to Straiton (B741), Straiton to Bargrennan (unclassified), and Bargrennan to Newton Stewart (A714). The hills of sections 1–3 run north and south parallel to each other, with the Awful Hand to the west of the Dungeon Range and the Kells Range in the east. The hills of section 4 spread across south of these ranges and are separated from them by the gap formed by Glen Trool, Loch Dee and Clatteringshaws Loch. Sections 5 and 6 have much looser constructions and consist of isolated hill masses. Section 5 lies to the south and south-east of sections 1–4, between the Solway Firth and the road from Newton Stewart through

New Galloway to Dumfries (A712 and A75). Section 6 lies to the west of the other 5 sections, between the sea and the hill road from Straiton to Bargrennan and Newton Stewart (unclassified and A714).

The geology of the region is rather complicated but the major hill areas are composed of sedimentary rocks, generally of Silurian Age, in a thick belt of shales, slates, greywackes, grits and conglomerates (sections 1, 3 and 4). Granite has been intruded into this area (section 2) causing metamorphism in the rocks of the surrounding sections. The isolated masses of Cairnsmore of Fleet, Bengairn, and Criffel (section 5) have also been formed from the granite.

The region contains in the Merrick 2764 ft. (842m.), the highest summit in the Southern Uplands. It also holds three other hills over 2500 ft. (760m.) and has the wildest scenery and roughest walking in Scotland south of the Highlands. The ranges of sections 1 and 3 rise considerably higher than the granite mass of section 2, which they surround. The granite intrusions of section 5 make the dominant hills in that area as the surrounding areas of softer rock have been eroded away.

Galloway lies to the west of the main routes between England and the Midland Valley of Scotland, and has to a large extent, been by-passed by travellers through the ages – whether war-like invaders, industrialists, or tourists. Numerous prehistoric relics have been found in the lowlands round the Solway Firth, but only a few in the uplands. Even the Romans appear to have found the region unattractive as evidence of their presence here is scanty and inconclusive.

Traces of a 'Deil's Dyke' are shown on large scale maps traversing the region. This was thought to stretch from Loch Ryan in the west to the Nith Valley (see also Steygail, chapter 3) and down past Annan to the Solway. The dyke's very existence is disputed by some people while others cannot agree on its origin. It is popularly thought to have been built around the time of the Romans to protect the Solway Plains from the warring tribes of Strathclyde. Traces of the dyke run across the southern edge of the Minnigaff Hills, but are being further obscured by new forests.

Robert the Bruce sought refuge among these hills in the fourteenth century, and three and a half centuries later it was the turn of the Covenanters. Bruce successfully harassed the English occupying army from here and turned the tide against them in the struggle for Scottish independence.

An extensive forest must have covered much of this region to allow

Bruce and his followers to escape detection. Any guerrilla band attempting the same today – outside of the recent forestry plantations – would be easily spotted on the barren hillsides, if it had not succumbed through exposure and starvation. The bleached roots of trees from this forest can be found preserved in the peat at several places – particularly to the south of Loch Doon. Glen Trool and other areas still contain fragments of natural forest while the area is being extensively replanted with conifers.

Most of the region is now owned by the Forestry Commission, who have established the Glen Trool Forest Park which embraces the hills of sections 1 and 2 and parts of the hill regions of sections 3–6. The Commission has the prime duty of growing timber economically, but is sympathetic to the recreational needs of the general public, and the obligation to conserve the scenic qualities of the region.

The Commission encourages hill-walkers to visit these hills, with the only regulations being those that responsible hill-walkers impose upon themselves anyway. A few forests are privately owned – notably the extensive Forrest Estate east of the Kells Range. Several of the numerous lochs in the region have been dammed to provide water for public supply and hydro-electric power, but here again there are few restrictions in force to hinder walkers. Unforested slopes are generally used for sheep-rearing.

The Glen Trool Forest Park covers approximately 230 sq. mls. (600 sq. kms.) and consists of the forests of Glentrool, Carrick, Garraries, Kirroughtree, and parts of Bennan, Clatteringshaws and Dundeugh. The neighbouring Fleet Forest, although outside the Park, is also of interest to walkers, while the hill masses of Bengairn and Criffel are partly owned and forested by the Forestry commission under the Solway Forest.

The Glentrool Forest itself covers approximately 80 sq. mls. (210 sq. kms.). About half of this area has been planted, while the remainder is either too rough or exposed for planting, or is required for sheep grazing.

The Forestry Commission has been much criticised for planting large blocks of close-growing conifers. It is claimed that this shuts out views, spoils the scenery, harms sheep-farming and interferes with wild life. Much of this criticism is unjust in Galloway, as some of the bleakest and most monotonous slopes have been enhanced by the forests, while the range of wildlife is increasing. The re-introduction of trees is returning the area to something like what it was, before factors like climatic changes, warfare, sheep-farming and sporting interests upset the vegetation.

The new forests are invariably in the valleys and on the lower slopes of the hills. These can prove serious obstacles to hill-walkers who do not know the area, but roads have been constructed through all the forests, and, if followed, make the journeys easier than before. The public are normally allowed to walk on the forest roads but are not permitted to drive over them. It is foolish to blunder blindly through the forests. These can be vast and are often extensively planted with Sitka Spruce, which have painfully sharp needles. Information on routes can be sought from people living in the area, or from the Caldons Camp Site in Glen Trool or local forest offices. These are listed in the telephone directory.

There are few paths in the region outside the forests. Walking in the valleys is often tiresome due to the long, coarse vegetation and the ill-drained nature of the ground. Extra time should be allowed for this in some expeditions – particularly around the Dungeon Range, where walking is rougher than on most Highland hills.

Large herds of deer and goats exist in the region. Roe deer are common in all the forests while red deer can be seen in the central hill region as well as in many of the forests, and around their fringes. A Galloway Deer Control Scheme was introduced in 1965, and 1432 Red Deer were counted in a census in that year. The Forestry Commission have set up a Deer Museum beside Clatteringshaws Loch.

There are at least 900 goats in Galloway, living in feral conditions, although they may be descended from domestic stock of earlier times. The goats do great damage to trees and are being excluded from the forests. The Forestry Commission have established a Goat Park near Talnotry on Craigdews Hill, which was stocked with 27 goats in 1970. This will help to ensure the survival of the feral goat, while making them readily visible to the general public, as the Newton Stewart to New Galloway road runs under this slope. Goats are also found on the slopes of Cairnsmore of Fleet, and in Glen Trool, where they have lost their shyness to become a tourist attraction at the car-park.

Adders are common in the Galloway hills. As Britain's only poisonous snake they excite loathing in many people, but they are scarcely a hazard to hill-walkers. The adder is a shy, retiring, and fairly slow-moving creature that shuns trouble. They are rarely seen since they sense the vibrations from approaching feet and move out of the way. Only when surprised or cornered will they hiss and strike. Their mouths are small and capable of biting only an exposed finger or toe, while their strike is limited to a few inches. Hillwalkers in stout boots who keep their hands out of the heather are in no danger. Even those who insist on walking barefoot are unlikely to die from a bite if they are in normal health. Those who wish to see adders can find them best by walking in 'line abreast' formation. Those who prefer never to meet them should adopt 'line astern' order.

Centres and Accommodation

The best centres for exploring sections 1–4 are Carsphairn, Bargrennan, Newton Stewart, Minnigaff, Dalry and New Galloway, which all provide overnight accommodation and are near, if not on, bus routes. New Galloway, Minnigaff and Newton Stewart can also be used for Section 5, while accommodation can also be found at Castle Douglas, Auchencairn, Dalbeattie, Creetown, Gatehouse of Fleet, Dumfries, New Abbey, Glenluce and elsewhere. Ballantrae, Barrhill and Barr are the most useful centres for Section 6.

Camping sites will be found at Castle Douglas, Dumfries, Gatehouse of Fleet, Kippford, Kirkcudbright, Balminnoch, Stranraer and Glen Trool. The camp site and caravan park at Caldons in Glen Trool (M.R. 403790) is run by the Forestry Commission and is open normally from April to September. It lies at the south-west corner of Loch Trool in a picturesque setting among the trees. It has a full range of facilities including a shop and is a splendid base for the hills. Camping is discouraged elsewhere in the Park.

Another Forestry Commission caravan site has been opened at Talnotry beside the New Galloway to Newton Stewart road. Eventually this should be available to campers as well.

Bothies

Numerous shielings and lodges existed among the Galloway Hills at one time. Most have now been reduced to their foundations, but the following still stand and may be of use to walkers:

Culsharg (M.R. 415821) lies to the north of Loch Trool in the valley of the Buchan Burn at the foot of the Merrick. It is now in a very poor state and is only of use in an emergency.

Tunskeen (M.R. 424906) is to the east of Shalloch on Minnoch and to the south-west of Loch Doon. It was recently restored by the Mountain Bothies Association.

18. The Afton Reservoir and Windy Standard from Craigbraneoch Hill.

19. Meikledodd Hill and Lorg from the Whigs Hole on Altry Hill.

20. Cairnsmore of Carsphairn and the Water of Deugh.

21. Shalloch on Minnoch from Craigenrae near Rowantree Toll.

22. Shalloch on Minnoch and Tarfessock above Tarfessock Farm.

23. Kirriereoch Hill (left) and Merrick from Laglanny.

24. The Spear of the Merrick from the col to Kirriereoch Hill.

25. Loch Trool.

26. Loch Trool and the Bruce's Stone.

Back Hill of Bush (M.R. 481843) is a gem of a bothy. It is very remote and in a fine area, as well as being in good condition. It is centrally situated between the Dungeon and Kells Ranges, and between Loch Doon and Clatteringshaws Loch. Two of its rooms are kept locked but the other two are open to walkers. A forest road runs near the door rather spoiling the sense of isolation, but it is well worth a visit and can be an overnight stop on some grand cross-country walks.

Orchars (M.R. 574734) is at the edge of the forest, off a forest road on the south side of the River Dee. In poor shape, but roofed.

Meikle Cullendoch (M.R. 559651) sits on the east bank of the Big Water of Fleet to the south-east of Cairnsmore of Fleet. It may be approached by path or forest road from the bridge or rail viaduct to the south.

Black Laggan (M.R. 469777) The Mountain Bothies Association plan to rebuild this ruin in 1972.

Youth Hostels
Kendoon, Minnigaff.

Some recommended cross-country walks
1. *Carsphairn to Bargrennan* 22 mls. (35kms.). Much shorter with transport at either end.
Leave the Dalmellington road at the Green Well of Scotland M.R. 556945, taking the road to the disused leadmines past Garryhorn. Ascend Bow by a path slanting up the hillside. Follow the ridge to Corserine then drop down to Backhill of Bush (overnight stop). Cross to the Nick between Dungeon Hill and Craignaw going north of the Round Loch of the Dungeon to avoid the Silver Flowe. Turn Loch Neldricken on the east and follow the Gairland Burn to Glen Trool to join the road (2 days).

2. *New Galloway to Loch Doon by Clatteringshaws Loch* 29 mls. (47kms.). Much shorter with transport at either end.
Leave the A712 on the road to Mid Garrary north of Clatteringshaws. Turn off this route once past Upper Craigenbay by the forest road on the left. Continue along this to Backhill of Bush (overnight stop). Carry on along road round Meikle Craigtarson. Leave this at the Riders Rig and cross moor to join another forest road (35 minutes away) going north to join Starr-Loch Head road on east side of Gala

Lane. Follow road along west side of Loch Doon to meet A713 at Mossdale (2 days).

3. *Bargrennan to Minnigaff by Loch Dee* 19 mls. (31kms.). Much shorter with transport at either end.
This route follows the road into Glen Trool then continues as a path beyond Glenhead, passing south-west of Loch Dee and through the gap between Bennan Hill and Millfore. It then descends the valley of the Pulnee Burn to Auchinleck where the public road is joined.

4. *Bargrennan to New Galloway* 23 mls. (37kms.). Much shorter with transport at either end.
By road into Glen Trool, then path from Glenhead to south side of Loch Dee. Walk round Cairngarroch and join public road at Craigencallie. For a shorter route look out for a new bridge over the River Dee at the pass between the Kells Range and Cairngarroch. By crossing the river here the forest road can be followed north of Clatteringshaws to the main road.

5. *Minnigaff to New Galloway by the Old Edinburgh Road* 17 mls. (27kms.).
This route starts off by following the road to the Penkiln Glen. Beyond Kirkland M.R. 424673 the path climbs between Risk and Barncaughlaw and runs parallel to the main road past the Loch of the Lowes, the Black Loch, and Lilie's Loch to Clatteringshaws Loch. Beyond here the route is never far from the main road, being at first south of, and then, north of it.

6. *Polharrow Bridge* M.R. 603843 *to Bargrennan* 20 mls. (32kms.). Much shorter with transport at either end.
By road up valley of Polharrow Burn. Turn off to Fore Bush and take path south of Bennan Hill to the col between Corserine and Millfire. Descend to Backhill of Bush (overnight stop). The route out is the same as for 1 (2 days).

7. *Polharrow Bridge to Straiton* 28 mls. (45kms.). Much shorter with transport at either end.
The start of this route is the same as for 6, stopping overnight at Backhill of Bush. Pass north of the Round Loch of the Dungeon to avoid the Silver Flowe and climb up to Loch Enoch around the south end of Dungeon Hill. Cut across the Eglin and Tunskeen Lanes to reach Tunskeen Bothy (overnight stop if wished). Continue by

Slaethornrig and Cornish Loch to join the Straiton road near Craiglure Lodge (2 or 3 days).

8. *Bargrennan to Loch Doon and Mossdale* 26 mls. (42 kms.). Much shorter with transport at either end.
By road to Glen Trool, then up the Buchan Burn to Loch Enoch turning it on the west. Cut across below the Awful Hand Range to Castle on Oyne and drop down to Tunskeen (overnight stop). Continue to the east end of Loch Riecawr to join the road to Loch Doon and the main road at Mossdale M.R. 494041 (2 days).

SECTION I

THE AWFUL HAND

(1)	**Shalloch on Minnoch north top**	2162 ft. (659m.)	M.R. 400920
(2)	**Shalloch on Minnoch**	2528 ft. (771m.)	M.R. 405907
(3)	**Tarfessock**	2282 ft. (696m.)	M.R. 409892
(4)	**Tarfessock south top**	2050 ft. (625m.) ap.	M.R. 413886
(5)	**Kirriereoch Hill**	2575 ft. (785m.) ap.	M.R. 420870
(6)	**Merrick**	2764 ft. (842m.)	M.R. 428854
(7)	**Benyellary**	2360 ft. (719m.)	M.R. 414838
(8)	**Buchan Hill**	1600 ft. (488m.) ap.	M.R. 428816

Maps: O.S. 1-inch, Seventh Series, sheet 73 (northern limit on sheet 67).
Bartholomew ½-inch, sheets 37 and 40.

The name, the Awful Hand, is suggested by certain views of the range from the west, when the ridges of the four main hills appear like long bony fingers, while Benyellary – a subsidiary top of the Merrick – supplies the thumb to this rather fanciful hand. The comparison is useful in that it distinguishes five high summits with five long ridges running west or south-westwards. All have much shorter and steeper slopes on the east. In addition there is a north top to Shalloch on Minnoch and a south top to Tarfessock, both listed in Donald's Tables, but they are of minor importance.

The range contains three hills over 2500 ft. (760m.) and gives rise to the Rivers Doon, Girvan and Stinchar, as well as supplying much of the water in the River Cree. The hills are wholly contained within the Glen Trool Forest Park and have been extensively planted with conifers on the lower slopes to the west and south-west.

The hill-road from Bargrennan to Straiton bounds this area on the west and offers access to all the summits. The north and central parts of the range can also be reached from Loch Doon, while the southern end is most frequently tackled from Glen Trool. Minor roads run to Ballochbeatties and Loch Bradan in the north while numerous forestry roads penetrate the hills. The Loch Bradan road is private from Knockdon as a new water scheme is being developed.

Apart from being hills, the names Shalloch on Minnoch, Tarfessock and Kirriereoch are also applied to the farms at their bases. These names are given here as shown on the 1-inch O.S. map but the locals know the last two as 'Tarrefessock' and 'Kirrieoch'.

Transport

Buses run between Ayr and Straiton, and Ayr, Girvan, Glen Trool Village and Newton Stewart. While these routes are a long distance from the hills they do allow the range to be traversed by strong walkers.

Western S.M.T. Co. Ltd.

Shalloch on Minnoch (the heel of the ridge over the Minnoch) 2528 ft. (771m.) is a rounded dome of a hill from the west, and the highest wholly within Ayrshire. It is situated at the northern end of the range and is mainly grassy, although the steep eastern face is quite broken and stony.

The quickest way to it is from the summit of the Bargrennan–Straiton road – a sign marks the spot at 1407 ft. (429m.) near a small pilot plot of trees. This route crosses the north top at 2162 ft. (659m.) but is dull. The Rivers Girvan and Stinchar have their sources very close together on this top, while one of the sources of the Doon also flows close to the Girvan.

A slightly more interesting route to the hill starts from Shalloch on Minnoch farm and ascends the ridge between the Shalloch and Knocklach Burns. There is a bridge over the Shalloch Burn near the junction. An O.S. pillar sits on the highest point of the hill with two cairns nearby. A slight dip to the east leads to another rise that is almost as high but has no cairn.

A large flat stone on the steep north-eastern slope above Tunskeen is known as the 'Maiden's Bed'. There is also a 'Session Stone' on the west bank of the Shalloch Burn under the rocky Shalloch Craig Face. This is a flat slab level with the turf and crossed by the path up the burn. It is said to have been used as a pulpit by the Covenanters and faces a small hollow on the other side of the burn.

The hill may also be climbed from Loch Doon by following the road to Loch Riecawr (there is a locked gate at the Loch Doon end). From the east end of Loch Riecawr the route is rather damp as far as Slaethornrig where the face of the hill is tackled.

Craigmasheenie 1769 ft. (539m.) and Shiel Hill 1665 ft. (507m.) to the west of Loch Riecawr, are rough little tops on a ridge running from the Awful Hand towards Loch Doon. There is a gap in the ridge beyond here that is occupied by Ballochbeatties Farm.

Tarfessock 2282 ft. (696m.) is the next finger of the range going south from Shalloch on Minnoch. The easiest route to the hill is from Shalloch on Minnoch Farm by the Knocklach Burn. Accordingly, it is usually climbed along with Shalloch on Minnoch across the Nick of Carclach. The direct approach from Tarfessock Farm is not recommended, as there is no longer a bridge across the Water of Minnoch. It may also be climbed with Kirriereoch Hill (for route see Kirriereoch Hill).

The summit is rough and stony and is marked by a cairn. There is also a prominent cairn of white quartzite boulders to its north and just west of the route along the ridge to Shalloch on Minnoch. South-east by south from the summit there is a south top at 2050 ft. (625m.) ap. in a region of interest to geologists. For on the eastern edge of this low ridge running to Kirriereoch Hill, there is a dyke of pinkish rock where the underlying granitic area comes to the surface. This, along with the light greys of other granitic slabs and erratic boulders, contrasts strikingly with the darker sedimentary and metamorphosed rocks of Tarfessock's summit. This ridge is undulating with numerous outcrops and lochan-filled hollows. It merges into a gentle grassy slope south of Carmaddie Brae then abutts the steep, rocky Kirriereoch Hill.

Kirriereoch Hill (the hill of the great corrie) 2575 ft. (785m.) ap. lies to the north of the Merrick, and is a long way from the road ends at Loch Doon and Loch Trool. It is more easily reached from the west and can be climbed along with Tarfessock. The route leaves the Bargrennan–Straiton road near the ruins of Suie Toll House just south of the Ayr–Kirkcudbright county boundary. A forest road crosses the Minnoch here and runs past the farms of Kirriereoch and Tarfessock. A large fire-break leads through the trees from Kirriereoch offering a straightforward way on to and off the hills by the Pillow Burn.

Kirriereoch Hill is a fairly narrow but rounded ridge, with steep, broken slopes to the north and south. The rusted remains of a fence follow the ridge, leading into a dyke which follows the county boundary across the summit cap. The summit is about two minutes walking south of the dyke at its highest point, and just east of a large cairn. Walkers going on towards Tarfessock have a steep drop from the summit to the flat expansive col. Those going in the other direction to the Merrick see its grandest face across a fine corrie.

Merrick (the branched finger) 2764 ft. (842m.) is a rather retiring hill to the north of Glen Trool and does not flaunt itself before the casual tourist. It is famed for the fact that it is the highest hill on the Scottish mainland south of the Highlands (there is none higher south of Ben Lomond, save for Goat Fell on Arran).

The ascent of the hill is not difficult and is an excellent introduction to Galloway. Glen Trool is the obvious base to start from, and between here and the summit, the hill-walker may sample some of the grandest scenery in Southern Scotland. Glen Trool is often compared to the Trossachs as it is highland in character. It has unique qualities though not a mini-version of a highland landscape. There is a large car-park above Loch Trool and cars should not be taken beyond this. Wild goats frequent the car-park shamelessly cadging food from the tourists.

The route to the Merrick is signposted and goes off to the left opposite the Bruce's Stone. It follows the west bank of the Buchan Burn on a good path and gives excellent views back across the glen. After crossing a stile, watch out for a junction and take the higher branch, indicated by an arrow painted on a rock. The high path winds its way through the forest and emerges at the ruined house of Culsharg.

The slopes have been planted above here, but a path goes up the right side of the dyke by the burn, and this dyke can be followed all the way to Benyellary (the hill of the eagle) 2360 ft. (719m.). Its summit has a moderate sized cairn. The Merrick looks a long way off from here across a dip known as the Neive of the Spit, but the ground is firm and grassy and the slope gentle.

The dyke continues across the Neive of the Spit to the steep, northern slopes of the Merrick about $\frac{1}{2}$ ml. ($\frac{3}{4}$km.) west of the summit. If the steep ground of the Black Gairy is kept on the left there is no difficulty in locating the summit in mist. The shortest route from Benyellary leaves the dyke just beyond the col and heads up the Broads of the Merrick. Thirsty climbers can contour round to the source of the Gloon Burn on the way.

The summit has a large cairn and an O.S. pillar, and several large erratic boulders are embedded near here. The return can be made across Benyellary again or down the steep spur of the Gloon Burn. The latter route involves some rough and boggy terrain in the valley. Those returning over Benyellary can stay with the ridge and follow it over the Bennan to the Fell of Eschoncan. This falls away precipitously to Glen Trool and is a superb viewpoint. The descent is easily made to the east.

Another route to the Merrick from Glen Trool is by the Gairland Burn, Loch Neldricken and its fictitious Murder Hole, and the Rig of Loch Enoch to the east ridge of the hill. This route goes through a wild and very interesting region with constantly changing scenery. The interest is maintained all the way and about 300 ft. (90m.) below the summit, there is a metamorphosed juncture of the rocks where the grey underlying granite meets the shale of the summit.

The Merrick can also be climbed on its western side from the hill-road to Straiton. The ascent from Palgowan is straightforward but unexciting. A much more interesting route is that from the Kirriereoch Farm, by the forestry road east of Kirriereoch Loch and up the Kirriermore Burn. This leads through the forest towards the Kirshinnoch Burn and gives access to the rocky slopes of the Black Gairy, or the shapely spur known as the Spear or Fang of the Merrick, which runs up from the col from Kirriereoch Hill and joins the Merrick right under the summit. This is the grandest side of the hill with fine corries on either side of the Spear. That to the east is known as the Howe of the Cauldron. The 2½-inch map shows the corrie to the west as the Fang of the Merrick. (Dick refers to the spur as the Fang, while McCormick calls the chasm by this name – see bibliography.) The slopes of these corries are steep and very broken but may be climbed almost anywhere by a competent hill-walker. Loch Doon is a long way from the Merrick, but the ascent from there is practicable by the Eglin Lane and the Rig of Munshalloch. The route starts on the road to Loch Riecawr until a branch is taken across the Whitespout Lane near Craigfionn. This forest road is followed until a fire-break leads to a bridge across the Eglin Lane under Craigmawhannal. The east bank of the Eglin is followed until the Rig is reached.

A rock outcrop on the Merrick bears a striking resemblance to a rather grim human face and is known as the Grey Man of the Merrick. It can be found at valley level on the south-east face of the hill in the gap leading to Loch Enoch from the Buchan Burn.

Buchan Hill 1600 ft. (488m.) ap. is the terminal summit on a long, low and very rough undulating ridge that forms the east side of the valley of the Buchan Burn north of Glen Trool. Walkers returning from the Merrick can use this ridge but it is a tiring route. The views are interesting with a fine climax in the prospect down Glen Trool. The Buchan Burn is confined in a hanging valley and escapes to Loch Trool by some fine cataracts above Buchan Farm. A dyke runs along Buchan Hill all the way from Loch Enoch to Loch Trool. Helen's Stone under the Rig of Loch Enoch marks the spot where a woman died.

The Bruce's Stone sits above Loch Trool just past the large car-park that marks the end of the public road. It commemorates a victory over an English force in 1307, by a small band led by Robert the Bruce in his campaign for Scottish independence which culminated at Bannockburn. The English soldiers were reputedly ambushed under the steep face of Mulldonach while traversing along the southern side of Loch Trool. The dead are said to be buried on the 'Soldiers' Holm' – a flat stretch at the east end of the loch.

Rowantree Toll is a lonely junction on the hill-road from Bargrennan west of the Awful Hand. One branch heads through the Nick of the Balloch to Barr while the other makes for Straiton over a shoulder of Shalloch on Minnoch. The foundations of a former inn and toll-house can still be seen here. Close by was the site of a 'Murder Hole' where a pedlar's body was dumped by two men who were later hanged for the murder. S. R. Crockett used the idea in 'The Raiders', although he transported the scene across the Merrick to the much more dramatic-looking Loch Neldricken.

Just north of the road junction there is a cairn capped with a relief model of the Galloway Hills. A plaque on it is inscribed 'In Remembrance of David Bell "The Highway Man" who knew these hills so well 1907–1965'. Davie Bell was a 'rough-stuff' cyclist. His accounts of his travels were published weekly in the Ayrshire Post for 30 years under the name of 'The Highway Man'. He was a legendary figure and made numerous cross-country journeys through the Galloway Hills, and to the summits of the Merrick and other hills – nearly always accompanied by his bike!

SECTION II

THE DUNGEON RANGE

(1)	**Craiglee, Loch Doon**	1715 ft. (523m.)	M.R. 471963
(2)	**Macaterick**	1637 ft. (499m.)	M.R. 438900
(3)	**Mullwharchar**	2270 ft. (692m.)	M.R. 454867
(4)	**Dungeon Hill**	2020 ft. (616m.) ap.	M.R. 461851
(5)	**Craignaw**	2115 ft. (645m.)	M.R. 459833
(6)	**Craiglee, Loch Dee**	1743 ft. (531m.)	M.R. 462802

Maps: O.S. 1-inch, Seventh Series, sheets 67 and 73.
Bartholomew ½-inch, sheets 37 and 40.

The hills of this range stretch in a roughly north to south line between Lochs Doon and Dee at the heart of the Galloway Highlands. Macaterick lies slightly west of this line, while Craiglee of Loch Doon is really part of a minor range on its own to the north.

The Dungeon Range has been formed from granite, and although not particularly high, it contains the wildest scenery to be found in the Southern Uplands. The ranges of the Awful Hand to the west and the Kells to the east are considerably higher, and effectively discourage any normal approaches from these directions. A direct assault on the range is possible from three directions – Loch Doon to the north, Glen Trool to the south-west, and from Clatteringshaws Loch in the south-east, although the last route is complicated by rivers, bogs and forests.

The central part of the range forms a very wild plateau around the rock basin of Loch Enoch, which is one of the highest lochs of this size in the country. This area is sometimes referred to as the Cauldron of the Merrick and was the seat of a glacier in a past age, whose ice moved northwards to Loch Doon and Ayrshire, and southwards into Cumberland and the Irish Sea. We may trace its tracks backwards today from the gigantic boulders perched on lowland farmlands to the chaotic wilderness of rock debris littering the Loch Enoch area. The evidence of glaciation is abundant around here in the corries, moraines, erratic boulders, scored rocks and over-deepened lochs.

The scenery is quite different from that of any other area in the Southern Uplands and is more akin to the wilder parts of the Highlands.

The three main summits are only a short climb above the level of Loch Enoch, and the impression of a range of hills is lost to some extent when seen from the west. The ridges are better defined on this side northwards of Mullwharchar and southwards from Craignaw. Beyond Snibe Hill at the southern limit of Craignaw, the deep glen from Loch Valley and Loch Narroch interrupts the range, which terminates south of this in the rocky little peak of Craiglee above Loch Dee.

The eastern side of the range is much more rocky and precipitous than the western, and consequently the views from the east are grander and more complete. An impressive line of cliffs extend from Hoodens Hill at the north end of Mullwharchar for most of the way past Dungeon Hill and Craignaw. These are broken in several places and an important pass known as the Nick of the Dungeon separates Dungeon Hill from Craignaw. It is something of a route centre for cross-country expeditions in this region.

Walking is generally much easier on the ridges of these hills than in the valleys surrounding them. There are many pleasant stretches of granite 'pavement' on the ridges of Mullwharchar and Craignaw which come as welcome relief after the rigours of the approaches. The valleys are generally wet and spongy with coarse tufted moor grasses cloaking a deep accumulation of peat. In many places along the Eglin, Gala and Cooran Lanes the vegetation grows so thick and high that it is not easy to see where you are placing your feet. It can be exhausting and exasperating negotiating these areas, never knowing whether your step is going to land on the top or edge, or in between the coarse clumps of grass – and even alarming when a deep watery ditch is suddenly revealed below you. Heather grows on many of the hill-slopes and can be a problem also where it masks the hollows around the granite boulders.

The most useful public roads serving the region terminate at Glen Trool, and at the south-west end of Loch Doon, where the Carrick Lane enters the loch. There are also several forest roads which are very useful to walkers, south-west and south of Loch Doon, east from Glen Trool, and north-west from Clatteringshaws Loch. Cars can be taken along the north side of Clatteringshaws as far as Mid Garrary. The forestry road (with locked gate) strikes off to the south before this and follows the east bank of the River Dee and the Cooran Lane up the valley to the east of the Dungeon Range. Keys for the gate are available to anglers for fishing on Loch Dee.

This road runs for 10 mls. (16kms.), passing the bothy of Back Hill of Bush, and ending on the northern slopes of Meikle Craigtarson not far from a forestry road at a lower level running from Loch Doon.

A public road runs round the south end of Clatteringshaws Loch to Craigencallie. There is a new bridge across the Dee north of here.

Warning

A raised bog known as the Silver Flowe stretches between Craignaw and the Saugh Burn. This is a dangerous area to cross and has claimed at least one life. It is now in the care of the Nature Conservancy who have included 472 acres (1·9 sq. kms.) in a National Nature Reserve. The safest route around it is from Back Hill of Bush – where there is a fire-break to the edge of the forest – following a line to the north end of the Round Loch of the Dungeon, or anywhere north of here.

Care should also be exercised in crossing many of the burns. The River Dee, the Black Garpel Burn, the Cooran, Gala, Eglin, Whitespout and Carrick Lanes deserve special respect as they are wide and deep over much of their lengths. A lane in Galloway is a name given to a watercourse connecting two lochs. They can be turbulent and rocky like the Eglin and Carrick on their descents to Loch Doon, or wide, slow-moving expanses of black, sinister water, like stretches of the Cooran and Gala Lanes, which are quite uncrossable for several miles.

Transport

Public transport stops a long way from this range. The nearest bus-points are Carsphairn and Glen Trool Villages. This almost rules out one-day expeditions for those without transport of their own unless they are strong walkers, but the bothies mentioned at the start of the chapter make two-or-more-day outings possible.

Western S.M.T. Co. Ltd.

Craiglee, Loch Doon (the grey crag) 1715 ft. (523m.) sits on a small ridge on the west side of Loch Doon. It may be climbed easily from

Loch Doon Castle and is a good viewpoint. It is worth going over the Wee Hill of Craigmulloch first as the prospect is even better from here.

Macaterick 1637 ft. (499m.) lies south-west of Loch Doon and points a bold rocky face to the north at the end of a long, low ridge running out as the Rig of Millmore from Kirriereoch Hill. It is quite a fine viewpoint for the Awful Hand Range and the northern lochs of Galloway, starting with Loch Macaterick spread out below. It makes a simple climb from Tunskeen Bothy although the moors between it and Loch Riecawr are rather damp. The site of a former bothy known as Cashernaw can be found in the sharp bend made by the Tunskeen Lane west of Loch Macaterick. Slaethornrig, and Anlon's Hut, other shielings to the north-west, have also ceased to exist.

Mullwharchar (the hill of the hunting horn) 2270 ft. (692m.) is a rounded, conical, and rather distant hill about midway between Loch Doon and Loch Trool. It stands just inside Ayrshire, due to the county boundary projecting around it up the Eglin Lane and Pulskaig Burn.

The ascent from Glen Trool is the more direct and involves following the Buchan Burn up past Culsharg to Loch Enoch and passing that loch on the west (for start of route see the Merrick). The route from Loch Doon starts at the road junction at its south-west corner where one branch crosses the Carrick Lane. The other branch should be taken through a locked gate for Loch Riecawr. This road should be left near Craigfionn and another branch road taken across the Whitespout Lane, branching again to the left to follow a road southwards through the forest. From its end, a firebreak leads to a bridge over the Eglin Lane to reach the east bank under Craigmawhannal. A steep little ridge leads up to Hoodens Hill above the impressive face of the Slock to the east. Thereafter, a pleasant level walk over granite slabs leads to a depression and the final rise to the cairn on Mullwharchar.

Those who don't mind wet feet and very rough walking can return by the Pulskaig Burn, south-east of the summit, which rises almost in Loch Enoch. This route returns to Loch Doon by the west bank of the Gala Lane and gives a close look at the cliffs on the east side of the ridge. Just opposite the Tauchers, there is a moraine that is prominent enough to be shown as a small ridge on the 1 inch map. This route also passes the ruins of a house called the Fore Starr to the north-east of the Slock. The Gala Lane can be forded at a point near the ruins to reach a forestry road east of the burn.

Dungeon Hill (the hill above the fastness ?) 2020 ft. (616m.) lies to the south-east of Mullwharchar and may be climbed along with it from Loch Doon, or tackled from Glen Trool by the Buchan or Gairland Burns. The route by the Buchan Burn and Culsharg (see Merrick) is slightly longer but less complicated, although the section around Loch Enoch crosses some very rough country.

The route by the Gairland Burn is one of the best outings in Galloway as the scenery is savage and constantly changing. Starting at the car-park in Glen Trool, descend to the bridge over the Buchan Burn and take a good path slanting upwards across the face of Buchan Hill. This turns into the hanging valley of the Gairland well above the burn. It is a sudden transition from the civilisation of Glen Trool to the barren, steeply enclosed glen. The rushing Gairland Burn is short and one of the most interesting of Galloway's streams. A sluice was once constructed across its head to improve the fishing in Loch Valley but floods have destroyed this.

Another quick transformation takes place as the moraines above the Gairland are passed and the confusion of the upland region is revealed. The way to Dungeon Hill is across the Mid Burn issuing from Loch Neldricken, and round that loch on its east bank. The journey is difficult in mist, but a cairn at the col between Dungeon Hill and Craignaw – the Nick of the Dungeon – is a good landmark. The summit of the hill is rocky and has a small cairn.

Below to the east lie the three lochs of the Dungeon, with the Dry Loch draining to Loch Doon, and the Round and the Long Lochs draining southwards to Clatteringshaws. Just south of the Dry Loch there is a massive boulder known as the Dungeon Stone.

Craignaw 2115 ft. (645m.) is a compact but complicated little hill to the north-east of Glen Trool that is well worth exploring. It is best ascended from Glen Trool by the Gairland Burn and the east shore of Loch Neldricken, working up past the outcrops and boulders of the Black Gairy. A small cairn built on an elongated boss of granite marks the summit.

A remarkable view is obtained from here of the watery network of ditches making up the Silver Flowe. A similar bog existed on the west bank of the Cooran Lane below the Brishie Burn, but the retaining bank burst allowing it to drain away and divert the Cooran to the west The former channel can still be seen.

The sites of two former shielings may be seen in the same area at the foot of Craignaw – one on the south bank of the Dow Burn and the other on the north bank of the Cornarroch strand.

Several small lochs lie high up among the rocks on the hill. The Dow Spout, originating in several of these, is a spectacular cascade after rain, as it plunges over the precipitous slabs of the east face. A large block of granite near the summit is known as the Deil's Loaf, due to its rectangular sides and rounded top. The Deil's Bowling Green may also be found, on the flat ridge running north-west from the summit and known as Little Craignaw. The Deil's Bowling Green is a level platform of rock with a chaos of boulders scattered about it as though strewn by Old Nick in a titanic game. A passage between two rock faces to the east is known as the Wolf's Slock.

The slopes south of Craignaw are broken but gently inclined, until they drop abruptly over the rocky nose of Snibe Hill.

Craiglee, Loch Dee (the grey crag) 1743 ft. (531m.) sits above Loch Dee and is a shapely little peak from the south and east. It is a very complicated piece of ground on the west in which the Long Loch and Round Loch of Glenhead appear surprisingly to the unsuspecting walker. The Rig of the Jarkness to their north, is a rough undulating ridge running parallel to Loch Valley. It offers a way to the summit from the Gairland Glen. Another route from Glen Trool is to follow the track past Glenhead until the south-west ridge can be gained. Both routes are of considerable interest and pass fine tracts of native oakwood in Glen Trool.

Loch Enoch

The size of this loch is extraordinary for its altitude – 1620 ft. (493m.) ap., particularly when it is considered that no burns feed it – save for a trickle here and there. It was formed in a rock basin in glacial times and is at least 127 ft. (39m.) deep from the soundings taken by J. M. McBain. The outlet or Sluice of Loch Enoch is to the north, into the Elgin Lane which feeds Loch Doon.

A small island near the west shore bears a lochan of its own, whose surface is slightly above that of the parent loch. It is known as the 'loch in loch'.

The white granite sands of Loch Enoch were very popular at one time with knife grinders and scythe sharpeners. It is said that fish taken from the loch have been found to have truncated fins due to the sharpness of the sand. The grave of a sand-vendor who expired among the hills lies under Craig Neldricken.

Loch Neldricken

The sands of this loch, like those of Loch Enoch, are famed for their sharpness in knife grinding. The loch is almost cut in two by a promontory running from the north. Its most famous feature is the 'Murder Hole' – a patch of water at its west end encircled by reeds. Crockett used the spot for the purposes of his novel 'The Raiders', and disposed of fictitious characters and almost his hero here. There is no evidence to suggest that any such events took place here. (See also Rowantree Toll in section 1.)

27. The Grey Man of the Merrick.

28. Mullwharchar and the Dungeon Range from Loch Doon.

29. The Gala Lane and Loch Doon.

30. Craignaw, Dungeon Hill and Mullwharchar from the Gala Lane.

31. Loch Doon from Mullwharchar.

32. The Merrick from Mullwharchar.

33. The Nick of the Dungeon between Craignaw and Dungeon Hill across the Saugh Burn.

34. Craignaw and Back Hill of Bush.

SECTION III

THE KELLS RANGE

(1)	**Coran of Portmark**	2042 ft. (622m.)	M.R. 509937
(2)	**Bow**	2002 ft. (610m.) a.p	M.R. 508928
(3)	**Meaul**	2280 ft. (695m.)	M.R. 501910
(4)	**Cairnsgarroch**	2155 ft. (657m.)	M.R. 515914
(5)	**Carlin's Cairn**	2650 ft. (808m.)	M.R. 496883
(6)	**Corserine**	2668 ft. (813m.)	M.R. 498871
(7)	**Millfire**	2350 ft. (716m.)	M.R. 508848
(8)	**Milldown**	2410 ft. (735m.)	M.R. 510839
(9)	**Meikle Millyea**	2455 ft. (748m.)	M.R. 516825

Maps: O.S. 1-inch, Seventh Series, sheet 73 (northern limit on sheet 67).
Bartholomew $\frac{1}{2}$-inch, sheet 37 (northern limit on sheet 40).

This range extends into the parishes of Carsphairn and Kells. From Corserine southwards it is known as the Rhinns of Kells, but the entire range has come to be known by usage as the Kells Range. The summits stretch in a fairly regular crescent-shaped ridge along the eastern edge of the Galloway Highlands. This is the best defined ridge of the Galloway ranges, but the regularity of the western contours has led to a monotonous type of scenery. The eastern flanks possess more character – as in the Awful Hand and Dungeon Ranges. These eastern slopes tend to be rocky and scree-strewn, whereas the western slopes are grassy and generally unbroken. Apart from some of the eastern faces, the range is much rounder, tidier and tamer than the adjoining granite region to the west.

The range is considerably higher than the Dungeon Range, and possesses in Corserine, the second highest hill in Galloway. The ridge-level does not fall below 1800 ft. (550m.) for 8 mls. (13kms.) presenting a formidable barrier to east-west movement. The high col between Corserine and Millfire is a useful pass to the outside world from the bothy of Back Hill of Bush.

Unlike the granite region (section 2), there are few lochs in the range. Apart from Loch Doon, Loch Dee and the Clatteringshaws

Reservoir on the fringes of the range, the only lochs of any size are Loch Dungeon, Loch Minnoch and Loch Harrow which are all in the one area. All other stretches of water are scarcely larger than puddles. Nevertheless, the range makes an important contribution to the drainage of the south-west. On the west side the Doon is draining northwards; on the east the Deugh and the Ken are draining southwards gathering tributaries from the Kells to reinforce the south-eastward flowing Dee. By 1936 all had been harnessed together in the establishment of the Galloway Hydro-Electric Scheme (now operated by the South of Scotland Electricity Board).

Travellers on the road between Dalmellington and Carsphairn can see a pipe-line emerging from the hills at Drumjohn and generally emitting a spectacular spout of water. This pipe has been tunnelled under Lamford Hill to the east to gather the waters of the Deugh and the Bow Burn, and under the northern end of the Kells to connect with Loch Doon.

Loch Doon is a large storage reservoir with dams at the north-west and north-east ends. According to supply and demand, water is gathered here, and some released northwards through the main dam to keep the River Doon flowing, and some southwards by the pipe under the Kells to the Carsphairn Lane to join the Deugh, the Ken and the Dee. The watershed, therefore, has been overridden, and the pipeline under the Kells controls the direction of flow.

Carsphairn stands 580 ft. (177m.) above sea-level, and this fact has been exploited in the scheme. Dams have been constructed to make reservoirs of Kendoon Loch, Carsfad Loch and Earlstoun Loch with associated power stations to generate electricity from the falling water. Similarly a power station at Glenlee exploits the head of water built up in the reservoir at Clatteringshaws Loch, before releasing it to swell the Ken and the Dee for further use at the power station at Tongland.

Another use was made of Loch Doon during the 1914–18 war when a rather ill-conceived scheme attempted to make a sea-plane base of it. Concrete relics of this project are to be found at the northern end of the loch.

Three large forests cloak the lower slopes of the Kells: the Dundeugh Forest to the north-east; the Garraries Forest to the west and south; and Forrest Estate to the south-east. The Forestry Commission control the first two while the Forrest Estate is run by a Norwegian company.

The range is quite well provided with access roads. The main road from Dalmellington to New Galloway passes to the east, but diverges quite a distance from it at the southern end. Several useful roads turn off from this: firstly the roads from Drumjohn and Brochloch to Lamloch, where there is a track to the Woodhead Lead Mines; the farm road to the Garryhorn which is public as far as the Carsphairn Lane and continues as a rough track to the lead mines; the next, travelling southwards, starts at Polmaddie Bridge, is not open to cars and is too far from the hills to be of much use to walkers; then comes the very useful road from Polharrow Bridge, which is public as far as the upper bridge near Forrest Lodge; and lastly, there is a public road from Glenlee to Drumbuie which is of use for reaching the southern end of the range.

This end of the range can also be tackled from Clatteringshaws Loch, where there is a public road to Mid Garrary. The forestry road up the Dee Valley to Back Hill of Bush may also be used although the gate near the road end is kept locked. Another route from this direction is from the end of the public road to Craigencallie, west of Clatteringshaws – as the Dee can be crossed north of here by a new bridge put up by the Forestry Commission.

The road down the west side of Loch Doon may be driven as far as the Carrick Lane and gives access to the north end of the Kells as far as Corserine.

Transport

This is one range where those without transport of their own need not feel at a disadvantage. The Ayr-Castle Douglas buses pass along the A713 between Carsphairn and Dalry, allowing walkers to be set down at one end of the range and picked up at the other, or somewhere in between. The timetable allows expeditions of over eleven hours.

Western S.M.T. Co. Ltd.

Coran of Portmark 2042 ft. (622m.) lies at the north end of the range and is easily reached from the disused lead mines at Woodhead north of the Garryhorn Burn. The mines were founded in 1839 to work galena for its lead and silver. Water-power was used to operate the mines and the community living here numbered about 300 at its peak. The scene is one of desolation now with most of the buildings reduced to their foundations amidst a wilderness of industrial spoil.

A hatch inside a slight depression covers a shaft over 300 ft. (90m.) deep. A gate in a dyke beyond the mines leads on to the hillside.

A path leads uphill from the gate but is indistinct and hard to stay with on the ascent. It is much more useful on the descent. A branch of this crosses the col between Coran of Portmark and Knockower, while the main path slants left of the Coran to the col to its south.

A moderate sized cairn marks the summit of this grassy hill. The ridge becomes more stony to the south at the col to Bow. Bow 2002 ft. (610m.) ap. is a longish ridge with no distinct summit. Three points vie for the distinction of being the highest. The most northerly wins and has been adorned with a fairly large cairn. The southern top has a smaller cairn.

The Coran of Portmark and Bow may also be climbed from the south end of Loch Doon.

Meaul 2280 ft. (695m.) gives a good view of the Galloway ranges and looks the entire length of Loch Doon which lies to the north-west. Coming from Coran to Portmark, there is a small lochan at the col after Bow. A dyke comes up from the left soon after this, and a fence carries on from it to cross north-east of the summit and abut a dyke coming in from Cairnsgarroch. This dyke continues almost to the summit where there is an O.S. pillar.

North-east of the summit is the King's Well, where, according to tradition, Robert the Bruce slaked his thirst. Several mines were tunnelled high up on the west side of the hill at one time in an attempt to exploit the haematite veins.

Cairnsgarroch 2155 ft. (657m.) is an outlying summit on the east of this range. The dyke from Meaul runs across its crown, with a small cairn to the south marking the summit, and a larger cairn to the north indicating the way back to the lead mines by the north-east ridge. There is an old mine shaft running into the hillside on this ridge. A series of moraines known as the Lumps of Garryhorn are worth seeing in the corrie to the north-west of the hill.

Carlin's Cairn 2650 ft. (808m.) to the south of Meaul, has been rather harshly treated in Donald's Tables where it is classed only as a top of Corserine. There is a fair drop on all sides, and with its fairly narrow ridge, it is the most distinctive peak in the range. The distinction is aided by the massive cairn crowning the summit. Legend attributes the building of this to a miller's wife, who aided Robert the Bruce in his fugitive days, and was rewarded later with a grant of land in the Polmaddy Glen. The cairn has been much altered in shape by visitors fashioning wind-breaks and seats from it.

The hill is usually climbed along with Meaul from the Woodhead Lead Mines, or the bridge over the Carrick Lane at the foot of Loch Doon. An old drove road from Loch Doon ran over the col between Carlin's Cairn and Meaul to Castlemaddy.

Corserine (the crossing of the ridges) 2668 ft. (813m.) is the central point of the range, and gets its name from the cross-formation of its four ridges. The east ridge divides further into a north-east and a south-east branch. The hill is a great rounded whale-back, but there are steep broken slopes on the faces to the north and east. Four air-craft are reported to have been wrecked on the hill.

The shortest ascent is from near Forrest Lodge to the east, starting at the end of the public road where a bridge crosses the Polharrow Burn. Private roads run off from here to Forrest Lodge, Fore Bush and Burnhead. Walkers should take the Fore Bush road past a sawmill. This goes through plantations around Fore Bush to Loch Harrow which has a ruined boat house and was a popular loch for curlers. The route then goes over North Gairy Top 2233 ft. (681m.) and on to Corserine, which is expansive with an O.S. pillar standing starkly on the highest point.

The hill can be reached from the foot of Loch Doon without too much effort if the correct route is taken. The important point is to avoid the energy-sapping bogs that lie along the Gala Lane. This can be done by following a forestry road which strikes south from the Loch Head road just east of the bridge over the Gala Lane. The road is followed for about 2 mls. (3kms.) until it turns to the right back to the burn, where it ends. The route to Corserine goes up the Riders Rig and over Meikle Craigtarson.

A house stood at one time between Little Craigtarson and the March Burn. This was called Hunt Ha' and was the meeting place for farmers and shepherds on days set aside for fox-hunting. The Rev. C. H. Dick refers to Hunt Ha' as one of Lord Kennedy's hunting lodges about the end of the fourteenth century.

The March Burn is the highest source of the River Dee as it starts just below the summit of Corserine. The bothy of Back Hill of Bush stands in a clearing in the forest on Downies Burn in this area.

Another house, known as Downies' Shiel, stood a short distance away on the other side of the burn but no longer exists.

Milldown 2410 ft. (735m.) ap. is situated to the south-west of Loch Dungeon. The route to Corserine from Fore Bush should be followed for this hill as far as Loch Harrow. Then, if Corserine is not to be included in the outing, follow a fire-break by a dyke through the gap west of Bennan Hill nearly to Loch Minnoch. Other fire-breaks lead south, then west to the edge of the forest under Millfire, with little climbing having been done.

On the north-east bank of the Hawse Burn, a circular dyke encloses a cairn marking the death of a shepherd when nearly home. A plaque on it is inscribed:

'Erected to the Memory of Ralph Forlow
The Brave Shepherd Boy who died in the blizzard
of 27th, January 1954 aged 17 years
'Gie him his place amang the great
The Men o'war or kirk or state
An add this message chiselled deep
The guid herd died to save his sheep.'

Steep, broken slopes west of Loch Dungeon (not to be confused with the three smaller Lochs of the Dungeon – section 2) lead on to the Kells. Some vegetatious scrambles on unreliable rock may be undertaken here, or easier slopes can be sought nearer to Corserine. There is a remarkable contrast between the black, craggy slopes of Millfire and Milldown, where the shale is exposed, and the smooth, grassy dome of Corserine. The gap between Corserine and Millfire is marked by a cairn on the route between the Fore Bush and Back Hill of Bush houses. A funeral party carrying the wife of a shepherd from the Back Bush ran into a blizzard in this pass, and had to dump the coffin here for three days before carrying on. There is a prominent group of moraines below the pass at the head of the Hawse Burn.

South-east of the pass, the ridge rises to Millfire 2350 ft. (716m.), which has two cairns slightly apart. This is the north-west top of Milldown. A dyke runs across the col south of this top, where another dyke leads from it to the summit of Milldown.

Meikle Millyea 2455 ft. (748m.) is the most southern of the major summits of the range. Most walkers will want to visit this hill along with Milldown. A gentle slope leads from the one to the other past the Lochans of Auchniebut. The north end of Meikle Millyea has a cairn and an O.S. pillar, but the south-west end with another cairn, is slightly higher.

The dyke from Milldown runs over Meikle Millyea and on down its south-west ridge. Those returning to the Polharrow Bridge should take the north-east ridge to a rocking stone, shown on the map, which no longer rocks. A steep descent leads to a gate at the corner of the forest. Fire-breaks running east lead to a road to Burnhead. There is a fork on this road – the left branch going to Loch Minnoch and the right to Burnhead.

Those heading for Glenlee should turn right at the rocking stone and go over the Rig of Clenrie to Drumbuie.

Loch Doon Castle

Several islands in Loch Doon were submerged in 1936 with the raising of the level for hydro-electric purposes. Loch Doon Castle had stood on one of these for over 600 years, and to preserve it, the Ministry of Works numbered each stone and dismantled the curtain wall and parts of the interior. They then rebuilt it higher up on the west bank of the loch with the same orientation, so that the gateway now faces into the hillside. The castle has eleven unequal sides and was a seat of the Lords of Carrick. The island, with the foundations of the castle on it, still shows above the water when the loch is low.

The Bruce's Stone

This stands a short distance north of the New Galloway–Newton Stewart road at the east end of Clatteringshaws Loch. It is signposted but is not quite so well known as the famous cairn of the same name in Glen Trool. This stone is a massive granite boulder and commemorates the Battle of Raploch Moss in 1307 when Bruce defeated an English force. It is in the care of the National Trust for Scotland and may be seen at any time.

SECTION IV

THE MINNIGAFF HILLS

(1)	**Larg Hill**	2216 ft. (675m.)	M.R. 425757
(2)	**Lamachan Hill**	2350 ft. (716m.)	M.R. 435770
(3)	**Curleywee**	2212 ft. (674m.)	M.R. 455769
(4)	**Millfore**	2151 ft. (656m.)	M.R. 478755
(5)	**Craignell**	1550 ft. (472m.) ap.	M.R. 510752

Maps: O.S. 1-inch, Seventh Series, sheet 73.
Bartholomew ½-inch, sheet 37.

This range is contained in the angle between the roads from Clatteringshaws Loch to Newton Stewart and Newton Stewart to Glentrool Village, and is bounded to the north by the trough of Glen Trool, the Glenhead Burn, Loch Dee, the River Dee and Clatteringshaws Loch.

Whereas the hills of the previous three sections lie in ranges running from north to south, these hills have adopted a more east to west order. The range is more divided than the previous three and is bisected at 1300 ft. (400m.) at the Loup of Laggan – the gap between the valleys of the Pulnee and White Laggan Burns. An old pony track followed this route into the hills, running from the Penkiln Glen to Loch Dee and Glen Trool. It is difficult to find in the Penkiln Glen now because of the forest, but a route from Drigmorn can be taken to the east of the trees.

The boundary of the Glen Trool Forest Park runs over the col between Larg Hill and Lamachan Hill. The summit of the former is outside the park and most of the slopes south and west of it are unforested, save for the pleasant deciduous woodlands fringing the minor road east of the River Cree. Large forests extend around much of the rest of the area, restricting access to a few well-defined routes.

The northern side of the range may be reached from the road into Glen Trool, starting either at the Bruce's Stone or the Caldons Camp

35. Loch Enoch from the summit of Craignaw. The Merrick is in cloud.

36. Benyellary and Loch Neldricken from the slopes of Craignaw.

37. Loch Enoch and the Awful Hand from the slopes of Craignaw.

38. The north end of the Kells Range from Loch Doon.

39. Cairnsgarroch from the lead-mines above the Garryhorn. Meaul is hidden by the trees.

40. Cairnsgarroch, Meaul and Bow from the road north of Carsphairn. Note the moraines around the Carsphairn Lane.

41. Glacial debris in the valley of the Gala Lane under Carlin's Cairn and Corserine.

42. *Opposite above.* Corserine and Carlin's Cairn from Meaul.

43. *Below.* Carlin's Cairn.

44. *Opposite below.* Loch Doon from Carlin's Cairn.

45. North Gairy Top of Corserine from Loch Harrow.

46. Approaching Corserine from Meikle Craigtarson. Benyellary, the Merrick, and Kirriereoch Hill are on the horizon above Dungeon Hill and Mullwharchar.

47. Millfire and the cairn to Ralph Forlow.

48. The Awful Hand and Dungeon Ranges from Meikle Millyea. The Merrick is seen above the Nick of the Dungeon.

49. Larg Hill from Lamachan Hill.

50. Curleywee (left) from the col from Lamachan Hill.

Site. A very useful road from Minnigaff leads up the Penkiln Glen on the south side of the range. This is public to Auchinleck Farm. The eastern end of the range may be reached from the Craigencallie road west of Clatteringshaws Loch, or from Craigdews on the Newton Stewart–New Galloway road.

Transport
The hills are a fairly long way from the bus routes. Newton Stewart, Clachaneasy, Glentrool Village and New Galloway are possible starting points for strong walkers relying on public transport.
Western S.M.T. Co. Ltd.

Larg Hill 2216 ft. (675m.) lies on the western edge of the range. The shortest route to it is by the forestry road running southwestwards from the Caldons camp site. There is a martyr's tomb near this road on the west side of the camp site where several Covenanters were surprised and killed. This road heads towards another coming up from the bridge over the Minnoch near Clachaneasy, and leads into the corrie north-west of the summit.

The best approach from the south is by the Penkiln Glen. A forest road runs 4 mls. (6½kms.) up the glen from a locked gate at the bridge over the burn south-west of Auchinleck. This route is direct and has an easy gradient. Fire-breaks lead on to the hill near the unroofed house of Lamachan, and a dyke is met which runs past the summit. A small cairn on the west side of the dyke marks the highest point. The hill also has a small top to the south-west at 2159 ft. (658m.) but this is not distinguished enough to merit a place in Donald's Tables.

In 'the Merrick and the Neighbouring Hills', J. McBain states that a small airship was wrecked on the face of Larg Hill during a storm in 1917. All of the crew survived.

Lamachan Hill 2350 ft. (716m.) lies to the south-east of Loch Trool and is usually climbed along with Larg Hill. A dyke runs from Larg Hill to the col, meets with a fence coming up from the right, and swings north-westwards off the ridge. The pass here is known as the Nick of the Brishie, and an old fence may be followed from here to the summit of Lamachan Hill, which is beside another dyke running west to east over it.

An interesting route from the Caldons is to follow the forest walk along the south side of Loch Trool (booklet available), and strike up at a convenient point over the rugged slopes of Mulldonoch 1827 ft. (557m.). This is the way an English force is said to have come to its doom in 1307, when the Scots under Bruce ambushed them. The English were proceeding in a file along the track when the waiting Scots let loose a landslide of boulders on them, and charged down to finish off the affair, at the Steps of Trool.

Mulldonoch is a fine little hill with good views of the Merrick and of the valley running from Glen Trool to Loch Dee. There is a short drop from it to the south to the Nick of the Lochans, where the north-east ridge of Lamachan Hill starts.

Curleywee (the hill in the wind) 2212 ft. (674m.), to the south-west of Loch Dee, is one of the most impressive hills in the Southern Uplands. This is due to its steep conical shape and the blackness of its shale screes, which contrast with the grassy slopes around it. The circuit of Larg Hill, Lamachan Hill and Curleywee makes a good outing from Glen Trool or the Penkiln Glen.

The route from Lamachan Hill is fairly rugged and goes over two small rises – one at the end of Lamachan Hill and the other in the col. A line of old fence posts from Lamachan Hill to the col below Curleywee is a good aid in mist. Then comes a steep pull-up past the screes of Curleywee to its summit, where there is a small cairn. A ridge runs north-eastwards from the summit over White Hill and is surrounded by steep slopes, but the way down to the north is fairly easy and obvious. The ruins of two bothies lie on the east side of the hill – the White Laggan and the Black Laggan. The path past the White Laggan leads back to Glen Trool.

If the start has been made from the Penkiln Glen the same path may be taken in the opposite direction from the col south-east of Curleywee. This path is boggy and indistinct in places but leads to the house at Drigmorn where a forestry road is joined for Auchinleck. Alternatively, the forestry road down the Penkiln Burn can be taken under the Nick of Curleywee. This gives a much less arduous walk.

Millfore (the cold hill?) 2151 ft. (656m.) lies to the south of Loch Dee and is easily reached from the Newton Stewart–New Galloway road starting from either the car park at Murray's Monument or Craigdews. The first route follows a path up the Grey Mare's Tail Burn, which has a fine waterfall – one of several Grey Mare's Tails in the Southern Uplands – and cuts round the back of Craigdews Hill to the Black Loch. The route from Craigdews is by a forest road on the other side of the hill and also passes the Black Loch. The Old Edinburgh Road also passes this loch, running parallel to the main road. It is overgrown in places but is an interesting track for walkers.

Continue on the forest road as it leaves the Black Loch and winds up the south-east ridge of Millfore. Leave it where it swings right over Poultrybuie Hill, and head straight for Millfore along a fire-break. Thereafter the ascent can be made from the corrie or by the ridge on its right. The forest road continues round the east side of Millfore and down the Fore Burn towards Craigencallie.

Craigencallie can be reached by a good but narrow road running along the west side of Clatteringshaws Loch. This road offers another starting point for the hill from the point where it crosses the Craigencallie Lane. From here, head up the Fore Burn on the forest road, until the steep and rocky north-eastern slopes of Millfore are passed.

The hill can also be climbed from Auchinleck in the Penkiln Glen or from Glen Trool by the path south of Loch Dee, but both these routes are longer.

There are several cairns on the main ridge. The highest point is shared by an O.S. pillar and a moderate sized cairn. The south-west shoulder of the hill exceeds 2000 ft. (610m.) and is listed in the appendix to Donald's Tables.

The White Lochan of Drigmorn is conspicuous to the west of the main summit. It is a large sheet of water for this elevation and used to be popular with curlers. A small building was erected beside it at the time of the Crimean War by military officers.

Millfore is fairly detached from the other Galloway Hills and is a good viewpoint for Cairnsmore of Fleet and the Lamachan, Dungeon and Kells ranges. Anyone thinking of penetrating to the heart of the Galloway Hills for the first time will benefit from a reconnaissance here first.

Cairngarroch 1829 ft. (557m.) is a stony mound of a top terminating the main ridge north-east of Millfore. Being farther to the north it gives an even better view into the wild region known as the Dungeon of Buchan which lies beyond the Cooran Lane. A large outcrop of granite cliff to its north-east is known as Craigencallie (the old wife's crag?) above the house of that name. According to tradition, Robert the Bruce was aided by an old woman and her three sons here and rewarded them with a grant of land.

Craignell 1550 ft. (472m.) ap. is a rocky and very broken hill lying to the north of the Newton Stewart–New Galloway road and to the west of Clatteringshaws Loch. It is best reached by fire-breaks from the road to Craigencallie west of the loch. Numerous small lochans fill hollows on the rough summit cap. Darnaw and Low Craignell are two tops to the north and east. Darnaw has a memorial cairn to the north-east of its summit commemorating the four occupants of the Daily Express aircraft 'Dragon Fly'. The plane crashed here on 2 February, 1937, and its wreckage is still strewn around the cairn.

Murray's Monument is a conspicuous landmark on the north side of the road between Newton Stewart and New Galloway. It is a tall granite obelisk set on a hillock above Talnotry and commands attention from those climbing Millfore or Cairnsmore of Fleet from this direction. It commemorates Alexander Murray, born in this area at Dunkitterick, whose facility with languages earned him the post of Professor of Oriental Languages at Edinburgh University from 1812 until his death the following year. The ruins of his birthplace can be found about 1 ml. (1½kms.) east of the monument on the south side of the road.

SECTION V

THE SOLWAY HILLS

(1)	**Cairnsmore of Fleet**	2331 ft. (710m.)	M.R. 502671
(2)	**Knee of Cairnsmore**	2154 ft. (657m.)	M.R. 509654
(3)	**Meikle Mulltaggart**	2000 ft. (610m.)	M.R. 512678
(4)	**Craignelder**	1971 ft. (601m.)	M.R. 505699
(5)	**Cairnharrow**	1496 ft. (456m.)	M.R. 533561
(6)	**Fell of Fleet**	1544 ft. (471m.)	M.R. 566707
(7)	**Cairnsmore of Dee**	1616 ft. (493m.)	M.R. 584758
(8)	**Bengairn**	1283 ft. (391m.) ap.	M.R. 771545
(9)	**Criffel**	1868 ft. (569m.)	M.R. 957619

Maps: O.S. 1-inch, Seventh Series, sheets 73 and 74.
Bartholomew ½-inch, sheet 37 (eastern limit on sheet 38).

The Galloway hills described in the previous four sections have all formed parts of fairly well-defined ranges. The hills of this section form a much more loosely-knit region in which uplands and lowlands are intermingled.

The region is bounded to the north by the roads between Newton Stewart and New Galloway (A712), and New Galloway and Dumfries (A712 and A75); to the west by Wigtown Bay and the River Cree; to the east by the River Nith; and to the south by the Solway Firth.

This is a much more fertile and populated region than those of the previous four sections, with a good balance between uplands and lowlands, farming and forestry, and rural and urban life – although unemployment, depopulation and cuts in public transport are major problems.

The upland areas of Criffel, Bengairn and Cairnsmore of Fleet are granite intrusions into a peaceful landscape. Only in Cairnsmore of Fleet does the ground rise above 2000 ft. (610m.). It is the largest and wildest area in the region, lies adjacent to the Minnigaff Hills, and may be considered as a continuation of the wild country forming sections 1–4.

The more lowland character of this region is reflected in its greater number of roads – which allow the hills to be climbed from a number of directions. Even the wild area around Cairnsmore of Fleet has numerous forest roads, and many of these are worth exploring for their own sakes, as they frequently pass through country that is out of sight from the public roads.

Transport
Buses between Dumfries and Stranraer pass through Gatehouse of Fleet, Creetown and Newton Stewart near to several of the hills. Bengairn can be reached by a service from Dalbeattie to Auchencairn and Kirkcudbright (A711) and by another from Castle Douglas to Kirkcudbright (B727).

Western S.M.T. Co. Ltd.

A service between Dumfries, New Abbey, Kirkbean and Rockcliffe is useful for Criffel.

Carruthers Bus Service (New Abbey).

Cairnsmore of Fleet (the great hill of Fleet) 2331 ft. (710m.) lies to the east of Newton Stewart. There are two short routes to this hill: the first from the road between Newton Stewart and Creetown; and the second from the road between Newton Stewart and New Galloway.

For the first, leave the main road south of Palnure and take the minor road past Muirfad. Fork right beyond the viaduct for Cairnsmore. At the next fork, veer right again, then pass left around the farm and take the second of two roads going off to the left. This leads into a field and continues as a track up the grassy slopes north of Crammery Hill. Emerging on the ridge of Cairnsmore of Fleet it turns left to the summit. This is a quick but unexciting route which allows the southern top to be visited on the way back – the Knee of Cairnsmore 2154 ft. (657m.).

The second route starts north-east of Newton Stewart where a forest road leaves the New Galloway road for Dallash and Corwar. Bear left on this road ignoring three branches going off to the right. This crosses the Palnure Burn by a low concrete bridge (a footbridge nearby leads only to the fields). Carry on past Corwar going through a gate and following the forestry road as it winds up the slope between the Crochan and Lauran Burns amidst pine and spruce plantations. The second bend to the right leads into a long straight slope approaching very close to the Lauran Burn. Abandon the road at this point and pass out of the forest to the burnside. The north-west ridge of the Cairnsmore rises from here and gives a straight-forward route to the summit.

The hill has gentle grassy slopes to the south-west and steep, rocky outcrops to the north and east. The ridge between them is broad and fairly level. The summit is crowned by a large cairn, an O.S. pillar and the ruins of a small stone building. The pilot of a Tiger Moth is said to have landed his plane on this summit and taken off again, but wreckage from another plane is strewn around the summit and down the rocks to the north. According to locals this was a German Heinkel bomber which crashed in 1941.

The north and east faces of the hill are chaotic with strewn granite boulders, and several of these are large enough to provide rough shelter for a night. There is also a large howff in the form of an underground cave at the north end of the hill. An iron bar projects from the boulder above it as a marker but it is still hard to find. The cave is said to have been used in the past by the notorious Galloway tinker Billy Marshall and his gang. On the other hand, tradition has it that Billy's Cave lies at the southern end of the hill.

There is another top ¾ ml. (1¼kms.) north-east of the summit – Meikle Mulltaggart 2000 ft. (610m.) ap. This has little character to it but it is on the round to Craignelder.

Craignelder 1971 ft. (601m.) is an outlying hill at the north end of the Cairnsmore of Fleet range. It has a steep imposing face to the south-west and is separated from the Cairnsmore by a very rough ridge. It can be climbed along with the Cairnsmore quite easily from the Newton Stewart–New Galloway road. The round is best accomplished from Corwar (see Cairnsmore of Fleet).

Craignelder on its own can be reached easily from Murray's Monument, although the shortest route involves fording the Palnure Burn. One point on the cliffs west of the summit is known as the 'flesh market' from the number of sheep that have fallen here. Wild goats can usually be seen in the area between Craignelder and Cairnsmore of Fleet.

Cairnharrow 1496 ft. (456m.) is the highest hill in the area between Cairnsmore of Fleet and the Cree estuary. Consequently it is a good hill from which to view the Solway coastline. It is easily climbed from Whiteside on the Corse of Slakes road between Creetown and Skyreburn Bay or from near Kirkdale on the coast road. The ascent may be combined with a visit to Cairnholy where there are two chambered cairns.

Fell of Fleet 1544 ft. (471m.) to the west of New Galloway Station is surrounded by forests, but may be reached easily from the south end of Clatteringshaws Loch. A forest road on the west side of the River Dee leads between the hill and Loch Grannoch.

Shaw Hill 1255 ft. (383m.) can also be reached from here across the Nick of Orchars. An obelisk to the south-east of Shaw Hill commemorates four Covenanters shot at the spot. It is difficult to find in the forest, but can be reached by fire breaks.

Cairnsmore of Dee (the great hill of Dee) 1616 ft. (493m.). This hill is also known as the Black Craig of Dee and rises steeply to the south of the Newton Stewart–New Galloway road east of Clatteringshaws Loch. It can be climbed quickly from this road but is a tougher climb than it looks.

The shortest route starts at the east end of the forest but requires a hefty jump to clear the Knocknairling Burn. The route then goes up the fence through boggy ground on to the steep heather slopes. It is better to slant left over these with the fence rather than tackle the thick undergrowth direct. Once the ridge is gained the summit will be found to the south. It has a large cairn and an O.S. pillar beside a small lochan.

The view is one of the best in Galloway. It takes in Cairnsmore of Fleet, Clatteringshaws Loch, The Minnigaff, Awful Hand, and Kells Ranges, the Carsphairn and New Cumnock Hills, the Lowthers, Criffel, Bengairn, the Lake District, Isle of Man, Ireland and the Mull of Galloway.

The hill can also be climbed from the Newton Stewart road by fire-breaks farther west. One of these leads to the col west of the summit, from which Benniguinea 1270 ft. (387m.) can also be climbed. It has a look-out tower above the forest and gives a fine view of Clatteringshaws Loch.

Bengairn 1283 ft. (391m.) ap. sits on a raised beach south of Castle Douglas and is a prominent hill from the Solway coast. It is best climbed along with its neighbour Screel Hill 1126 ft. (343m.) although

51. Lamachan Hill, Curleywee and Benyellary from Millfore.

52. Goats at Craigdews above the New Galloway road. Murray's Monument is on the right near the skyline.

53. Cairnsmore of Fleet across Clatteringshaws Loch.

54. Cairnsmore of Carsphairn from Cairnsmore of Dee.

55. Sunset over the Lamachan Range and Clatteringshaws Loch from Cairnsmore of Dee.

56. Bengairn and Screel Hill from Kippford.

57. Rough Firth and Orchardton Bay on the Solway from Screel Hill.

58. The summit of Criffel looking south-west.

59. Carsethorn and the Solway Firth from Criffel.

this is a longer outing than the map suggests. The ascent of Screel Hill is complicated since it is almost surrounded by Forestry Commission plantations.

The shortest round starts from the Gelston–Kirkmirran road which runs north and east of the hill. This should be left opposite Potterland Mill and a forest road taken through a gate. This leads to two more gates at both of which the road splits. Take the left fork at the first and the right fork at the second. Higher up fork right again heading north of Screel Hill, then take a left fork to cross over the ridge to the Glen of Screel Burn. There are no more problems and the road continues almost to the col south-west of Screel Hill. This hill is steep and rugged with numerous outcrops of rock amongst the thick heather. A large cairn is situated at the west end of the hill but the east end appears just as high. The views are good particularly to the Solway.

The Mid Hill rises between Screel Hill and Bengairn. In coming from Screel Hill it is better to bypass the Mid Hill altogether as it is almost completely forested. This can be done by following the dyke westwards from Screel Hill although this appears to be heading down the Linkins Glen in the wrong direction. Little distance is being lost though, and once the forest is passed, there is a short and straightforward climb on to Bengairn. It has a large cairn and an O.S. pillar and was at one time a beacon hill for summoning the men of Galloway to arms.

The return can be made to the south-east to Bengairn Farm but it is shorter and easier to return past Screel Hill by the same route unless the weather is bad. A vein of amethyst quartz is exposed in the Screel Burn.

Criffel (boundary hill? Split hill?) 1868 ft. (569m.) lies to the south of New Abbey and is a very famous hill in the south of Scotland despite its comparatively modest height. This is because of its commanding position over the Nith estuary and the Solway Firth. Most routes to it start fairly near sea-level.

The usual approach is from the Dumfries–Kirkbean road about 2 mls. (3 kms.) south of New Abbey. Turn off to the west on the road to Ardwall Mains and Ardwall. Cars are allowed to just short of Ardwall where a sign to the left indicates the way to Criffel. Cars should be left here and this track taken around Ardwall and over a style into the forest. The path passes a wooden hut and leads into a wide fire-break where a burn comes down between larch plantations. The burn rises in a small corrie beyond the forest with the summit above it to the south. The summit slopes are rather rough and damp in places with granite boulders projecting from the coarse grasses.

A stone dyke crosses the summit which has two cairns and an O.S. pillar. The larger cairn is known as Douglas's Cairn, after the Black Douglas, who, it is said, was killed when his horse stumbled crossing a trail below at a spot called the Fox Hole.

The easiest route to Criffel, though not the shortest, starts from Kirkbean and follows the Kirkbean Burn. This leads to the south-west shoulder of the hill where easier slopes, among large boulders, rise to the summit.

The view from Criffel is exceptional as it is the southernmost hill of this magnitude in Scotland. The prospect encompasses Carlisle and the coast of Cumberland, Skiddaw and other Lake District Hills, the Isle of Man, Galloway, Dumfries, the Lowther, Moffat and Ettrick Hills, and the plains around Annan, dominated by the four giant cooling towers of the Chapelcross nuclear power station. Nearer at hand lies Loch Kindar and Shambellie Wood where some fine specimens of Scots Pine date from 1775–80. Loch Kindar has two islands – one with the ruins of a church on it, and the other smaller one a crannog. Beyond the loch lies Sweetheart Abbey, whose monks once tended sheep on Criffel. But it is the vast expanse of the Solway Firth which holds the attention. If the tide time-tables are studied beforehand, the view can be enhanced by showing off the tides advancing or retreating over the mud and quicksands.

There is a monument on a northern shoulder of Criffel to commemorate the Battle of Waterloo. This is not seen from the summit but it is very conspicuous when climbing the hill from the east. The monument is about 50 ft. (15m.) high and has a winding stair inside it. The route to the hill from New Abbey passes close to it and goes up the north ridge to Knockendoch. This narrow ridge is a prominent feature of the hill and has a dyke running all the way up it which renders it even more conspicuous.

An outcrop of quartzite on the north-east slopes of Criffel is known to the locals as 'the diamond' from the brilliant reflection it gives after rain.

SECTION VI

SOUTH-WEST AYRSHIRE

(1) **Craigenreoch** 1854 ft. (565m.) M.R. 335911
(2) **Knockdolian** 870 ft. (265m.) M.R. 113848
(3) **Beneraird** 1439 ft. (439m.) M.R. 136785

Maps: O.S. 1-Inch, Seventh Series, sheets 72 and 79.
Bartholomew ½-inch, sheet 37.

This region is bounded on the west by the Firth of Clyde and Loch Ryan; on the south by the Stranraer–Newton Stewart road (A75); on the east by the Newton Stewart–Bargrennan–Straiton roads (A714 and unclassified); and on the north by the Straiton–Girvan road (B741).

These boundaries enclose a large tract of thinly populated country used mainly for sheep and cattle-rearing and forestry, with some arable crops grown in the valleys. The region has no hills of great importance to hill-walkers and much of the territory is indeterminably between lowland and upland in character. Only the most significant summits are mentioned here but numerous short hill-walks are available. Some of these are very rewarding scenically, such as the traverse of the Byne and Grey Hills between Girvan and Lendalfoot, or Penderry Hill and the range west of Glen App.

Transport

The Glasgow–Stranraer bus service passes through Glen App and buses from Stranraer to Dumfries pass through Glenluce. There are also services between Girvan, Colmonell and Ballantrae; Girvan, Barrhill and Newton Stewart; and Girvan, Crosshill, Straiton and Maybole.

Western S.M.T. Co. Ltd.

Trains between Glasgow and Stranraer sometimes stop at Barrhill.

Craigenreoch 1854 ft. (565m.) is the highest point on the ridge running south-west from the Nick of the Balloch, on the road from Crosshill which joins the Straiton–Bargrennan road at Rowantree Toll. The main assets of this ridge are that it is easily reached – the Nick of the Balloch reaches 1280 ft. (390m.) at the Brandy Well – and that it gives a fine uninterrupted view of the Awful Hand Range across the forests.

The ridge continues from Craigenreoch to Polmaddie Hill, and Pinbreck Hill then drops to the Nick of Darley, Cairn Hill, beyond the col, has a large prehistoric cairn at its north end. The Nick of Darley is a narrow slit between the hills at the summit of an old drove road. North of here, in the Howe of Laggan beyond the Lead Mine Burn, there is a cairn marking the spot where a shepherd died in a blizzard.

Knockdolian 870 ft. (265m.) is a superb little peak lying between Ballantrae and Colmonell. It is often mistaken for Ailsa Craig from the Stinchar Valley and hills to the east, and is also known as 'the False Craig'. It is best climbed by its north east ridge from the road north of the River Stinchar. The views are excellent to Ailsa Craig, Ireland, Arran, Ballantrae, the Stinchar Valley and the Galloway Hills.

Beneraird 1439 ft. (439m.) is the highest hill in the area to the east of Glen App. The approach to it is by the Lagafater Track (see below), as the summit lies just three minutes walking north-east of the track. An O.S. pillar crowns the summit. The near views are rather bleak in this grassy area but the far views are good. Two cairns are conspicuous on Kilmoray to the east having been constructed from a much more ancient cairn.

Hill Paths

Ballantrae to Glenluce by the Lagafater Track 21 mls. (34kms.). Much shorter with transport at either end.
This route runs south-east from Ballantrae, leaving the Stranraer road by the second road on the left once across the River Stinchar. This minor road is taken for Auchairne and Kilwhannel but keeping on between them up the hill. This was an ancient route to the south and has no padlocked gates or private signs to deter travellers on this side. Motorists should not be deluded into attempting the crossing by

car though as the going quickly becomes impassable beyond Smirton Hill. A fence at the summit contests the existence of a Right of Way.

The track rises to 1392 ft. (424m.) where it passes just to the south-east of the summit of Beneraird, then it drops down the Black Glen into the valley of the Main Water of Luce. Lagafater Lodge and its loch stand among trees here and are conspicuous on the moorland. A 'private' road is joined at the lodge leading past Barnvannock to Shennas. Beyond here the road is public at the county boundary and leads to New Luce and Glenluce.

Several variations are possible to this walk. Altimeg in Glen App or Craigcaffie at the south-east end of Loch Ryan are alternative terminal points.

SELECTED BIBLIOGRAPHY

Highways and Byways in Galloway and Carrick, Rev. C. H. Dick – 2nd. ed., MacMillan, 1938.

Transactions of the Dumfriesshire and Galloway Natural History and Antiquarian Society, XLIII, 1966 – Landscape Evolution in Galloway, W. G. Jardine.

Glen Trool Forest Park Guide, H. L. Edlin – H.M.S.O., 1965.

Rambles in Galloway, Malcolm McL. Harper – Thos. Fraser, Dalbeattie, 1896.

The River Doon, Wilson MacArthur, Cassell, 1952

The Merrick and the Neighbouring Hills, J. McBain – Stephen and Pollock, Ayr.

Galloway, Andrew McCormick, 2nd complete ed. – John Smith, Glasgow, 1947.

Carrick Gallovidian, J. Kevan McDowall – Homer McCririck, Ayr 1947.

The Place Names of Galloway, Sir Herbert Maxwell – Jackson Wylie, Glasgow, 1930.

Scottish Field – April 1966. *The Galloway Diamond*, K. M. Andrew.
March 1968. *High and Low in Galloway*, Tom Weir.

Scottish Mountaineering Club Journal –
Vol. I *The Highlands of Galloway*, Colin B. Phillip.
Vol. II *Galloway and Ayrshire Hills*, H. B. Watt.
Vol. VI *A Gallowegian Wander*, Edred M. Corner.

Vol. XXI *The Galloway Hills*, John Dow.
Vol. XXV *Back Bearings on Merrick*, Ian W. Craig.

The Scots Magazine –

May 1956 *The Forests of Galloway*, T. C. B. Phin.
Oct. 1956 *Call at the Dikers' Tent*, Leonard Fluke.
Dec. 1958 *The Castle that Crossed a Loch*, P. A. MacNab.
April 1961 *Days on the 'Awful Hand'*, K. M. Andrew.
Dec. 1961 *Return to Loch Trool*, Tom Weir.
Dec. 1966 *Taming High Galloway*, Benington Marsh.
Feb. 1968 *White Galloway*, K. M. Andrew.
Dec. 1968 *In Billy Marshall's Kingdom*, Maurice Fleming.
Jan. 1969 *A Hunt for Two Caves*, Maurice Fleming.
May 1969 *The Other Dee*, T. C. B. Phin.
Jan. 1970 *Hill and Shore in Galloway*, Tom Weir.
Mar. 1970 *Footprints in the Scythe-Sand*, Benington Marsh.

Fiction

The Raiders, S. R. Crockett.

EASTERN HILLS

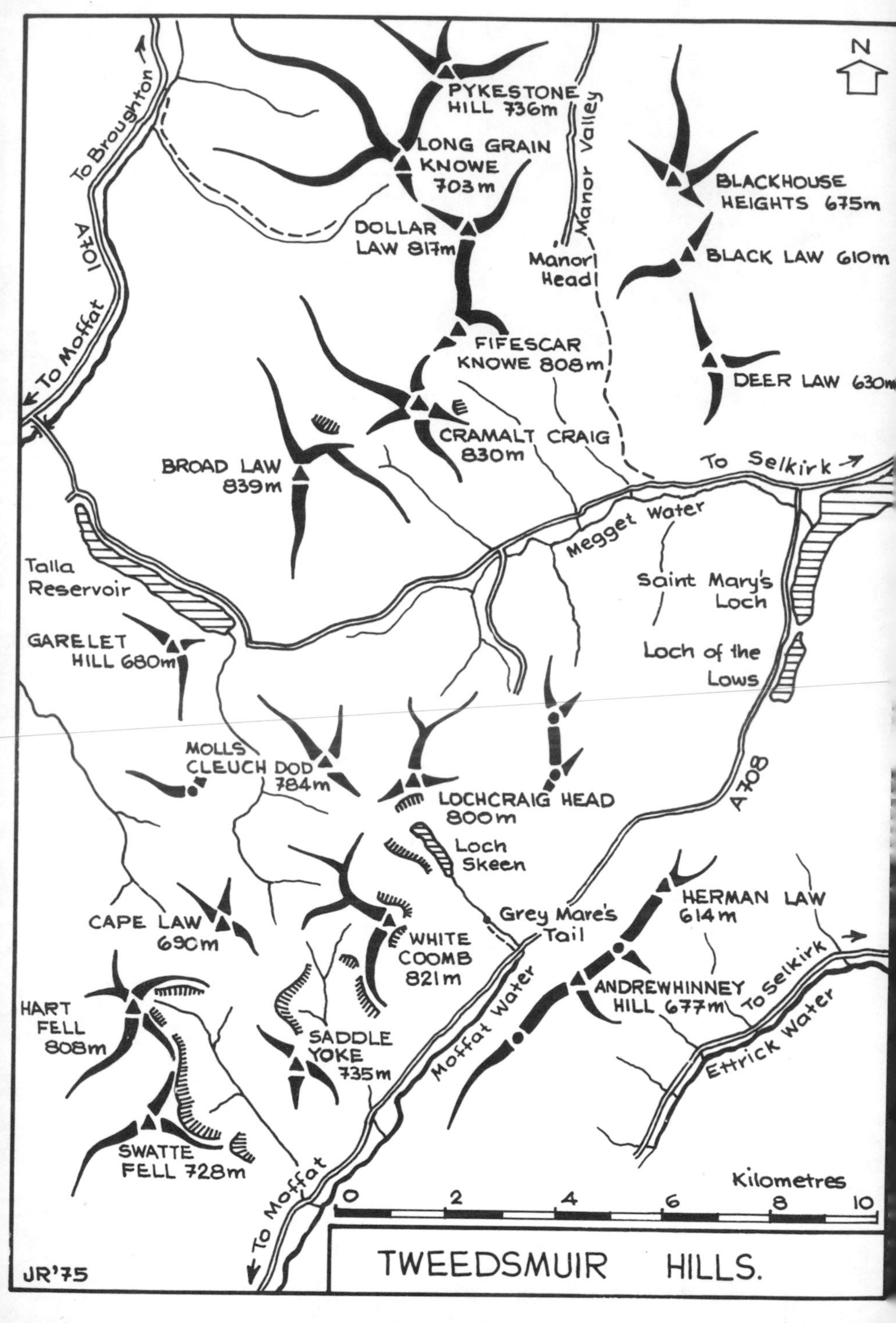

TWEEDSMUIR HILLS.

6

The Pentland Hills

(1)	**Scald Law**	1899 ft. (579m.)	M.R. 192611
(2)	**Carnethy Hill**	1890 ft. (576m.)	M.R. 204619
(3)	**West Kip**	1806 ft. (550m.)	M.R. 178606
(4)	**The Mount**	1763 ft. (537m.)	M.R. 144576
(5)	**East Cairn Hill**	1839 ft. (561m.)	M.R. 122596
(6)	**West Cairn Hill**	1844 ft. (562m.)	M.R. 108584
(7)	**Byrehope Mount**	1752 ft. (534m.)	M.R. 110548
(8)	**Craigengar**	1700 ft. (518m.)	M.R. 090551

Maps: O.S. 1-inch, Seventh Series, sheets 61 and 62.
Bartholomew, ½-inch, sheet 45
Bartholomew's 'Pentland Hills' Map, 1½-inch to the mile.

The Pentland hills stretch for some 15 miles (24kms.) to the south-west from the outskirts of Edinburgh and provide excellent hill-walking country within easy reach of the city centre. The A702 road through West Linton lies immediately to the south of the hills with the parallel route to Carnwath (A70), providing easy access to the north. There are no motor roads cutting through the Pentlands, a point of some importance since any one of the many footpaths through the hills swiftly takes the walker out of earshot of motor traffic. None of the hills reaches the 2000 ft. (610m.) mark, but the list above contains all the principal hills.

From the top of East Cairn Hill the main mass of the Pentlands can be seen, stretching to the north-east in two main ridges on either side of the Logan Burn. The southern ridge contains the higher summits and the more attractive shapes, but a traverse of this route brings the walker down to Glencorse reservoir where the valley must be crossed to reach Castlelaw Hill for a finish over Allermuir and Caerketton.

West of the two Cairn Hills are more rounded shapes and more open high moorland with, perhaps, for some people, the added benefit of less frequented paths. Byrehope and Craigengar, lying between two recognised hill tracks, represent the western limit of the Pentlands and lie further from a road than any of the other hills.

Scald Law 1899 ft. (579m.) is the highest point in the Pentlands. It lies on the ridge on the south side of the Logan Burn and the top is less than one mile from the A702 road. Access from this road is by either of two public paths, one on the west and one on the east side of the hill. The western approach leaves the road by a track to Eastside Farm, a second signpost reads 'Public path to Balerno'. The track contours round the southern slopes of South Black Hill and passes over the western shoulder of West Kip 1806 ft. (550m.) at a height of 1500 ft. (457m.) A way may then be made to the east over the West Kip and the East Kip to Scald Law, slightly more than one mile from the top of the pass. There is a triangulation pillar on the top.

The eastern approach leaves the main road one-and-a-quarter miles further east, the path being signposted 'Public path to Colinton and Balerno'. There is a car park a few yards away. The track passes over the eastern shoulder of Scald Law before descending to the Logan Burn, where the way divides. The left branch follows the burn then turns north to cross the northern ridge and descend to Balerno and the A70 road. The right-hand branch follows the Logan Burn to Glencorse reservoir then turns north to pass to the west of Capelaw Hill and descend to Colinton. A branch track at Glencorse also runs to Balerno.

Carnethy Hill 1890 ft. (576m.). This hill lies one mile to the north-east of Scald Law and forms the end of the continuous line of hills on the south side of the Logan Burn. It is ascended very readily from the path from A702 already described under Scald Law, the two hills rising on either side of the highest point reached by the track. An ascent from the road which encircles Glencorse reservoir to continue along the lower reaches of Logan Burn is also possible, but it should be noted that this road is closed to motor vehicles.

Carnethy Hill forms a ridge one-and-a-half miles in length culminating in a subsidiary top – Turnhouse Hill 1650 ft. approx. (503m.), whose northern slopes descend directly to Glencorse reservoir. The cairn on Carnethy measures 70 ft. (21m.) in diameter and some 8 ft. (2·4m.) in height and, like that on East Cairn, is of archaeological interest.

West Kip 1806 ft. (550m.) lies one mile south-west from Scald Law and its sharp top forms one of the most readily identifiable points in the group. It is easily ascended by way of the track over the western shoulder already described under Scald Law. An alternative path to this same point on the shoulder begins near the hotel at Nine Mile Burn where there is a signpost, erected by the Scottish Rights of Way Society, marked 'To Balerno by Broad Law'. (There is a difference of spelling here since both the O.S. and Bartholomew refer to the hill as 'Braid Law'.)

The traverse of the three miles of ridge between the West Kip and Turnhouse Hill forms a delightful, if all too short, walk which may be readily extended to more than double the distance by descending from Turnhouse and walking round Glencorse reservoir to reach Allermuir Hill either by way of a direct route over Castlelaw Hill or by way of the Colinton path to Capelaw Hill. Caerketton, with its rocky northern front, forms an interesting finish.

Caerketton crags offer some rock climbing. The rocks are lichen covered and somewhat friable. They can give some exhilarating winter climbs. There are sounder rocks even nearer to the centre of Edinburgh, but Caerketton is remote in more senses than one and the challenge to the climber here is not likely to be a human voice.

The Mount 1763 ft. (537m.). This hill lies three-and-a-half miles (6kms.) south-west from Scald Law and forms the highest point on the ridge dividing the North Esk and Lyne Water valleys and their reservoirs. The access road to the North Esk reservoir may be taken from Carlops and left at any suitable point on the eastern slopes of the hill. An alternative path to the same slopes begins on the old road, parallel to the A702, which runs to Nine Mile Burn. A signpost on this road, erected by the Scottish Rights of Way Society, indicates a path to Balerno via the Bore Stane; this joins the Carlops route near the foot of the reservoir.

From West Linton the road to Baddinsgill reservoir may be followed until a turn on the right leads to Stonypath. This track continues round the southern tip of the main ridge and a starting point here leads the walker to Mount Maw 1756 ft. (535m.) and a ridge walk of rather more than one mile to The Mount. It is then no great distance to cross Wether Law and reach East Cairn Hill. A return may then be made down the track to Baddinsgill or the traverse continued to West Cairn Hill and Byrehope Mount, returning to West Linton by the reservoir road. The complete circuit is almost fourteen miles (22kms.) and will require seven hours walking.

East Cairn Hill 1839 ft. (561m.). **West Cairn Hill** 1844 ft. (562m.). These hills, whose tops are little more than one mile apart, are prominent on the northern slopes of the Pentlands, to the south of Harperrig Reservoir. The pass between the two hills is the Cauldstaneslap, possibly the best known stretch of the drove road which ran from Falkirk to the Border crossing. A little to the west of the point where the power cables pass over the A70 road lies the ruin of the old toll house which was a feature of the drove road. A path begins at this point and follows a line over the moor, defined by poles at one or two points. From the path, the track descends past Baddinsgill to West Linton. The drove road continued to Peebles by a route described in detail as one of the rights of way in the 'Moorfoot Hills' (chapter 7).

The hills lie rather more than two miles from the A70 road and the Cauldstaneslap route provides the easiest access. East Cairn is fractionally the lower of the two but possesses an added interest in that the large cairn on the summit is of archaeological interest, being of the type assigned to the second millennium B.C.

More interesting, perhaps, to the average hill walker is the view, particularly the shapely ridge formed by the West and East Kips, Scald Law and Carnethy. Three-and-a-half miles (6kms.) of open moorland lie between the East Cairn and the West Kip and the route does not fall below the 1300 ft. (396m.) mark of the Bore Stane.

An approach from the A702 road at West Linton requires a five mile (8km.) walk to the top of the Cauldstaneslap.

Byrehope Mount 1752 ft. (534m.). This hill lies two-and-a-quarter miles south from West Cairn and three miles from the A702 road. The easiest access is by way of the road to Baddinsgill reservoir from West Linton.

Craigengar 1700 ft. (518m.) is the most westerly hill of any significant height in the Pentlands and lies 2 miles south by west from

West Cairn Hill. The A70 and A702 roads at this point are rather more than 7 miles (11kms.) apart, Craigengar being slightly nearer the A70 or northern road.

Short as the distance is between these two roads, it is hardly possible to remain unaware of the difference in the atmosphere of the two routes. To traverse the northern side of the Pentlands along the A70 road is to sense all the bare and open spaciousness of a northern moorland landscape. Here the wind seems colder, the distances greater, the trees fewer than on the southern slopes through West Linton. The greater flow of traffic along the southern road helps to emphasise the difference and the steeper slopes of the hills on this side disguise the fact that the road itself is little lower in altitude than the northern route.

Right of way. None of the paths across the Pentland Hills are defined as rights of way by Midlothian County Council, despite the fact that a number are identified by direction posts erected by the Scottish Rights of Way Society. These paths have been used by walkers for many years and it seems unlikely that dispute will now arise over their use for this purpose.

The Pentland Hills map, published by Bartholomew, is supplied with a leaflet listing all the principal walks across the hills.

There are eight main footpaths and these are described from west to east, using the A70 road as a starting point in each case.

1. *To Dunsyre and West Linton*

At map reference 021516 on the A70 road there is a Scottish Rights of Way Society signpost indicating Dunsyre and West Linton. Two miles south-east from this point the path divides, the left branch crossing the moor to the south of Bleak Law and continuing the line to Medwinhead and North Slipperfield. The right-hand branch continues southward past Stonypath Farm to the road 1 mile west of Dunsyre; this is followed, holding an easterly direction to cross West Water and Medwin Water. The track continues past North Slipperfield to West Linton. An extension of this walk may be made to Carlops by turning left instead of right on the final approach to West Linton and turning right again at the signpost indicating 'No through road'. This continues as a track to Carlops. The distance to West Linton is slightly over 10 miles (16kms.).

2. *To Dolphinton*

At map reference 052578 on the A70 road a farm road on the south side bears a sign to Crosswoodburn and Aberlyn. This road is followed to a track which climbs the moor to Henshaw Hill, crosses the west branch of Medwin Water and continues over Black Law to descend and follow the left bank of West Water to the footbridge over Medwin. The track then passes to the east of Garvald House and joins the Dolphinton road.

A variation to the start of this walk begins at the Tarbrax road end on A70 (M.R. 040547). There is no signpost but if the fence is climbed, a route may be made eastwards to join the track from Crosswoodburn on Henshaw Hill. The distance from the start at Crosswoodburn to the A702 road is 8 miles (13kms.).

3. *To Cauldstaneslap*

The remains of the old toll house mark the start of the old drove road called Cauldstaneslap and lie on map reference 102628 on the A70 road. There is a signpost indicating a public footpath to West Linton and the route is well enough marked to the crossing of the Water of Leith, where higher ground and drier going are soon reached. After crossing the ridge at 1400 ft. (427m.) the route descends over the Cairn Muir to the foot of the reservoir and Baddinsgill Farm. A turn to the left may be made here and a path on the east side of Lyne Water followed to West Linton. The distance is 8 miles (13kms.).

4. *Buteland to Carlops via the Bore Stane*

A turning off the A70 road at map reference 129655 leads to a 'T' junction, near Buteland Farm and a right turn here brings the walker to a track running southwards and signposted by the Scottish Rights of Way Society as a public footpath to Nine Mile Burn and Carlops. This is at map reference 133642. The route continues southwards, crosses the ridge with the Bore Stane on the right and descends past the North Esk reservoir to a division of the path. The left fork goes via Spittal to Nine Mile Burn, while the right branch curves round the shoulder of Fairliehope Hill to descend to Carlops and the main road. The distance is 7 miles by either route (11kms.).

5. *Balerno to Nine Mile Burn*

After crossing the western end of Threipmuir reservoir, a right turn brings the walker to the start of a path at map reference 164628.

This runs south over the moor then to the neck below the West Kip where a branch path runs to the left to join the main road at map reference 197597. The way to Nine Mile Burn continues the line to the south, rising slightly to Cap Law, then descending the ridge to Nine Mile Burn. The distance from the reservoir is 5 miles (8kms.).

6. *Balerno to Penicuik*
The starting point for this walk is also from the western end of Threipmuir reservoir. From the reservoir road, a right turn leads to the start of a path at map reference 166627. This runs east then south-east to pass through the gap between Hare Hill and Black Hill before descending to the Logan Burn. This is crossed and a track followed over the second ridge to pass to the east of Scald Law and descend to the A702 road at map reference 211608.

The distance from the reservoir is 4 miles and a further 2 miles brings the walker to Penicuik. A short distance eastwards along the main road is the turning to Coates Farm (M.R. 215611). This road runs through an attractive wood and the line continues across the road directly towards Penicuik.

7. *Balerno–Currie to Glencorse*
This short walk to Glencorse from the north has alternative starts from Balerno and Currie. A farm road, beginning at Currie at map reference 182678 leads south-east to Middle Kinleith and Wester Kinleith farms and a track continues the line at the crossroads. The route from Balerno skirts the eastern end of Harlaw reservoir and the two ways join at reference 192653. Three miles then take the walker over the ridge to Glencorse reservoir and the A702 road. The road to the reservoir is closed to vehicles.

8. *Glencorse to Colinton*
There is a route to Colinton from Glencorse reservoir which branches east from the Currie–Balerno route at reference 213643. This passes to the east of Bonaly reservoir and descends the moor to join the road at Bonaly Tower (M.R. 214678). From the A702 road to this point is a little over 4 miles.

Kaimes Hill; Dalmahoy Hill. These two hills lie to the north of the A70 road near Balerno and are worthy of mention despite their lack of altitude. There is a quarry on Kaimes Hill and a rocky escarpment on the north side of Dalmahoy, and as both offer an excellent viewpoint, in addition to the possibility of some modest climbing, they are well worth a visit on a summer evening. The farm road at map reference 135659 offers easy access.

Another of the less obvious features of the district worth a visit is the railway between Balerno and Colinton, now closed to trains. Railway cuttings and embankments have for long been happy hunting grounds for botanists because of the variety of plant life springing from the straw carried in such quantity and the exclusion of grazing animals. The paper mills at Balerno and Currie were supplied with imported grasses as raw material and in consequence the plant life along the route contains a higher proportion of exotics than might normally be expected.

Bus routes. Access by public transport to the Pentlands follows the pattern of the traffic on the two roads, A70 on the north side and A702 on the south. The southern road carries a good deal more traffic than the northern road, which runs through more open country. Balerno is well served, but there is only one bus each way by this route to Carnwath and that at a very early hour on weekdays.

The service to West Linton is at a fairly high frequency.

Accommodation. Again the north side is somewhat inhospitable compared with the south, where there are hotels at West Linton, Carlops, Nine Mile Burn and Glencorse road end.

There are two caravan sites in Edinburgh – one being Municipal. Map references are 145726 and 212768 respectively. There is a third site on the A701 road at 264648. Edinburgh also possesses a Youth Hostel of many years standing.

BIBLIOGRAPHY

The Pentland Hills; their Paths and Passes, W. A. Smith – Scottish Rights of Way Society, 1885.

Pentland Walks, Robert Cochrane – Edinburgh, 1938.

The Breezy Pentlands, G. M. Reith – Edinburgh, 1910.

The Call of the Pentlands, Will Grant – Edinburgh, 1951.

Pentland Days and Country Ways, Will Grant – London, 1949.

The Pentland Hills, W. A. Anderson – London, 1926.

60. The Ballantrae end of the Lagafater track.

61. The Nick of the Balloch from the Stinchar Valley at North Balloch, Craigenreoch is on the right.

62. Changue Forest and the Lead Mine Burn from Pinbreck Hill.

63. Windlestraw Law to Eildons.

64. The Broch at Edinshall, looking north-east over the Whiteadder Valley.

65. Drumelzier Law to Tinto.

66. Talla Cleuch Head from Garelet Hill.

67. Talla Reservoir from Garelet Hill.

7

The Moorfoot Hills

(1)	**Jeffries Corse**	2040 ft. (622m.)	M.R. 275491
(2)	**Bowbeat Hill**	2050 ft. (625m.)	M.R. 292469
(3)	**Blackhope Scar**	2137 ft. (651m.)	M.R. 315484
(4)	**Whitehope Law**	2038 ft. (621m.)	M.R. 330446
(5)	**Windlestraw Law**	2162 ft. (659m.)	M.R. 372431

Maps: O.S. 1-inch, Seventh Series, sheet 62.
Bartholomew, ½-inch, sheet 41.

The Moorfoot Hills lie on the north side of the Tweed valley, neatly enclosed by the A703 road (Peebles–Penicuik) on the west and by the A7 (Galashiels–Dalkeith) on the east. This stretch of some 100 square miles (256 sq. kms.) is further divided by the B709 road running north from Innerleithen. This road reaches an altitude of 1250 ft. (381m.) and forms a convenient access route with excellent car-parking facilities on both sides of the highest point. Cars may also be taken to Portmore Loch or Gladhouse reservoir, both of which lie on the northern fringe of the Moorfoots, north and east of Eddleston. The road to Portmore Loch is very rocky but passable; the road on the south side of Gladhouse is narrow but well surfaced.

There are five hills of 2000 ft. (610m.) and above. The 1-inch O.S. map shows the name 'Jeffries Corse' as half-a-mile north-east from point 2042 ft. (2040) where there is a triangulation pillar and the name 'Dundreich'. Jeffries Corse is the name used in the table of 2000 ft. hills in 'Munro's Tables' and is therefore adhered to. The apparent discrepancy in height is similarly explained.

There are, additionally, several points only slightly less than 2000 ft. (610m.), notably Dunslair Heights, above Glentress Forest 1975 ft. (602m.) M.R. 288436; Rough Moss 1965 ft. (599m.) M.R. 329479 and Eastside Heights 1944 ft. (593m.) M.R. 355459 which lie respectively on the west and east sides of the B709 road.

The brief article on the Moorfoot Hills in Volume 9 of the S.M.C.

Journal (May 1907) referred to Blackhope Scar 2137 ft. (651m.) as the highest point in the group and this is, in some degree, supported by the 1-inch O.S. map which appears to define the hills as lying to the west of the B709 road (Innerleithen–Heriot). This would be to cast Windlestraw Law into geographical obscurity since it can hardly be associated with the Lammermuirs so far to the east, nor can it reasonably be considered as a separate hill. The long summit ridge, which offers such superb views over the Tweed valley and the impressive ridges which descend on the south and east sides invest Windlestraw Law with a character no less satisfying than any of the hills further to the west. There is, moreover, a record of long association with the Club, for an article on the hill appears in Volume 1 of the Journal.

The Midlothian–Peebles border runs along the whole ridge of the Moorfoots, passing slightly to the south of the top of Blackhope Scar and joining the Selkirk boundary below the top of Windlestraw Law. These county march fences have their uses as guide lines for the walker but a point of equal interest, perhaps, regarding the association of hills with counties is that Peebles, of all the counties of Scotland has the highest average height above sea level.

The two most notable features of the Moorfoots, perhaps, are the straight line of the northern escarpment falling to Gladhouse reservoir and the flat ground near Gorebridge and the equally straight trench, which contains the Dewar Burn, and the upper reaches of Glentress Water flowing north and south respectively. Near the top of the road at this point a stone at the side of the road marks 'The Piper's Grave', and the story goes that a piper undertook to play from Peebles to Lauder, but expired at this point! The hills to the west of the road consist substantially of two stretches of high moorland where the tops, with one exception, are not very sharply defined. These areas are joined by a ridge on which stands Bowbeat Hill and Emly Bank.

The stretch of moorland, a little to the east of Blackhope Scar, bears the name of Garvald Punks, surely one of the strangest hill names to be found in the area. It is the sort of name which may well become etched in the memory of the walker who finds himself crossing this stretch in conditions of high wind and driving rain.

To the south of this area runs the deep valley of Leithen Water, accessible only on foot and offering, in its higher reaches, all the visual and aesthetic rewards of a remote mountain glen, for in the narrow upper reaches the retaining walls stand at a high angle, some 800 ft. (244m.) above the floor of the glen.

The hills between Leithen Water and the Tweed Valley form a narrow and winding ridge and offer the walker more striking foreground views than he will find on the wider stretches of the hills to the north. Nor is the difference in altitude excessive since Dunslair Heights, at about the central point of the ridge, is less than 200 ft. (61m.) lower than Blackhope Scar to the north. The hills on the lower stretch of Leithen Water are also shapely enough to warrant interest, and Lee Pen and its twin hill, Kirnie Law, on the east side stand prominently above the point where the Leithen enters the Tweed. The ridge terminates in the plateau at a point less than one mile from the top of Jeffries Corse.

On the east side of the B709 road the dominating hill is Windlestraw Law, for not only is it the highest point in the area but its summit ridge almost 2 miles in length and the steep and complex ridges on the south and east sides invest it with a character at once apparent to the visitor. East of Windlestraw the hills gradually decrease in height as far as the natural boundary of Gala Water beyond which is a further area of open hill country, which eventually steepens into the western edge of the Lammermuirs.

Jeffries Corse 2040 ft. (622m.), which is shown as 'Dundreich' on the 1-inch O.S. map, stands less than one mile to the south-east from Portmore Loch and may be reached by walking half-way round the east side of the loch before striking up hill. Access may also be gained from Eddleston, on the A703 road, by following the track to Boreland. The South Esk valley, draining into Gladhouse reservoir, offers a somewhat more lengthy approach. The Peebles – Midlothian boundary fence passes a few hundred yards east of the triangulation pillar which marks the summit.

Bowbeat Hill 2050 ft. (625m.). This lies south-east from Jeffries Corse and $1\frac{1}{4}$ miles distant. The approach from the South Esk valley is straightforward since the hill lies clearly in sight. A slightly more distant approach is from the south along Leithen Water, where a walk of four miles from the B709 road brings the summit underfoot. At the time of writing, this approach involves some poor walking conditions since a track has been cut through the glen for the heavy-tracked vehicles used for preparing the ground for forestry planting. This track has not been surfaced so that bad weather reduces it to deep mud and there are several crossings of the river which involve wading. The upper reaches of Leithen Water run through a deeply cut glen, remote and impressively wild in character. The deep trenches cut by the mechanical ploughs in readiness for tree planting march with a depressing and misplaced precision up most of the slopes on the northern side of the glen.

Blackhope Scar 2137 ft. (651m.). This hill lies 1¾ miles north-east from Bowbeat Hill and rather more than 2 miles north-west from the summit of the B709 road. This is the shortest approach and offers the advantage of a start from 1250 ft. (381m.). A walk along the upper reaches of the South Esk from Gladhouse is slightly longer but the upper eastern branch runs directly towards the summit of Blackhope scar. There is a triangulation survey pillar here and a junction of four fences. Having reached the top, the return walk may be extended to include Bowbeat Hill and Jeffries Corse, returning to Gladhouse by the final north-facing slopes of the plateau. Five hours should suffice for this round.

Whitehope Law 2038 ft. (621m.) lies at the southern edge of this section of the Moorfoots and rises directly above the division in the glen where Leithen Water is joined by Glentress Water. It is easily ascended from this point or from a starting point on the road 1½ miles further north. Both this hill and Glede Knowe, at the southern end of the Windlestraw ridge, form superb viewpoints.

Windlestraw Law 2162 ft. (659m.). This long ridge lies on the eastern side of the B709 road and represents the highest ground in the Moorfoots. The most direct approach is by the Glentress Rig shoulder, which rises from the road a mile from the Leithen Water branch. The summit is 2 miles to the east from this point and is marked by a triangulation pillar and by the county boundary fence which turns east at this point. A subsidiary fence runs south-west along the ridge and little height is lost in following this to the end at Glede Knowe. This forms an excellent viewpoint, for both the Tweed valley and the valley of the Leithen Water are narrow and steep sided so that the eye rests not on the streets of Innerleithen but on the slopes of the Minch Muir and the hills of Glen Sax, stretching south to Dollar Law.

A route may also be made to Windlestraw Law from Innerleithen or Walkerburn by walking up the ridge of Pirn Craig and Priesthope

Hill to reach the top after 5 miles (8kms.) of continuous ascent. A longer walk is from the summit of the B709 road and along the line of the county boundary fence over the plateau from Eastside Heights to Windlestraw. This is a wet moor, gashed with peat hags and the walk to Glede Knowe, the southern tip of the Windlestraw ridge, will require five hours for the round trip.

Eastwards from Windlestraw lies an attractive area of ridges not a great deal lower, and valleys both steep sided and unfrequented. Gala Water forms the eastern boundary, but the Lugate and Caddon Water valleys and their associated ridges offer an area well away from the beaten track for the walker who sets a value on solitude. There is one route through this district which is claimed as a right of way. This is Blackhaugh to Stagehall, described in the appropriate section.

There are two brochs in the region, one at Torwoodlee (O.S. sheet 69, map reference 465384) two miles north-west from Galashiels and the other only two miles to the north at Bow Castle on Gala Water (M.R. 461417). The Torwoodlee remains were excavated twice, first in 1891 and again in 1950–51, the conclusions of the work being that a broch had been built within the ramparts of an Iron Age hill fort. The date of the fort has been placed at the beginning of the first century A.D. and it was apparently abandoned before the broch was built. The excavations disclosed a large number of Roman relics, including a silver penny of Titus (A.D. 79–81). All this material can be firmly dated to about A.D. 100 and it is considered that the relics were looted from the Roman fort at Newstead when this was captured and sacked, in the reaction to a temporary withdrawal of the occupying forces. The Romans returned to Newstead when southern Scotland was re-occupied and it appears that the broch was systematically destroyed.

The broch at Bow Castle, high above the east bank of Gala Water, although ruinous, has slightly more to offer the visitor but is in no way to be compared with Edinshall broch, near Preston (see page 138). Pictish brochs, as they are often called, are normally associated with the far north and north-west of Scotland and it may not be widely known that there were ten brochs built between the Tay and the Tweed and four in Wigtownshire.

Rights of Way. There is a right of way running north-west from Peebles to West Linton, which may well form the line of the old drove road, the Cauldstaneslap, which ran between the East and West

Cairn Hills. Peebles was a staging post on this road, since there were grazing rights on the Kingsmuir.

Taking the route in the northerly direction we go along the Rosetta road from Peebles to Standalane Farm (M.R. 244416) and continue along the track on the east side of Hamilton Hill. A turn to the west brings the walker to the farm road to Upper Kidston and this is followed in a northerly direction until the ridge of White Meldon can be crossed and the Meldon road is reached. This is crossed and a track (at M.R. 216440) is followed to Nether Stewarton and Upper Stewarton. The track then turns west and enters the Eddleston Water Forest, the line continuing to curve round the southern slopes of Green Knowe. The Flemington and Fingland Burns are crossed and the main A701 road reached ¾ mile north of Romanno Bridge. The exact line of the remaining section to West Linton is obscure. The distance from Peebles to the A701 road is 8¾ miles (14kms.).

Soonhope to Leithen Water

The Soonhope Burn runs under the main Peebles–Galashiels road (A72) ½ mile east of the town centre and the route runs up the east side of the stream to Shieldgreen (M.R. 273431). From here a way is made to a track which runs north-east over the ridge and down to Craighope on Leithen Water. An alternative route turns to the right shortly after leaving the main road and climbs through the forest on a zigzag track to Caresman Hill (M.R. 288427) on the ridge and then descends the moor, on a track running north-east, to reach Leithen Water at Williamslee. The walk to Craighope is 4½ miles (7kms.) and that to Williamslee slightly longer at about 5¼ (8kms.). Both of these routes constitute rights of way, while Glentress Forest stretching for more than 2000 acres, offers the walker many miles of forestry paths.

Blackhaugh to Stagehall

Blackhaugh is in the Caddon Water valley at map reference 424383 and a route begins here by crossing the stream and taking a course north-west along a track which climbs the shoulder of Black Law before turning north to Caddonhead and Scroof. Here the route turns east and climbs the ridge. A long descent follows to a crossing of Lugate Water and a finish at Stagehall (M.R. 454444). The distance is 8 miles (13kms.).

Apart from these rights of way, two extended ridge walks may be made in the area. The first is Jeffries Corse to Glede Knowe with a start at Gladhouse reservoir or Portmore Loch. Jeffries Corse lies rather less than 1 mile east from Portmore Loch. A south-easterly course along the main ridge will bring the walker to the county boundary fence at a point where it runs due east and then south for Bowbeat Hill. The fence is then followed over the narrowing ridge to Blackhope Scar after which a moorland traverse of 1½ miles brings the walker to point 1921 ft. (585m.) on the 1-inch O.S. map where a decision must be made either to follow the fence down to the road and cross at the highest point (1250 ft. 381m.) or to include Whitehope Law in the excursion and accept the extra 300 ft. of descent (91m.) which is entailed.

If the higher road crossing is taken then the fence is followed over the open moor to Eastside Heights and Caddon Head. From Whitehope Law the best route is to go south-east from the top so that the descent to Glentress Water is made at a point opposite the narrow ridge called Glentress Rig, which offers the best approach to Windlestraw Law. If the river crossing proves difficult, there is a bridge ½ mile downstream at Whitehope Farm.

From Windlestraw Law the ridge to Glede Knowe provides excellent going and excellent views. The walk may be completed by continuing the descent over Priesthope Hill to Kirnie Law and the convenient ridge which descends to the road junction at Innerleithen. The route as described, omitting Whitehope Law, covers 17½ miles (28kms.) and would require 7½ hours.

The second walk traverses the ridge forming the southern retaining wall of the Leithen Water valley, and a start may be made from Innerleithen by the approach road to St Ronan's Lodge on the western edge of the town, or from the Leithen Water valley at the bridge near the golf course. The narrow stone bridge near Leithen Lodge also offers access to the lower slopes of Black Law but this means that an attractive stretch of ridge is omitted.

Lee Pen at map reference 326387, forms the southern extremity of the ridge and, once this point is gained, a walk of 10½ miles (17kms.) to Portmore Loch is possible along a winding ridge which does not fall below 1400 ft. (427m.). The route runs north to Black Law, above the striking turn in the narrow valley, where Glentress Water joins the Leithen, then north-west to Dunslair Heights with the higher reaches of Glentress Forest close on the left. The ridge then runs due north and offers attractive walking as it rises and falls to the final ascent to the Jeffries Corse plateau. A brief acquaintance is then made with the county boundary fence as it passes over Jeffries Corse, when a descent to the north-west brings the walker to Portmore Loch. The route as described covers 12 miles (19kms.) and 6 hours should be allowed.

The walker wishing to make a round trip and return to his car might combine these two excursions in a single walk, which covered Jeffries Corse, Bowbeat Hill, Blackhope Scar and Black Law. A start and finish at Portmore Loch would involve 19 miles (31kms.) and require not less than 9 hours. A start from Leithen Lodge would shorten the time since rather less ascent is required.

Bus routes. No public transport runs over the B709 road through the Leithen valley.

Edinburgh to Peebles and Galashiels. There is a frequent service on this route from St Andrews Square in Edinburgh.

Accommodation. There is accommodation of all grades in both Peebles and Innerleithen and both towns have caravan sites.

There are two Youth Hostels within a reasonable distance, Broadmeadows, three miles west of Selkirk and Priorwood at Melrose.

BIBLIOGRAPHY

Windlestraw Law, W. Douglas – S.M.C. Journal, Vol. I.
The Moorfoots, William Douglas – S.M.C. Journal, Vol. II.
Moorfoots, F.S.G. – S.M.C. Journal, Vol. X.
The Moorfoot Hills, R. M. Gall Inglis – S.M.C. Journal, Vol. XXIII.
Glentress, Forestry Commission Booklet – H.M.S.O., 1953.

68. Talla Cleuch Head.

69. Megget Water.

70. The Glensax Burn.

71. White Coomb from Loch Skeen.

72. The Devil's Beef Tub, near Moffat.

73. *Above left.* The Grey Mare's Tail.

74. *Above centre.* The Gorge of the Midlaw Burn on Donald's Cleuch Head.

75. *Above right.* Loch Skeen from Lochcraig Head.

76. *Opposite.* White Coomb from the East. Forestry Planting on the floor of the corr

77. White Coomb from Priest Craig.

78. Saddle Yoke and Raven Craig.

79. Swatte Fell.

80. Moffat Water Valley.

81. Looking north-east from Donald's Cleuch Head.

82. The steep flanks of Saddle Yoke from the small spur ot Nether Coomb Craig.

8

The Lammermuir Hills

(1)	**Meikle Says Law**	1755 ft. (535m.)	M.R. 581618
(2)	**Lammer Law**	1730 ft. (527m.)	M.R. 524618
(3)	**Seenes Law**	1683 ft. (513m.)	M.R. 557597
(4)	**Crib Law**	1670 ft. (509m.)	M.R. 525598
(5)	**Lowrans Law**	1631 ft. (497m.)	M.R. 555611
(6)	**Willie's Law**	1626 ft. (490m.)	M.R. 568608
(7)	**Hunt Law**	1625 ft. (495m.)	M.R. 575583

Maps: O.S. 1-inch, Seventh Series, sheet 63.
Bartholomew, ½-inch, sheets 41 and 46.

The Lammermuir Hills form an eastward extension of the Moorfoots and the escarpment, stretching continuously along the northern edge of the two groups as far as the coast, represents the beginning, in a geological sense, of the Southern Uplands as distinct from the Central Lowland valley. The district forms a considerable stretch of high moorland with no really outstanding summits, but the above mentioned seven hills may be selected, all grouped at the western end.

The general character of the Lammermuirs is of long stretches of moorland and somewhat indefinite tops rather than steep slopes and hills of pronounced character. The ground is mainly heather-covered, relatively dry and forming somewhat easier and more predictable walking conditions than the wet peat and thick heather found on some stretches of the Cheviot hills. The simultaneous sighting of 15 mountain hares on a December day emphasises this, for under some conditions even a white hare might not be readily seen. Another important characteristic of the group is that, like the Pentlands, it is not spoiled by a network of roads and it is very easy to achieve a long day's walking out of sight and sound of motor traffic. Here lies a good deal of the charm of these hills, for there are wide and empty horizons, almost endless slopes and, withal, a rainfall of half the amount found on the Ettricks or Moffat Hills.

The hills continue eastwards, at diminishing height, to the coast and here, where the 500 ft. (152m.) contour comes close to the cliffs, lies another attractive area. Some rock routes have already been recorded at Fast Castle Head (M.R. 858711) and further possibilities exist. (Details of these routes are in the chapter on rock climbing.)

This section of coast offers some delightful walking for it is heavily indented and there are fascinating views down to the stacks and skerries, which have been produced by erosion of the rocks. The best area is that between St Abb's Head and Fast Castle.

Further westward, some 2 miles north-west from Preston, is the Edinshall Broch (M.R. 772603), by far the most impressive of the brochs which are known in the area of Scotland south of the River Tay. The site is a delightful spot overlooking the White Adder; the walls of the broch, now about 5 ft. high, enclose a circular court of 55 ft. (17m.) diameter. The walls are some 15–20 ft. (5–6m.) in thickness and the whole structure stands on the site of a fort of much earlier date. The site is maintained by the Ministry of Works and it is so attractive in its own right that it is worth a visit apart from the intrinsic interest of the remains of the broch. If the Gifford road is followed from Preston, an unclassified road turns right after some 2 miles and this should be left where it makes a sharp left-hand turn on the descent to the river. After crossing the stream a stretch of open moorland follows until the broch comes into sight on a shelf overlooking the river. There are very clear traces of both a fort and a settlement on the same site.

At the western extremity of the Lammermuirs are traces of Dere Street, the Roman road which ran from the borders to Newstead and continued to Dalkeith and the shores of the Forth, probably at Cramond. The best defined sections are at Kedslie Hill, south of Lauder at map reference 536400 and further north at map reference 465564, where the line continues from the camp at Kirktonhill to cross the Armet Water. This road passes to the west side of Soutra Hill and it is ironic to think that the traveller, safe as he doubtless was under the protection of Roman law, might well have feared for his life in this same area some 1600 years later. It was here, on the Lauder road, that the infamous 'Lowrie's Den' was to be found, a place feared by every respectable traveller for its reputation of robbery, violence and murder.

Meikle Says Law 1755 ft. (535m.). This hill represents the highest point of the Lammermuirs and lies some two miles north from the headwaters of Dye Water, the stream which runs through Longformacus to join the White Adder. The nearest approach by road is from the minor road which runs north-west from Longformacus towards Gifford. Leaving the road at Faseny Cottage, a walk of 2¼ miles up the left-hand branch of the stream will bring the top under foot. A much longer approach is from the west along the county boundary fence. This crosses the track between Longyester and Tollishill, which is described as a right of way later in the chapter, and a walk of 4½ miles (7kms.) from this point will bring the walker to Meikle Says Law.

The top of the hill is unique in its own small way, since it is marked by an O.S. triangulation point on a small island surrounded by a circular moat. The fence runs to the top.

Willie's Law 1626 ft. (496m.). This hill lies one mile south-west from Meikle Says Law and is reached very quickly from that point. The top is flat and featureless and the boundary fence, which encircles the hill on the north, may become a useful guide.

Seenes Law 1683 ft. (513m.). Two miles south-west from Meikle Says Law lies Seenes Law, another slightly defined hill on the flat ridge which defines the course of Dye Water. The boundary fence passes ½ mile to the north and a walker following the line of the fence from the west would leave it at the centre of the ridge.

Lowrans Law 1631 ft. (397m.). This lies rather less than one mile north from Seenes Law, near the edge of the plateau where it runs down a uniform slope of almost 800 ft. to the Hopes reservoir. It may be approached from that direction or from the west, lying 2 miles from the Longyester–Tollishill track.

Hunt Law 1625 ft. (495m.). 1½ miles south-east from Seenes Law lies Hunt Law, the last point on the ridge which tops the 1600 ft. (488m.) level. The easiest route of access is from the head of the road running along Dye Water, but it should be noted that the road is gated at Byrecleugh, where there is a 'No admittance' notice. There is, however, a right of way from this point and this is referred to in greater detail later in the chapter.

Continuing the south-eastern line from Hunt Law, a distance of four miles (6kms.) would bring the walker to Twinlaw Cairns 1465 ft. (447m.) a hill which deserves mention because of the unique summit cairns. As the name indicates, there are two cairns, built in the form of circular towers some 11 ft. high. The cairns face east of south and each contains a seat to hold one person. Once esconced in this regal perch, the visitor may gaze his fill over the wide expanse of the Tweed valley, no less content, perhaps, that his companion is comfortably out of earshot, so well sited are the cairns. Cheviot lies twenty-seven miles (43kms.) away in the direct line of sight and, on a day when that distance can be covered by the eye, either cairn will offer a noble perch indeed.

The history of the cairns is obscure, but it seems beyond reasonable doubt that they are of considerable age. The easiest route to Twinlaw Cairns is via the unmetalled road which runs from Dye Cottage to Wedderlie. After crossing Watch Water, the road goes over the eastern ridge of the hill and should be left at the point where the fence crosses the road. The top lies 40 minutes away, west by south.

Lammer Law 1730 ft. (527m.). This hill lies less than ½ mile west from the highest point reached by the track between Longyester and Tollishill and is more easily reached than any of the other Lammermuir hills of comparable height. A walk of 3 miles from either end of this track will bring the summit underfoot, but an extra 3¼ miles is required to reach the main road at Carfraemill from Tollishill.

A notice near the head of Kelphope Water reads, 'Parking 3/–; Vans, etc. prohibited; Camping prohibited'.

Two routes which would cover most of the high ground in the western area of the Lammermuirs can be made by starting either at Longyester or Tollishill and following either of the two major ridges to Kilpallet or Longformacus.

Longyester–Longformacus. Take the track which begins at Longyester (M.R. 545652) and follow it to the 1600 ft. (488m.) contour line, from which point Lammer Law may be reached by a short excursion to the west. Continue on the track to the point where the East Lothian–Berwickshire boundary fence crosses and follow this to the east. In two miles the fence passes between Lowrans Law and Seenes Law and the route turns south to follow the ridge. After a further mile another fence is joined which continues the line of the route until it passes to the north of Twin Law Cairns and finally descends to the

Wedderlie–Dye Cottage track. This is followed to the north, over the Watch Water, until a track on the right or east leads of Watch Water reservoir and the Longformacus road. The route is some 16½ miles (27kms.) and 7 hours should be allowed.

Longyester to Kilpallet. This route follows the same ground but continues eastwards along the fence to the right angle at map reference 565606, where a diversion is made to cross Willie's Law. The fence is rejoined to Meikle Says Law and Little Says Law; another corner is straightened out until Kilpallet Heights is reached and a descent made, either direct or along the fence, to the Longformacus–Gifford road at map reference 635612. This route covers rather more than 11 miles (18kms.) and 5 hours should be allowed.

Not all of the Lammermuirs consists of widely-spaced contours and uniform stretches of moorland. The eastern seaboard has already been mentioned and the country between these two types of scenery offers further contrasts with its engaging mixture of cultivated land with open moor. Northwards from the Whiteadder valley lies some 50 square miles (121 sq. kms.) of excellent walking country deeply cut with unfrequented water courses and well out of sight and sound of motor traffic.

Rights of way. The rights of way over the Lammermuirs are of more than usual interest. Taking the routes in order from west to east, we have first the route already described:

1. *Longyester to Tollishill*

Longyester lies some two miles south-east from Gifford at map reference 545652. The track runs south, to pass over the eastern shoulder of Lammer Law and continues to Tollishill (M.R. 519580) at which point a metalled road is joined for Carfraemill on the A697 road.

2. *The Old Herring Road*

This is the route by which saut herrin' were taken from Dunbar to the Border Abbeys and, while there are many variations to the route, the most walkable one is via Halls (M.R. 653727) and over Watch Law and Friardykes Dod to Beltondod (M.R. 660678). The way then runs south-west and south to the B6355 road at Gamelshiel and continues to Kilpallet (M.R. 629606). Crossing the county boundary, the walker reaches Byrecleugh (M.R. 620580) where there is a division, the westerly branch going to Braidshawrig (M.R. 581529) and Wanton Walls (M.R. 548483) and Lauder and the easterly crossing Watch Water to join the Dye Cottage–Wedderlie track at map reference 641546 and finish at Wedderlie (M.R. 644519).

There is a further variation to the Herring road, which appears in the Berwickshire records. This runs from Little Says Law (M.R. 597616) to North Hart Law (M.R. 563588), then continues south to join (at M.R. 558567) a faint track, marked on the 1-inch O.S. map, which continues to Lylestone Hill (M.R. 539530) and joins the A697 road (M.R. 532503).

This variation, like the other in the county of Berwickshire, is referred to as an assumed right of way.

3. *Dye Cottage to Wedderlie*

This route starts from the right bank of the Dye Water at the road bridge (M.R. 650581). An unmetalled road runs south from this point over the ridge then descends to cross Watch Water by a wooden bridge of uncertain years. Continuing the line, the road is joined, at reference 641545, by the right of way track from Byrecleugh. Wedderlie is reached 1½ miles further south (M.R. 644519).

4. *Lodge Wood to Hardens Hill*

A short route with a start some 2½ miles east from Longformacus. From Lodge Wood on the B6365 road (M.R. 735591) the route runs south through Commonside, over Black Hill to join the Longformacus – Duns road at map reference 741541.

5. *Oxton to Stow*

Here we are somewhat outside the area of the Lammermuir Hills with a route which closely follows the western border of Berwickshire, but since the route crosses ground of about 1200 ft. (366m.) it has been deemed worthy of inclusion. O.S. sheet 62.

From Oxton an unclassified road runs south-west, beginning at map reference 497535. This line is followed until it turns south at map reference 480519; the route then continues to Inchkeith and Inchkeith Hill to join the B6362 road 1½ miles east of Stow at map reference 482456.

The following route, though not claimed as a right of way, forms an important and interesting route over the eastern Lammermuirs –

Elmscleugh to Harehead

A minor unclassified road begins at Elmscleugh (M.R. 696718) and runs south-west to climb the moor and descend to the upper reaches of Monynut Water. This line is followed for a short distance, then the road ascends again to follow the ridge for 2 miles, finally descending to Harehead (M.R. 693631). The whole distance is some 6½ miles (10kms.).

Bus routes. The perimeter of the district is well served by public transport from Edinburgh.

Accommodation. Longformacus is the most obvious geographical centre for walking over the Lammermuirs and there is one hotel in the village. On the northern slopes, Gifford also offers accommodation in a most attractive setting. Dunbar, with its wealth of choice, might attract the walker content to snatch odd days of exercise during a family holiday.

There are Youth Hostels at Edinburgh and Coldingham.

BIBLIOGRAPHY

A bit of the Berwickshire Coast and its Birds, W. Douglas - S.M.C.J., Vol. VIII.

9

The Manor Hills

These hills are enclosed by the roads between Tweedsmuir, Talla, St. Mary's Loch, Traquair, Peebles and Drumelzier.

There are three hills of over 2500 ft. (762m.)

(1)	**Broad Law**	2754 ft. (839m.)	M.R. 146235
(2)	**Cramalt Craig**	2723 ft. (830m.)	M.R. 169248
(3)	**Dollar Law**	2680 ft. (817m.)	M.R. 178278

Ten hills of 2000 ft. (610m.) and above:

(4)	**Birkscairn Hill**	2169 ft. (661m.)	M.R. 275332
(5)	**Drumelzier Law**	2191 ft. (668m.)	M.R. 149313
(6)	**Dun Rig**	2433 ft. (743m.)	M.R. 254316
(7)	**Middle Hill**	2340 ft. (713m.)	M.R. 159294
(8)	**Glenrath Heights**	2382 ft. (726m.)	M.R. 241323
(9)	**Black Law**	2285 ft. (610m.)	M.R. 218275
(10)	**Stob Law**	2218 ft. (676m.)	M.R. 230333
(11)	**Talla Cleuch Head**	2264 ft. (690m.)	M.R. 134218
(12)	**Greenside Law**	2110 ft. (643m.)	M.R. 198256
(13)	**Pykestone Hill**	2414 ft. (736m.)	M.R. 174313

and seven tops of 2000 ft. (610m.) and above:

(14)	**Blackhouse Heights**	2214 ft. (675m.)	M.R. 222290
(15)	**Fifescar Knowe**	2650 ft. (808m.)	M.R. 176269
(16)	**Deer Law**	2007 ft. (630m.)	M.R. 223256
(17)	**Hunt Law**	2094 ft. (638m.)	M.R. 150265
(18)	**The Scrape**	2347 ft. (715m.)	M.R. 176325
(19)	**Clockmore**	2105 ft. (641m.)	M.R. 183229
(20)	**Taberon Law**	2088 ft. (636m.)	M.R. 146289

Maps: O.S. 1-inch, Seventh Series, sheets 68 and 69.
Bartholomew, ½-inch, sheet 41.

At Drumelzier (pronounced Drumeelyer) at the eastern end of the Biggar–Broughton Gap the River Tweed changes direction and begins the eastward course which takes it to the sea at Berwick upon Tweed. The first tributary of any size on the right bank is Manor Water, which joins the main stream about a mile to the west of Peebles. The Manor valley runs south for some 9 miles (14kms.)

and gives its name to the group of hills which lie to the north of the road between Talla reservoir and St Mary's Loch, and which are bounded on the west and north by the River Tweed. The group forms a natural continuation of the Moffat Hills for the road through the Megget valley forms the only break in an otherwise continuous belt of high ground stretching for sixteen miles (26kms.) and even this obstacle only involves a descent to 1483 ft. (452m.). The name 'Tweedsmuir Hills' is used on some maps to describe the whole area between Peebles and Moffat. The main features are the high ridge which runs northwards from the Megget watershed along the west side of Manor Water with a somewhat lower ridge running north-east to divide and form Glen Sax. There are none of the striking corries which descend from White Coomb and Saddle Yoke in the Moffat hills, nor are there any crags; the slopes lie at a modest angle and the going is good. Yet the charm of the hills is undeniable. It may be true that it would be possible for a nursemaid to wheel a perambulator along the summit ridge of Broad Law, but it is no hardship to encounter long stretches of excellent going and with a height only a little less than the highest hill in Southern Scotland, a walk over Broad Law brings its own reward. Excellent going is also a feature of the ridge between Cramalt Craig and Dollar Law, but the whole area offers superb opportunities to the hill walker.

Some of the most shapely ridges are those which descend to the upper Tweed valley in the stretch between Talla and Drumelzier and these present a constant invitation when seen from the road. Nor is access any problem here, for there are bridges over the Tweed at a number of points. The Peebles–Selkirk county boundary crosses the Megget–Talla road at the watershed (Megget Stone) and runs over the top of Broad Law and Cramalt Craig to Dollar Law, where it turns east to curve round the compact and shapely head of the Manor Valley and continue along the ridge north-east to Dun Rig at the head of Glen Sax. This is an area of more gently rolling moorland running with a gradual dip to the east where the Douglas and Kirkstead valleys wend their modest ways to Yarrow. To the north of this area are somewhat steeper slopes and more shapely ridges. Hundleshope Heights and Stob Law descend abruptly to the dry valley to the south of Cademuir Hill and offer a most attractive scene under favourable lighting conditions. The width of this valley and the absence of any stream of significant size points to the possibility of it having been formed by Manor Water with the present course of the river representing a later diversion. Another notable feature of the Manor valley is the isolated hill of 1101 ft. (336m.), which stands like a gigantic drumlin in the centre of the valley opposite Glenrath. The 1-inch O.S. map indicates a fort on the summit with the intriguing title of 'Macbeth's Castle', but the origin of this remains obscure and there is no obvious connection with the Thane of Cawdor.

To the east of the Yarrow–Traquair road (B709) lies an area of attractive hill country generally referred to as the Minch Moor from the name of the highest point. It is crossed by a number of tracks, some of great antiquity, and offers some rewarding and worthwhile routes even in an area so richly endowed. The Traquair and Yair Hill Forests which stretch over so much of the northern and eastern slopes add to the attractions of the area.

Talla Cleuch Head 2264 ft. (690m.). This hill is not named on the 1-inch O.S. map. It lies 1¼ miles south-west from the summit of Broad Law and is the highest point of the ridge enclosing Talla reservoir on the north side. The ascent from Talla side is uniformly steep unless the ridge running down to the embankment is taken; the route from Megget, with its added altitude, is even easier. The hills enclosing the head of Talla are impressive on both sides and with suitable lighting conditions and a low cloud ceiling offer a sight a good deal more dramatic than might be expected from their comparatively low height.

Broad Law 2754 ft. (839m.). This is the highest summit in the Manor group and is within ten feet of the height of Merrick the highest point in Southern Scotland. The top of Broad Law may be reached very easily by a two mile walk from the Megget Stone, which marks the highest point of the road between Tweedsmuir and St Mary's Loch. The fence marking the Peebles–Selkirk boundary crosses the road at this point and runs almost directly north to the summit. There is now a car park on the north side of the road between the Megget Stone and the bridge over the Talla burn.

The top of Broad Law carries a radio beacon station, which is served by a road running up from the Tweed valley at Tweedsmuir, but this is not normally available for public use.

Also starting in the Tweed valley is a very shapely ridge which leads directly to the top of Broad Law. This lies a short distance downstream from the bridge at Hearthstane Farm, the end of the ridge being shown on the 1-inch O.S. map as Great Hill. This west-facing slope has recently been planted with conifers and some divergence may be necessary at the start.

Cramalt Craig 2723 ft. (830m.). This hill lies 1½ miles (2·4kms.) to the north-east of Broad Law and represents a climb of over 500 ft. (152m.) when approached from that direction. This south-west face is very wide and lies at an easy angle with the fence continuing the direct line to the top. Here a large cairn stands at the point where the fence turns from east to north. Cramalt Craig sends out a long ridge to the north-west into the Tweed valley. This forms the twin ridge to the much narrower ridge beginning at Great Hill and running to Broad Law. 1½ miles from Cramalt Craig lies Hunt Law 2094 ft. (638m.), one of the two subsidiary tops. It lies on the ridge 3 miles (5kms.) from the road and may be reached by using the bridge at Patervan Farm. The bridge at Stanhope, a short distance downstream, is marked as a private road.

Clockmore 2105 ft. (641m.). This is the second subsidiary top of Cramalt Craig, lying 1½ miles to the south-east from the cairn and forming the terminal point of the ridge which runs in that direction to the Megget valley. Its ascent from that point presents no problem for it rises directly above the Megget road.

Dollar Law 2680 ft. (817m.) has a very long and almost level summit ridge, on which two named tops are shown on the 1-inch O.S. Map – Dun Law 2585 ft. (788m.) and Fifescar Knowe 2650 ft. (808m.)

The map also shows a spur to the south-east, extending for ½ mile which bears the name Notman Law 2409 ft. (734m.). Of these three tops only Fifescar Knowe is listed in *Munro's Tables*. Dollar Law rises directly above and to the west of Manorhead Farm, which lies ½ mile beyond the end of the metalled road along Manor Water. The ascent from this point is straightforward but steep and rises for over 1500 ft. (457m.). The slopes facing west towards the Tweed are much less steep but an approach walk of some 2½ miles (4kms.) up the Stanhope glen is a necessary preliminary if a start is made from that side.

At a point about half way along the summit ridge between Dollar Law and Dun Law, the fence marking the county boundary turns a right angle to the east while the parish boundary fence continues the northward line. A descent then follows to a col which forms a natural pass between the Tweed valley and Manor Water, which at this point are both flowing north-east. The western slope of the pass shows traces of a wide grass road, while the col itself is marked by several high rectangular stone cairns, a fact acknowledged on the 1-inch O.S. map, which bears the name Newholm Cairns Hill at this point.

The line of the grass road continues along the eastern slope of Long Grain Knowe avoiding the ascent to the summit, which, at 2308 ft. (703m.) is some 350 ft. higher than the col.

Middle Hill 2340 ft. (713m.). This offers slightly more complexity than most of the other hills in the group for the name does not appear on the 1-inch O.S. map and there is some doubt as to the accuracy of the contours shown. Lying ½ mile west from the boundary fence at Long Grain Knowe on the main ridge, the hill top covers an area of some size, further complicated by the omission of Long Grain Knowe and Glenstivon Dod from the list of subsidiary tops, for both these names appear on the map. The contours of the western slopes follow the curve of the ridge forming the Hopecarton glen and Middle Hill at the very head of the glen certainly appears to represent the highest point. Continuing northward along the ridge west of Manor a walk of 2 miles from Dollar Law brings us to –

Pykestone Hill 2414 ft. (736m.) whose top rises gently from the level of the ridge and is easily reached on a stretch of excellent going. A flat-topped ridge runs from the top to the north-east before descending steeply to Manor. This ridge is marked Posso Craig on the 1-inch O.S. map and its ascent offers no problems; an alternative route from this side is by way of the track to Old Kirkhope.

The Scrape 2347 ft. (715m.) is ¾ mile north of Pykestone Hill and forms a subsidiary top. The most pleasant ascent is by the grass road which leaves the Manor valley 1 mile to the south of the ruined tower at the roadside which marks Castlehill Farm. This road runs up to a small plantation of Scots pine and the line continues to the ridge and down to the Tweed valley at a point opposite Stobo Castle. From the highest point of this path less than two miles walking over easy slopes leads to The Scrape. The line is marked by a dry-stone wall which forms the parish boundary. The hill marks the end of the main ridge on the west bank of Manor for the hills further north gradually diminish into the minor slopes above the Tweed. For this reason The Scrape is another notable viewpoint, for Tweeddale is an attractive area by any standards and the curves of the river form an entrancing foreground to the northern prospect.

Drumelzier Law 2191 ft. (668m.). When the narrow upper portion of the Tweed valley is entered near Drumelzier the first glen on the left or eastern side of the road has some visual claim to be the most attractive. This glen contains the Hopecarton Burn and Drumelzier Law lies on the northern ridge. It is an attractive hill and shares with other nearby vantage points the advantage of enabling the viewer to look over almost all the ground to the north and north-west for a considerable distance. Access to the ridge may be made by taking the grassy track which leaves the road just before the river bridge on the west of Drumelzier. This track runs along the foot of the ridge to rejoin the main road above a ford. It may be useful to note that there is a footbridge a little way upstream from this ford, for the top of Drumelzier Law is then within 1½ miles.

Taberon Law 2088 ft. (636m.). This is a subsidiary top of Middle Hill and lies on the southern arm of the ridge enclosing the Hopecarton Burn and 1½ miles south from its 'twin', Drumelzier Law across the glen. The hill may be approached directly from the Tweed valley by way of the ridge or traversed by an excursion over both ridges and Middle Hill itself.

Greenside Law 2110 ft. (643m.). This hill lies immediately south of Manorhead Farm and is one of the two hills enclosing the head of the Manor Water valley. The opposite hill, Shielhope Head, merges into the eastern slopes of Dollar Law and does not appear in Section 3 of 'Munro's Tables', either as a hill or as a subsidiary top. The top of Greenside Law may be reached by following the line of Manor Water from the head of the valley until the ridge is gained; the top is then 250 ft. higher on the east side. The alternative, and no less satisfying, route is to take the footpath which begins at the end of the surfaced road in Manor and is marked as a right of way to St Mary's Loch. This track rises on easier slopes and offers excellent going, passing less than ½ mile to the east of Greenside Law. The track continues to join the Megget road, 1½ miles from the junction with the main road at Cappercleuch on St Mary's Loch.

Black Law 2285 ft. (610m.) lies 1½ miles east of Manorhead Farm. It begins the ridge which runs north-east for some 5 miles to Birkscairn Hill above Glen Sax. The ascent may be made by taking the track from Manorhead to a point where the fence may be seen on the left and following this to the top. An alternative approach is by the Kirkstead Burn at the east end of St Mary's Loch; the head waters of this stream rise from the eastern slopes of Black Law. A similar but much longer valley approach is by the Douglas Burn, past Blackhouse Farm and Muttonhall to the head of the glen where the left hand branch runs south-east to within ¾ mile of the top.

Blackhouse Heights 2214 ft. (675m.) is a subsidiary of Black Law 1 mile to the north.

Deer Law 2067 ft. (630m.) is a second subsidiary top slightly more than one mile to the south. From its top the ground slopes down to Cappercleuch at the foot of Megget Water. The ascent from this point requires less than 1½ miles of walking.

Glenrath Heights 2382 ft. (726m.) lies at the head of the Glenrath valley which drains westward into Manor. The ascent is most easily made by this route since there is an excellent track to Glenrathope where one is less than one mile from the top. A much longer approach from the south begins with the 4 mile approach walk up the course of the Douglas Burn to Muttonhall. This house lies at the foot of the ridge marked Drycleuch Law on the 1-inch O.S. map and the ascent of this leads to the long ridge of Dun Rig. From here a northerly course for 1 mile brings Glenrath Heights underfoot.

The ridge continues north from Glenrath Heights to Hundleshope Heights, which is not recognised as a subsidiary top, and terminates in ridges which point like the fingers of a hand towards Peebles.

Stob Law 2218 ft. (676m.) branches to the west from the main line of the ridge running to Hundleshope. It may be ascended either from Glenrath or via the Hundleshope Burn from the north. Either of the two ridges of Canada Hill behind Hundleshope or Cademuir farms provides a more satisfying route.

Dun Rig 2433 ft. (742m.). This is the highest summit in the eastern section of the Manor hills. It lies only three-quarters of a mile south-east from Glenrath Heights and, with that hill, encloses the head of Glen Sax. It represents, so far as the Manor hills are concerned, the most northerly point reached by the Selkirk–Peebles boundary fence. It may be reached from Muttonhall on the Douglas Burn or by taking the well-defined track which leaves this stream at a point ½ mile west from Blackhouse.

Birkscairn Hill 2169 ft. (661m.) lies 1½ miles north-east from Dun Rig on the east side of Glen Sax. The ascent by the eastern ridge of this glen is straightforward and the top on a clear day will be found a most rewarding viewpoint, since it should be possible to see both the Pentlands and Cheviot. There is a fence running from Dun Rig to Birkscairn Hill and this continues over Kirkhope Law and towards Peebles, although the going on the northern stretch is made somewhat tedious by the ploughing which accompanies forestry planting. A descent to Glen Sax is to be recommended before this point is reached.

Mention has already been made of the fence which marks the Peebles–Selkirk boundary. This forms an important feature of the Manor hills, since it runs in an unbroken line from the Megget Stone over Broad Law, Cramalt Craig, the ridge of Dollar Law, Greenside Law and the remaining heights to Dun Rig. Since the parish boundary fence continues along the ridge of Dollar Law and over Pykestone Hill and the Scrape, it will be seen that these fences constitute an invaluable guide in conditions of poor visibility.

It is hardly possible to contemplate a continuous line of this type over such attractive country without the thoughts turning to the fence as a basis for a long distance walk. To traverse the whole line, starting at the Megget Stone above Talla and finishing via Birkscairn Hill at Peebles would involve a walk of some 19 miles (31kms.) and not less than 8 hours.

The Manor Water valley. The road up the Manor Water valley forms an important access route to the Manor hills. The approach road leaves the A72 main road about 1 mile to the west of Peebles and there is a well surfaced road to within ½ mile of Manorhead Farm at the valley head, at which point we are within three miles of the Megget Valley road. There are bridges across Manor Water at the commencement of the track to St Mary's Loch from the head of the valley, at the point where the road crosses a cattle grid and enters open grassland and below Castlehill Farm, which is identified by a ruined tower at the side of the road. This particular bridge, visible from the road, is a useful crossing for the walker bound for Peebles, since it gives access to a grass track on the east side of the valley which leads to Cademuir Farm. From this point the most direct route to Peebles is over Cademuir Hill by a grass track which leads behind the plantation and continues to the town. The western end of Cademuir Hill contains two Iron Age forts with the lower of the two still showing traces of the original dry-stone walling at one point on the perimeter, while in the same area the pointed stones set upright in the ground are considered to have been set there for defensive purposes. Yet a further example of these forts may be seen across the valley on a prominent spur to the south of Hundleshope Farm; the assiduous seeker after antiquities will not lack for interest in this neighbourhood.

Another grass road of interest to the walker leaves the Manor valley on the west side near the turning for Glen Rath (M.R. 206343) and goes up the side of a plantation some distance above the road. This track continues to the B712 road near Stobo Castle where there is a bridge over the Tweed (M.R. 176363).

Rights of Way. The following routes in the Peebles–Manor district are recognised as rights of way:

1. *Manorhead to Megget*

The track from the head of the Manor valley has already been mentioned. The commencement is at M.R. 199286, where there is a signpost erected by the Scottish Rights of Way Society 'To St Mary's Loch'. The route is well graded, fairly well defined and cairned on the higher stretch. The track terminates at Glengaber in the Megget valley (M.R. 217232). Distance is 4 miles (6kms.).

2. *Manor–Glack–Stobo*

Another crossing of the ridge between Manor and Tweed begins at Glack (M.R. 213379). Keep to the left of the farm and pass along an enclosed road until opposite Stobo station, where there is a bridge over the Tweed (M.R. 182374). Distance 2 miles (3kms.).

3. *Cademuir*

The track over Cademuir Hill has already been described, but since it constitutes a right of way, the following additional details are given. Starting from the south side of Tweed Bridge, Peebles, continue

83. The Auchencat Burn flowing from Hart Fell. Queensberry in distance.

84. Bodesbeck to Saddle Yoke.

85. Gameshope and the Gameshope Burn.

86. The car park and start of the gorge of the Grey Mare's Tail—the famous beauty spot by the Moffat Water in Dumfriesshire.

87. Gorge of the Grey Mare's Tail.

88. Hart Fell (right) from A701.

89. *Below left.* Bodesbeck Law.

90. *Above right.* The head of the Selcoth Burn looking to Ettrick Head.

91. *Opposite right.* The Moffat Water looking towards the Birkhill Pass.

92. The Culter Water from slopes of Knock Hill.

93. Culter Reservoir.

94. Kilbucho Glen looking east.

95. The Hen Hole, Cheviot.

96. Upper Hindhope at the Head of Kale Water.

97. River Breamish Valley, Cheviots.

along Caledonian Road and at the end turn left and follow Edderston Road up to the private entrance to Tantah (M.R. 246394). On the right is a gate leading on to the moor with a sign indicating that it is a right of way. This path rejoins the road near Cademuir Farm (M.R. 230371). Distance 3 miles (5kms.).

4. *Peebles to Dryhope*

Another important right of way in the district is Peebles to Dryhope Tower in Selkirkshire. Cross Tweed Bridge in Peebles to the south bank and turn right into Springhill Road. Follow this to the end of the metalled road, where a bridle path continues the line (M.R. 262390). This path is the line of the main drove road through Southern Scotland from Falkirk Tryst to the border, King's Muir in Peebles being a resting place for the cattle, with rights of common pasture dating back to 1506.

The route continues over Kirkhope Law to Birkscairn Hill after which the route from Glen Sax is joined and the path turns south to curve round the head of the Quair Water valley and Loch Eddy. A rise over Whiteknowe Head brings a descent to the Douglas Burn and Blackhouse and the route finishes by traversing rising ground to the south-west to reach Dryhope Tower, near the eastern end of St Mary's Loch at map reference 267246.

The continuation of the line of the Douglas Burn from Blackhouse (M.R. 281273) to Craig Douglas (M.R. 292240) is also a right of way. Distance is 11½ miles (19kms.) to Dryhope, slightly less to Craig Douglas.

5. *Kirkhouse to Dryhope*

A further variation begins at Kirkhouse (M.R. 322336) from which point there is a right of way along Quair Water to the end of the road at Glenshiel Banks, from which point a track leads over Peat Hill and joins the main right of way on the descent to the Douglas Burn and Dryhope. Distance – Kirkhouse to Dryhope 9 miles (14kms.).

6. *Damhead to Deuchar*

Damhead lies (on M.R. 329341) to the south of Traquair and is the starting point for one of the rights of way which cross the tract of hill country between Selkirk and Innerleithen. The route runs south from Damhead to Glengaber, then crosses the col between Glengaber Hill and Peatshank Head to descend to Deuchar (M.R. 360281) on Yarrow Water. Distance is 5 miles (8kms.).

7. *Traquair Rig to Philiphaugh*

This route stretches some ten miles between Traquair and Selkirk and forms the longest and possibly the most rewarding crossing of this stretch of hill country, since the main ridge is followed for much of the way. Starting at Traquair Rig (M.R. 331346) the route climbs towards Minch Moor summit through the forest and passes to the north of the top. The county fence is followed for a distance until it turns north, the route then continues along the ridge until a descent is made along the line of the Philip burn, the main road being joined at M.R. 456287. Distance is 10 miles (16kms.).

8. *Broadmeadows to Yair House*

This route offers yet a third right of way over this country and crosses the Traquair Rig–Philiphaugh track at the eastern end. Leaving the A708 road at M.R. 413300 the route passes the Youth Hostel (Broadmeadows) then leaves the line of the stream to turn east and cross the ridge. The way then crosses a second ridge to descend through the forest to Yair and join the road ½ mile east of the bridge over the Tweed at M.R. 458325. Distance is 4 miles (6kms.).

Another useful and attractive link with the Philiphaugh route begins at Yarrowford (M.R. 407300) with a track which climbs the ridge towards Brown Knowe. There is no evidence that this represents a right of way, although it is marked 'Minchmoor Road' on the 1-inch O.S. map. Distance, Brown Knowe to Yarrowford is 2½ miles (4kms.); Traquair Rig to Yarrowford is 6½ miles (10kms.).

The route over the Minchmuir to Selkirk was at one time a drove road and formed an alternative way southwards from Peebles to that via Kirkhope Law and Dryhope. From Selkirk the cattle were driven towards the border either by way of Buccleuch and Teviothead, or more directly through Hawick and southwards to either the North or South Tyne valleys.

Bus Services. There is no public transport in the Manor valley, but there are excellent bus services between Peebles and Edinburgh and Glasgow. There is, therefore, a good service along the B712 road to Peebles–Broughton and Drumelzier. The A708 road from Moffat to St Mary's Loch and Selkirk is covered by an infrequent service.

Accommodation. There are hotels at Tweedsmuir, St Mary's Loch and Innerleithen, while accommodation of all grades may be found in Peebles. There is a Youth Hostel at Broadmeadows, three miles west of Selkirk and caravan sites at Peebles and Innerleithen.

BIBLIOGRAPHY

Minchmoor, W. Douglas – S.M.C. Journal, Vol. I.
Peebles to St Mary's Loch by Glen Sax, S.M.C. Journal, Vol. IV.
The First Official Meet – Crook Inn 27th *February*, 1891, Thos. H. Bryce – S.M.C. Journal, Vol. XXII.
The Peeblesshire Hills, W. L. Coats – S.M.C. Journal, Vol. XXIII.

10

The Moffat Hills

These hills lie in the triangle formed by the three roads – Moffat–St Mary's Loch (A708); Moffat–Tweedsmuir (A701); Taila reservoir–St Mary's Loch.

There are four hills of over 2500 ft. (762m.):

(1)	**Hart Fell**	2651 ft. (808m.)	M.R. 114136
(2)	**Lochcraig Head**	2625 ft. (800m.)	M.R. 167175
(3)	**White Coomb**	2695 ft. (821m.)	M.R. 163151
(4)	**Molls Cleuch Dod**	2571 ft. (784m.)	M.R. 152180

six hills of over 2000 ft. (610m.):

(5)	**Erie Hill**	2259 ft. (688m.)	M.R. 124188
(6)	***Under Saddle Yoke**	2445 ft. (745m.)	M.R. 142127
(7)	**Garelet Dod**	2263 ft. (690m.)	M.R. 125173
(8)	***Whitehope Heights**	2090 ft. (637m.)	M.R. 095138
(9)	**Cape Law**	2364 ft. (690m.)	M.R. 131151
(10)	**Swatte Fell**	2390 ft. (728m.)	M.R. 118114

and eleven tops of over 2000 ft. (610m.):

(11)	**Garelet Hill**	2231 ft. (680m.)	M.R. 124201
(12)	**Din Law**	2182 ft. (665m.)	M.R. 124157
(13)	***Laird's Cleuch Rig**	2237 ft. (682m.)	M.R. 125197
(14)	**Firthhope Rig**	2627 ft. (801m.)	M.R. 153154
(15)	**Carlavin Hill**	2383 ft. (726m.)	M.R. 140190
(16)	**Carrifran Gans**	2452 ft. (747m.)	M.R. 158137
(17)	**Nickie's Knowe**	2492 ft. (759m.)	M.R. 165192
(18)	**Saddle Yoke**	2412 ft. (735m.)	M.R. 144124
(19)	**Great Hill**	2540 ft. (774m.)	M.R. 145165
(20)	***Falcon Craig**	2373 ft. (723m.)	M.R. 123127
(21)	**Nether Coomb Craig**	2373 ft. (723m.)	M.R. 129110

* not marked on 1-inch O.S. Map.

Maps: O.S. 1-inch, Seventh Series, sheets 68 and 69.
Bartholomew, $\frac{1}{2}$-inch, sheet 41.

To the northbound traveller on the Carlisle–Glasgow road the group of hills lying to the north of Moffat form the first really impressive area of high ground to be seen in Scotland, and if the short diversion is made to Moffat not only do the slopes of Hart Fell form an impressive background, but the character of the town is quickly conveyed to the traveller with a sensitive eye for landscape. Hart Fell and the continuation ridge to Swatte Fell represent the southern extremity of a belt of high ground of a character unusual in southern Scotland. The hill tops are flat and offer excellent walking conditions, mainly on grass yet the eastern slopes are almost continuously steep and broken. The beauty of these hills may be readily appreciated if the journey is continued north-eastwards from Moffat along the Selkirk road for a most impressive landscape is encountered immediately. The road is narrow and winding between Moffat and St Mary's Loch and for the first two or three miles it is not easy to leave a car off the road. A large plantation covers the lower slopes for some distance but when Capplegill is reached at the foot of Blackhope Glen the view opens out and it is possible to see, even from the road, how attractive is the wild valley which runs westwards towards Hart Fell. The left-hand side of the glen contains long stretches of broken crags, divided by sharp ridges. There is too much grass and loose shaly rock to interest the rock climber, but the wild and impressive nature of the valley is at once apparent. The north side of the glen is less precipitous but still steep enough to make a satisfying mountain landscape when seen from Swatte Fell; indeed the view from here towards Whirley Gill on the northern slopes has been praised by at least one writer as an excellent example of mountain form, small in scale but not in proportion.

Another attractive feature of Blackhope Glen is the beautiful narrow curve of the grassy ridge which ascends to Saddle Yoke almost from the road. This is a route which holds a perpetual invitation to the walker and the ascent and circuit of the glen should not be missed.

At the head of the glen and close under the summit of Hart Fell is a stretch of crag of some 100–150 ft., which offers some attraction to the rock climber, being notably cleaner and less broken than the lower crags.

A short distance further north lies the entrance to the Carrifran Glen, the second of the three rocky valleys which add so much to the character of the Moffat Hills. It is only from a viewpoint on Bodesbeck Law, on the eastern side of the valley, that it is appreciated how high the tide of forestry has begun to lap around these hills and how harshly the hard edges of the plantations disrupt the natural curves.

The Carrifran glen penetrates less deeply into the plateau than Blackhope, but yields nothing in interest and character. The steep face of Carrifran Gans on the north side and the rocks of Priest Craig and Raven Craig at the head of the glen combine to form a harmonious and satisfying whole.

The corrie to the north of Carrifran Gans is easily entered and its gentle slopes offer ready access to the col between this hill and White Coomb. The continuation of the walk to Raven Craigs and Saddle Yoke offers as rewarding an experience as the circuit of Blackhope.

A short distance further north we enter National Trust property at the point where the Tail Burn from Loch Skeen forms the Grey Mare's Tail waterfall, only a short distance from the road. There are extensive car parks at this point, as the falls are sufficiently well known as a tourist attraction to draw considerable crowds in the summer months, so that the walker arriving here in search of a little peaceful hill walking may view the scene without enthusiasm. However, the track up the right-hand (true left) side of the stream is steep, there are notices warning tourists of the danger and it may well be found that a few minutes steady ascent brings the scene into better perspective. The track continues to Loch Skeen, winding in its higher reaches through the area of glacial debris which is so much in evidence near the foot of the loch and on the lower slopes of White Coomb across the burn.

Loch Skeen is ¾ mile long and lies in a magnificent setting, enclosed by the steep face of Lochcraig Head and the even more broken ridge which runs eastwards form Firthybrig Head towards the foot of the loch. A flat and somewhat featureless moor stretches eastwards towards St Mary's Loch.

There is little to choose between the routes on either bank of the loch but, having reached the northern end, a short ascent of only 500 ft. (152m.) brings the walker to the col between Firthybrig Head and Lochcraig Head. A descent to the north from this point enables the Megget Stone on the Talla–St Mary's Loch road to be reached very quickly. So excellent is the going on the ridge of Lochcraig Head that it is probably even quicker to accept the slight altitude penalty incurred and descend to Megget by this route, so avoiding the wet ground in the glen.

The area of the National Trust property around Loch Skeen is quite extensive, being defined by the line of the Peebles–Dumfries county boundary from the summit of the road at Birkhill Pass across the moor to the east of the loch and over the tops of Lochcraig Head, Firthybrig Head, Donald's Cleuch and Firthhope Rig. Here it turns east away from the county boundary, and goes along the ridge to White Coomb and Carrifran Gans, finally traversing the eastern corrie of White Coomb to descend to the road down the south bank of the ravine.

The stretch of road between the Grey Mare's Tail and Birkhill Pass is perhaps the most impressive few miles in the whole of the Southern Uplands, for the steepness of the hills on both sides is maintained as the valley narrows. Once over the pass a wider valley is entered and the road descends to St Mary's Loch. The hills continue on both sides, the highest point being a somewhat neglected hill 1½ miles to the east of the neck of land between Loch of the Lowes and St Mary's Loch.

The Wiss 1933 ft. (589m.) M.R. 264207. The unmade road between this neck and the Yarrow–Ettrick road curves round the southern ridge of this hill and offers ready access.

At Cappercleuch, half way along St Mary's Loch (A708), a turning may be made into the Megget Valley. This road has been re-surfaced and offers an ideal access route to both the Manor and Moffat hills, particularly since a car park has been provided a short distance to the west of the summit. From this point two ridges may be seen on the south side of the road, enclosing the upper reaches of Talla Water. Either of these offers easy access to the main ridge and the possibility of a continuous high-level walk to Hart Fell.

From the top at 1483 ft. (452m.) the road descends much more steeply to Talla reservoir and joins the A701 road at Tweedsmuir. The ascent of the Tweed valley from this point leads past the Devils Beef Tub and descends to Moffat and the A74 road. Some two miles to the north of the Beef Tub is a signpost indicating the source of the River Tweed about ½ mile away on the east side of the road.

The summit of this road at Tweedshaws is almost as high as Megget and at 1334 ft. (407m.) is often the scene of heavy drifting during snowstorms. It was here that the guard and the coachman of the Dumfries–Edinburgh mail coach died in a determined attempt to carry the mail over the hill on foot when the task proved too great for the horses. This tragedy, in February 1831, made a great impression on the public conscience, an impression by no means wholly removed for the Moffat road seems even now associated with these two men and their devotion to their task.

MacGeorge, the guard of the coach, had an overwhelming sense of duty and it was he who urged the coach forward from Moffat in a snowfall heavy enough to justify delay. When it became impossible to force the coach further through the drifts, the horses were taken out and two of them, loaded with mail bags, were led forward up the hill. Then it became clear that even the horses were not able to face the drifting snow and MacGeorge and his coachman shouldered the bags and went on. The mail bags were found next day tied to a post but the bodies of the two men were not found for several days.

Hart Fell 2651 ft. (808m.). This is the highest point of a fairly complex hill which sends down several ridges towards the Annan valley and Moffat. The ascent may be made by two routes from Moffat; first, by what is called locally 'The Well Road'. This leaves the town in a northerly direction to Archbank and Moffat Well and the ascent may be made by following this line over Greygill Head to Swatte Fell 2390 ft. (728m.) and continuing a delightful ridge walk to Hart Fell itself. The alternative route, which leads directly to the top of Hart Fell is to walk along the road on the east or true left bank of the Annan river for some 3 miles (4·8kms.) until a signpost and footpath are reached to Hart Fell Spa. Marker posts indicate the route to the Well which is at 1150 ft. (351m.) on the left fork of the stream. The top of Hart Fell is reached in 1½ miles from this point.

Yet another and very interesting route is via the Beef Tub at Annanhead. There is a car park at this point, often well patronised in winter since the slopes of Black Fell on the west side of the road attract quite a number of skiers. The route to Hart Fell curves round the undulating rim of the Beef Tub and picks up the line of the Peebles–Dumfries county boundary, a fence which leads to the top of Whitehope Heights before descending to a col at 1750 ft. (533m.) and beginning the final climb to Hart Fell.

An excellent view rewards the walker, for clear weather at the summit seems to disclose a plain of infinite size to the south and one gains an impression of standing on the very edge of all the hills. Sunlight over the Solway Firth adds to the sense of distance.

Whitehope Heights 2090 ft. ap. (637m. ap.). This hill is not named on the 1-inch O.S. map nor is the height quoted in detail. It lies a little over 1 mile west by north from Hart Fell and is most easily ascended by the route from the Beef Tub already described or from Ericstane Farm on Annan Water.

Swatte Fell 2390 ft. (728m.). This hill lies less than 1½ miles from Hart Fell, being south by east from the higher summit. A more interesting route to the top than the long plod from Moffat may be made from Capplegill in the Moffat Water valley. It is possible to get a car off the road at this point and the ascent may be made by either ridge of the Blackhope burn, according to the time available. An alternative route for hard winter conditions, but only for the experienced, is the ridge which descends to Blackhope between Upper and Nether Coomb Craig.

Nether Coomb Craig 2373 ft. (723m.). This point is a subsidiary top of Swatte Fell and lies ¾ mile southeast from that point, being the southern tip of the crescent-shaped ridge forming the east face of Swatte Fell.

Falcon Craig 2373 ft. (723m.) is also a subsidiary top and forms the northern tip of this ridge, rather more than a mile from Nether Coomb Craig. Neither of these tops is named as such on the 1-inch O.S. map but the steep face below the southern top is named.

Under Saddle Yoke 2445 ft. (745m.). This name is taken from the 6-inch O.S. map and does not appear on the 1-inch. The hill lies on the opposite side of the Blackhope burn to Swatte Fell and forms a short ridge of a ¼ mile running northwest–southeast. The subsidiary and slightly lower top at the southern end is named on the 1-inch map as Saddle Yoke 2412 ft. (735m.). Both these hills may be ascended from Capplegill by way of the attractive ridge running south-east from the top down to Moffat Water. This ridge terminates in an engaging little peak before broadening into the main summit and the keen photographer will scarcely need the advice to begin on this side of the Blackhope glen rather than the Swatte Fell side for the morning sun will add shape and shadow to the facing slopes as he ascends. The rising sweep of the ridges in this glen shows a balance of mountain form not readily appreciated by the passer-by on the road.

Carrifran Gans 2452 ft. (747m.). This hill lies on the northern side of the Carrifran Burn and shows a steep and broken face to that glen. It forms a subsidiary top to White Coomb, which lies a mile to the north but its ascent and the circuit of the Carrifran Glen forms a very pleasant expedition in its own right. The lower slopes of the hill facing Moffat Water have been planted with conifers and some restriction on access is therefore unavoidable, but an easy route may be found from the corrie on the south side of White Coomb. A track will be found on the side of the burn flowing from this corrie and the easy northern slopes offer no obstacles. The top is flat and grass covered, a replica of White Coomb, some 450 ft. (137m.) higher. Seen from Raven Craig at the head of the glen, the Carrifran Burn makes a steep and picturesque descent in a series of water slides and a walk round the rim of this glen from Carrifran Gans to Saddle Yoke should on no account be missed.

White Coomb 2695 ft. (821m.). This is the highest summit in the Moffat group of hills, overtopping Hart Fell by some 40 ft. Its ascent may be made from Moffat Water by way of the wide corrie on the east side of the hill or, alternatively, by the track which goes up the north bank of the Tail Burn at the Grey Mare's Tail fall, crossing the stream above this obstacle. Some care may be advisable here since there are several smaller falls above the Grey Mare's Tail, which are not very obvious from above. The eastern shoulder of the hill is steep and broken and an easier route may be found by traversing west towards Loch Skeen. The walker traversing the whole group from Hart Fell northwards will find that the diversion of White Coomb from his route where it crosses Firthhope Rig requires a walk of only ½ mile and a very slight rise.

Firthhope Rig 2627 ft. (801m.). This represents the second subsidiary top of White Coomb and lies ½ mile west by north from the main summit. As already indicated, it lies on the main trade route running from Megget to Hart Fell and Moffat and is more likely to be ascended on that traverse than in its own right.

Great Hill 2540 ft. (774m.). The third top of White Coomb lies 1¼ miles north-west from the main summit. Its west and north west facing slopes run down into the Gameshope valley, whose stream flows into Talla reservoir and this route offers the easiest ascent. There is an excellent track as far as the empty house marked Gameshope on the 1-inch O.S. map and the top is 1½ miles south-east from this point.

Cape Law 2364 ft. (690m.). This hill represents the southern end of the ridge which runs from Talla Linnfoots along the west side of the Gameshope valley. The top lies 2 miles west of White Coomb and 3½ miles from Talla Linnfoots. The ascent may be made by taking the track up the Gameshope valley running south from Talla or by the slightly shorter route from Moffat Water up the ridge leading to Saddle Yoke which begins near Capplegill. From the top of Saddle Yoke bear right along the crags which fall to the Carrifran Burn until the top of the ridge is reached. Cape Law is then 1 mile to the north-west.

Din Law 2182 ft. (665m.). This hill is a subsidiary top of Cape Law lying a little over ½ mile to the north-west. It is most easily ascended by walking up the Gameshope valley from Talla to the small plateau containing Gameshope Loch. A short ascent leads to Din Law. The walk up this valley is attractive and well worthwhile, but the walker of normal ambitions and energy is hardly likely to be satisfied with so minor an objective and may well feel that the circuit of the Gameshope valley by the east and west ridges is a more satisfying objective for a day's walk.

Garelet Dod 2263 ft. (690m.). This hill continues the line of the ridge forming the west side of the Gameshope valley and the top lies 2 miles south by west from Talla Linnfoots. It should not be confused with Garelet Hill which is a top at the northern end of the same ridge. Garelet Dod is most easily ascended from the Gameshope valley and rises above the house of that name at the end of the track. The top is of considerable area with the summit lying at the western edge. The hill would be equally accessible from the Fruid glen to the west of Talla but the road along the reservoir now completed in that valley is not a through route and the approach is not recommended.

Erie Hill 2259 ft. (688m.). This is the highest point on the final section of the ridge, here running due north and south. Erie Hill is 1¼ miles south west from Talla Linnfoots and is most easily ascended from that point. It should be noted that a wall runs from the county boundary on Cape Law over Din Law, Garelet Dod and Erie Hill to the end of the ridge at Garelet Hill, a feature which may be of direct assistance in bad visibility.

Laird's Cleuch Rig 2237 ft. (682m.). This point is not named on the 1-inch O.S. map but is a subsidiary top of Erie Hill, appearing on the 6-inch O.S. map. It lies a little over ½ mile north of Erie Hill, the route of ascent being from Talla Linnfoots.

Garelet Hill 2231 ft. (680m.). This is also a subsidiary top of Erie Hill, lying slightly more than ¾ mile north from the main summit. The ridge descending east to Talla Linnfoots is an attractive route in either ascent or descent being easier in angle than the slopes running directly down to the water on the northern face. The walker who is under no necessity to return to a car might well elect to finish his walk by the north west ridge running above Talla towards the Tweedsmuir road. This gives a very pleasant route of some 3½ miles (8kms.) but it may be noted that extensive forestry planting has recently been carried out on the slopes at the end of this ridge.

Molls Cleuch Dod 2571 ft. (784m.). This hill is the highest point on the ridge forming the east side of the Gameshope valley. It lies 1¾ miles south-east from Talla Linnfoots and has a ridge running north towards the Megget Stone. The easiest line of ascent is by this ridge but the top lies only ½ mile north-west from the angle of the wall marking the county boundary on Firthybrig Head. A wall runs from this angle to Molls Cleuch Dod and continues to Carlavin Hill further north.

Carlavin Hill 2383 ft. (726m.). This is a subsidiary top of Molls Cleuch Dod, lying about ¾ mile from that point. The ascent may be made, very steeply, from Talla Linnfoots but a more reasonable starting point is the bridge where the road from Talla crosses the stream. There is a car park a little higher which offers an advantage of 350 ft. compared with the lower starting point.

Lochcraig Head 2625 ft. (800m.). This hill rises very steeply to the north of the head of Loch Skeen and lies 1½ miles north by east from White Coomb. The ascent from the Megget Stone, two miles to the north, offers a pleasant route over excellent going. Another attractive approach is from the north-east via the Winterhope valley. This enters the Megget Valley some 2 miles downstream from Megget Stone with a bridge somewhat further downstream. The wall marking the Peebles–Dumfries boundary runs over Lochcraig Head roughly east–west, being joined at the summit by the fence representing the Peebles–Selkirk boundary. This fence continues north to Megget and Broad Law. There is a junction on the ridge to the north of the summit and the left-hand or western fence should be followed if bound northwards in bad visibility.

Nickie's Knowe 2492 ft. (759m.). This is a subsidiary top of Lochcraig Head, lying one mile north by west from the summit. It may be easily ascended from the Megget Stone. The county boundary fence runs over the top from Lochcraig Head and continues to Megget.

Perhaps the most rewarding of the long distance walks which are possible in this district is the journey between Moffat and Peebles by a route which takes in as many tops as possible. The exact point of starting may well be dictated by the necessity to arrange transport at both terminal points; there is little advantage to be gained so far as altitude is concerned since Peebles is the higher by only 184 ft. (56m.).

If the northbound walker elects to start from Moffat he will make first for the summit of Hart Fell by either of the routes already described. This point lies on the county boundary Dumfries–Peebles, a line which is marked by a stone wall. It is important to remember that this boundary mark, in the form of either a wall or a fence is continuous almost to the summit of Dollar Law, 13 miles (21kms.) to the north east. At Lochcraig Head, above Loch Skeen, the Dumfries boundary turns east with the fence continuing north as the Peebles–Selkirk boundary. The route continues east from Hartfell, over Hartfell Rig to Rotten Bottom, an area of decaying peat where running water may be found in even the driest weather. The dip immediately east of Hartfell Rig represents, at 1950 ft. (594m.) the lowest point of the hill traverse apart from the road crossing at the Megget Stone. From Rotten Bottom the route goes over Firthhope Rig from which point a very easy diversion may be made to include the summit of White Coomb 2696 ft. (822m.). A stretch of really superb going now follows to Firthybrig Head where the wall turns east. The enthusiastic collector of hill tops will hardly have missed the chance to take in the top of Great Hill, a diversion of ½ mile to the west but the lover of mountain form will be more than content with glimpses of Loch Skeen and the eastern corries.

From Firthybrig Head the direct route goes via Molls Cleuch Dod and descends to the Megget Stone at the highest point of the Talla–St Mary's Loch road but this means that Lochcraig Head, which is the higher summit, will be missed. The purist will be able to follow the boundary fence from Lochcraig Head over Nickie's Knowe and down to the Megget Stone. This stands on the south side of the cattle grid at the highest point of the road, 1483 ft. (452m.) and is a little over three feet high. Some indefinite markings remain but the stone has apparently no other significance than to serve as a boundary mark.

Continuing in a northerly direction the summit of Broad Law is reached in 2 miles where the radio beacon station may provide welcome shelter from the wind on a winter's day. Cramalt Craig is the next summit and here the fence turns from east to north at a point marked by a large cairn. Excellent going continues over Dun Law to the summit of Dollar Law from where a descent to the east takes one to the Manor Water road and so to Peebles. To abandon the high level walk at this point, however, is to miss a very rewarding stretch of hill walking and a route on either the east or west side of the Manor Valley is much to be preferred. For the east route turn right at the junction of two fences on the ridge between Dun Law and Dollar Law. The fence may then be followed to the col between Manor Water and Craigierig Burn from which point a north east course will take the walker over Redside Head and Black Law to Blackhouse Heights. Continuing this line brings one to another angle of the fence at a point marked as 2311 ft. (704m.) on the 1-inch O.S. map. From this point the walker may go either down the west ridge of Glen Sax over Hundleshope Heights or take the east side of the same valley and descend to the Glen Sax road at Waddenshope. The other possibility is to finish over Canada Hill and down the beautiful ridge which leads to Hundleshope Farm. From here, if the nobility of his spirit still rises supreme to his stiffening leg muscles, the walker will face the 300 ft. rise of Cademuir Hill and descend direct to Peebles. To continue on the west side of the Manor Valley, the route from Dollar Law descends from the summit north west to the col marked as Newholm Cairns Hill on the 1-inch map. This col contains a number of rectangular and quite high cairns which form an unmistakable point of identification. A track leads from this col along the east flank of Long Grain Knowe and Pykestone Hill and the Scrape follow in easy succession. Barely 2 miles northward from The Scrape is a grass road connecting the Stobo–Drumelzier road with the Manor Valley and the walker is quickly down to the Manor road. Turning right after 1 mile at Castlehill Farm, marked by a ruined tower, a bridge over the Manor Water leads to a track to Cademuir Farm and the route over Cademuir Hill already described.

The southbound walker descending the track from Cademuir Hill will find his eye drawn constantly to the beautiful curve of the ridge which rises from behind Hundleshope Farm to Canada Hill and may well feel tempted to take the eastern side of the Manor Valley and leave Dollar Law for another occasion. He will, however, cover an extra 2 miles as compared with the western route over The Scrape and Pykestone Hill.

Other variations to this walk will readily suggest themselves. A start may be made, for example, from the A701 road where it passes the Devil's Beef Tub. There is a car park at this point which is only 4½ miles (7kms.) distant from Hart Fell compared with the 6½ miles (10kms.) between that point and Moffat. The apparent advantage of over 900 ft. in altitude dwindles to an insignificant 200 ft. when the rise and fall of the ground is accounted for.

For most people the biggest problem to be solved in organising this walk is the transport involved. To the giants of the past with their great walking traditions, the problem would have been small indeed. A night stop at either Moffat or Peebles would have enabled the return walk to be completed the following day but lesser mortals may appreciate the bus services in some detail. For the months of July and August, a bus leaves Peebles High Street at 19.05 hours each day, reaching Moffat (en route for Dumfries) at 20.26 hours. The north bound bus leaves Moffat at 19.19 hours each day, reaching Peebles at 20.46 hours. For the remaining ten months of the year, the times are unaltered but the bus leaves Peebles on Fridays, Saturdays and Sundays only and Moffat on Saturdays and Sundays only. The route, Moffat, Hart Fell, Lochcraig Head, Dollar Law, Pykestone and Cademuir Hill covers some 31 miles (50kms.) and involves 7000 ft. of ascent. Fourteen hours should be allowed including normal stops.

For shorter excursions, the most spectacular area is the eastern side of the group overlooking Moffat Water. The round of either the Blackhope or the Carrifran glens is very rewarding and the walk may be further extended by starting up the track at the Tail Burn and continuing over White Coomb to traverse Raven Craig. A descent may then be made by Saddle Yoke or the walk continued round the Blackhope Glen to Hart Fell and a descent by Swatte Fell to Capplegill. For the full round, allow 4½ hours road to road.

A similar time should be allowed for the ascent of Hart Fell from the Beef Tub, descending by Hart Fell Spa and the Auchencat Burn and walking into the Beef Tub to climb back up to the road.

A starting point at the Megget Stone (M.R. 151203) offers some excellent exercise in a deserted landscape, particularly in winter. A start up the ridge of either Molls Cleuch Dod or Lochcraig Head is to be preferred to the wet approach by the burn which descends between these two ridges. The going improves still further over the long ridge to Firthhope Rig and White Coomb. For this walk to White Coomb, allow 4 hours road to road.

Gameshope Valley: Apart from its importance as an access route to the hills enclosing it on both sides, the Gameshope Valley forms an attractive walk in its own right. The empty house at the head of the tract would offer shelter for the night if necessary. Gameshope Loch (M.R. 135185) lies in the open, upper portion and at 1850 ft. (564m.) is almost the highest sheet of water in Southern Scotland.

Loch Skeen: This lies at a height of 1700 ft. (518m.) on the moor below Lochcraig Head in a very wild setting. The loch is National Trust Property and may be reached by taking the track on the right hand side (looking upstream) of the Tail Burn where it enters Moffat Water. There is a large car park at this point, much patronised in summer when the Grey Mare's Tail Waterfall becomes a tourist attraction of some note. The fall may be seen to advantage by taking the left hand path from the same point. During continuously cold weather in February 1969 a route was made up each side of the fall by two Edinburgh parties, a climb of 450 ft. which is unlikely to be often repeated.

The walker with geological interests will find much for his diversion in Dobb's Linn which lies on the west side of the road near Birkhill Pass.

There are two minor hills in the group of somewhat more than topographical interest. 1½ miles north east from the Devil's Beef Tub is a hill of 1766 ft. (598m.) which bears the name 'Crown of Scotland' M.R. 081180. Many explanations have been offered for the origin of this name but none seem wholly convincing.

The north western spur of Garelet Dod terminates in a hill of 1546 ft. (741m.) called Strawberry Hill and the origin of this somewhat unlikely name is described by Will Grant in his book 'Tweeddale'.

At the foot of the hill once stood the ancient castle of Fruid, built by the Frazers. This family was said to have come from France and bore the 'fraises' or strawberry leaves of nobility, on their shields from the time of the Crusades. The name has remained as 'Strawberry Hill'.

The Devil's Beef Tub marks the source of the river Annan which flows south to Moffat and the meeting with Moffat and Evan Waters at Threewater Foot. This was the site of a Roman Camp on the line of the road from Carlisle to Crawford and Edinburgh which was one of the two main Roman routes into Scotland. The Beef Tub itself is an impressive sight for its grassy slopes descend at a uniformly high angle for almost 500 ft. There is a story of a young Covenanter escaping from his redcoat captors by leaping suddenly on to the slope as the party approached the edge and rolling over and over to the flat ground at the bottom. The day was misty and he was able to hold his advantage and run to safety over ground he knew. A man who could leap to his feet and run after such a descent surely deserved his freedom.

Rights of Way. The following routes are recognised as rights of way in Dumfriesshire:

1. *Annan Water road to Hartfell Spa*
A track leaves the unclassified road along Annan Water, some 3 miles from Moffat at M.R. 075104. The track runs north-east to Hartfell Spa at 1200 ft. (366m.) and M.R. 098116. The distance is rather less than two miles.

2. *Ericstane to Earlshaugh*
Ericstane Farm (M.R. 073110) lies at the northern end of the road along Annan Water from Moffat. A track begins here and goes via Corehead farm up the slopes of Great Hill 1528 ft. (466m.) to pass to the west of the summit and cross the moor to Earlshaugh on the Powskein Burn at M.R. 071148. Forestry planting has recently been made on this moor and some alteration to the route seems likely as time goes on and trees mature. Distance is 3 miles.

3. *Moffat Water to Loch Skeen*
The track leaving the road along Moffat Water (A708) at the Grey Mare's Tail (at M.R. 181646) forms a right of way to the foot of Loch Skeen (M.R. 174160). The district has already been described on page 168. The distance is 1¼ miles.

Accommodation. Accommodation of all grades may be found in Moffat and there are also hotels at St Mary's Loch and one at Tweedsmuir. There is a camp/caravan site at Peebles with further opportunities in upper Tweedsdale and along Moffat Water.

Bus Services. There is an infrequent bus service between Moffat and Peebles during July and August and a more restricted service for the remainder of the year. An infrequent service also runs between Selkirk and Moffat via St Mary's Loch. Moffat may be reached by bus from Glasgow, Edinburgh and Dumfries.

BIBLIOGRAPHY

The Club Meet at the Crook Inn, J.G.S. – S.M.C. Journal, Vol. I.
A Day on the Moffat Hills, W. Cowan – S.M.C. Journal, Vol. I.
Moffat in the Seventies, Scott Moncrieff Renney – S.M.C. Journal, Vol. XV.
The first official Meet – Crook Inn, 27 February, 1891, T. H. Bryce – S.M.C. Journal, Vol. XXII.
The Peeblesshire Hills, W. L. Coats – S.M.C. Journal, Vol. XXIII.

11

The Ettrick Hills

There are nine hills of 2000 ft. (610m.) and above:

(1)	**Ettrick Pen**	2270 ft. (692m.)	M.R. 199077
(2)	**Wind Fell**	2180 ft. (664m.)	M.R. 178062
(3)	**Loch Fell**	2256 ft. (688m.)	M.R. 170048
(4)	**Croft Head**	2085 ft. (636m.)	M.R. 153057
(5)	**Capel Fell**	2223 ft. (678m.)	M.R. 164069
(6)	**Bodesbeck Law**	2173 ft. (662m.)	M.R. 169103
(7)	**Bell Craig**	2046 ft. (624m.)	M.R. 187129
(8)	**Andrewhinney Hill**	2220 ft. (677m.)	M.R. 198139
(9)	**Herman Law**	2014 ft. (614m.)	M.R. 214157

and six tops of 2000 ft. (610m.) and above, three of which are not named on the 1-inch O.S. map:

(10)	**Hopetoun Craig**	2075 ft. (632m.)	M.R. 188068
(11)	***Loch Fell W.**	2196 ft. (669m.)	M.R. 164053
(12)	***Smidhope Hill**	2111 ft. (643m.)	M.R. 168077
(13)	**White Shank**	2035 ft. (620m.)	M.R. 169082
(14)	***Mid Rig**	2018 ft. (615m.)	M.R. 180124
(15)	**Trowgrain Middle**	2058 ft. (627m.)	M.R. 208149

* not shown on 1-inch O.S. map.

Maps: O.S. 1-inch, Seventh Series, Sheet 69.
Bartholomew, ½-inch, sheet 41.

The high ground represented by the Moffat hills continues eastwards from the deep trench of the Moffat Water valley to form a group of hills lying in a rough horseshoe formation round the head of Ettrick Water. Ettrick Pen, the highest point, lies on the east side of Ettrick Water and has gentle grass-covered slopes on all sides. The hills on the opposite side of Ettrick are similar in character but form much steeper slopes on the western side and the uniformly high angle on this side adds much to the impressive character of the Moffat Water valley as the road climbs towards Birkhill Pass. Croft Head and Loch Fell lie south of the head-waters of Ettrick and, together with Capel Fell, form a group of impressive steepness at the head of the Selcoth Burn. There is a good deal of forestry planting in the area and, while many stretches now covered with young trees will become impassable as growth proceeds, there should be sufficient access roads and forestry rides to permit reasonable movement. It is normally permissible for walkers to use forestry access roads unless otherwise stated.

The Ettricks offer the walker even more isolation than the Moffat Hills, which can hardly be said to be over-populated at any time. The somewhat daunting sight of the 1500 ft. (457m.) slope which faces the walker on the Moffat Water road serves to emphasise this fact, but more reasonable access is achieved by driving up the higher reaches of Ettrick Water on the narrow but well surfaced road which runs as far as Potburn Farm.

It is well to note that the Selkirk–Dumfries boundary runs continuously either as a fence or a wall, from Herman Law, above Birkhill Pass to Ettrick Pen.

Ettrick Pen 2270 ft. (692m.). This is the highest point of the group, lying five miles due south from Birkhill Pass. It is best approached from the upper reaches of the Ettrick valley, either by crossing the stream to the foot of Birnie Brae and walking southwards up the ridge or by walking further up the valley road to a point west of the summit at Over Phawhope and following the burn to the ridge. The top is cairned and carries the county boundary fence.

Hopetoun Craig 2075 ft. (632m.). This is a subsidiary top of Wind Fell and lies almost 1 mile south-west from Ettrick Pen. It sends a shapely ridge to the north and may be ascended by this route from Over Phawhope. The fence crosses the summit.

Wind Fell 2180 ft. (664m.). This hill lies rather more than 1½ miles south-west from Ettrick Pen and the same distance south from Potburn Farm. It may be ascended by taking the track from the end of the road at Over Phawhope to the watershed at Ettrick Head 1700 ft. (518m.) and following the line of the fence eastwards to the top. It may also be ascended from the south from Loch Fell.

Loch Fell 2256 ft. (688m.). This hill lies 2½ miles south-west from Ettrick Pen and south of the main curve of the ridge. Like Wind Fell, it may be ascended from Ettrick Head or by an alternative route from

Moffat Water. This begins either at Craigbeck Farm, a little over a mile north of the river junction at Threewater Foot, where there is a footpath or from the bridge over Moffat Water, a short distance north of the farm. At this point an unmetalled road, passable to a car, leads for some miles to the head of Wamphray Water, being joined by the footpath from Craigbeck. At a point where the road curves round the foot of Coomb Cairn and begins to descend, a faint track will be seen on the left leading up to the ridge of Cowan Fell. The fence may then be followed to the left up easy slopes to the top of Loch Fell and the fence continues to join the county boundary on that hill.

Loch Fell West 2196 ft. (669m.). This is a subsidiary top of Loch Fell, lying ½ mile north-west from the main summit. The name does not appear on the 1-inch O.S. map.

Croft Head 2085 ft. (636m.). This hill lies 1¼ miles north-west from Loch Fell. A fence runs from the higher summit, over Loch Fell West and continues to Croft Head. The ascent may be made from Craigbeck Farm as described, or by a track following the line of the Selcoth Burn from Moffat Water. This is reached by a short approach road, which is not signposted, leading from the Moffat Valley road at the northern end of the long plantation, 4½ miles from Moffat. The bridge over Moffat leads to Sailfoot Farm and the road continues downstream to Selcoth Farm. The track to Ettrick Head begins at the farm and follows the line of the stream. The north-eastern shoulder of Croft Head should be ascended from the point where the track contours the broken face of Capel Fell before the final rise to Ettrick Head.

Capel Fell 2223 ft. (678m.). This hill lies on the west side of Ettrick Head, the 1700 ft. (518m.) col at the head of the Ettrick valley. It is 1 mile north-west from Wind Fell and may be ascended by easy slopes from the col along the line of the county boundary fence. An approach may also be made by the track along the Selcoth Burn from Moffat Water.

Smidhope Hill 2111 ft. (643m.). This is a subsidiary top of Capel Fell, unnamed on the 1-inch O.S. map, lying ½ mile north-east by north from the main top. The boundary wall crosses the summit.

White Shank 2035 ft. (620m.). This is also a subsidiary top of Capel Fell, lying rather less than a mile north of the main top and ¾ mile west from Over Phawhope, which forms the easiest point of access. The wall crosses the top.

Bodesbeck Law 2173 ft. (662m.). This hill lies 1¼ miles north-west from Potburn Farm at the head of the Ettrick valley road. It marks the beginning of the ridge which runs for 4½ miles to Herman Law and which forms so steep a retaining wall for the Moffat Water valley.

The top may be reached from Potburn by following the track leading up the hill from the farm until the county boundary wall is reached. This may be followed to the top. An alternative route from Moffat Water is to cross the river by the bridge at Bodesbeck Farm, opposite Capplegill and, keeping the stream on the right hand, follow the path to the ridge. The boundary wall may then be followed northwards to Bodesbeck Law.

Mid Rig 2018 ft. (615m.). This is a subsidiary top of Bell Craig and is not named on the 1-inch O.S. map. It lies 1¼ miles north-east from Bodesbeck Law and to the south of Bell Craig. It should not be confused with the point marked 'Mid Rig' on the 1-inch O.S. map between Andrewhinney and Trowgrain Middle. Mid Rig may be ascended from the Ettrick valley by way of Range Cleuch where a track leads from the road bridge over that stream. It may also be ascended, much more steeply, from Moffat Water, crossing by the bridge at Polmoody.

Bell Craig 2046 ft. (624m.). This lies 2 miles north by east from Bodesbeck Law and within ½ mile of Mid Rig. The fence crosses the summit, access routes being similar to those for Mid Rig. The main stream of the Kirkhope Burn leads from Ettrick in a direct line to the top.

Andrewhinney Hill 2220 ft. (677m.). This hill lies one mile north-east from Bell Craig. The top is also ¾ mile from the car park at the Grey Mare's Tail in the Moffat Water valley by a route which, if steep, is at least obvious. The walker who has gained the ridge by a less strenuous route may well find that the sight of the motor coaches gathering in the car park adds length to his stride and exhilaration to his spirits for he is unlikely to find any other disturbing influence on this group of hills.

On this part of the ridge the cloudberry (Rubus Chamaemorus) grows in unusual abundance.

Trowgrain Middle 2058 ft. (627m.). This is a subsidiary top of Andrewhinney, $\frac{3}{4}$ mile north-east from the main top and even closer to Birkhill Pass which lies 950 ft. (290m.) lower.

Herman Law 2014 (614m.). This hill lies $1\frac{1}{2}$ miles north-east from Andrewhinney and is the point where the county boundary fence turns westwards to cross the main road at Birkhill and rise to Lochcraig Head. The northern and north-western slopes are a good deal less steep than those further south and an ascent from Yarrow Water presents no problem.

The most rewarding excursion in the Ettrick Hills is the round of the county fence from Ettrick Pen to Herman Law, so traversing all the listed hills except Loch Fell and Croft Head. The best starting point would be from the Ettrick valley, leaving a car where the road loops round Range Cleuch, rather over 1 mile short of Potburn Farm and $1\frac{1}{4}$ miles beyond the bridge leading to Nether Phawhope.

From this point the stream may be crossed and a way made up Birnie Brae, and south up the ridge to the cairn on Ettrick Pen summit. From this point the fence may be followed south-westwards over Hopetoun Craig and Wind Fell to the col at Ettrick Head. An ascent of 520 ft. (158m.) follows to gain the top of Capel Fell, the route then turns north to cross White Shank and the moor at the head of Bodesbeck Burn. This is at 1550 ft. (472m.) and is the lowest point on the circuit. When the top of Bodesbeck Law is reached a splendid ridge walk follows to Herman Law and superb views are enjoyed into the corries of the Hart Fell–White Coomb plateau, particularly under morning lighting conditions.

The return to the valley may be made either by walking back along the ridge to Bell Craig, then turning south-eastwards to cross Black Knowe Head and descend direct to the starting point or by taking a southerly route from the top of Herman Law. This will lead to the upper reaches of Back Burn, and this may be followed to reach the road at a point 3 miles downstream from the car.

The round, as described, covers $17\frac{1}{2}$ miles (28kms.) and $7\frac{1}{2}$ hours should be allowed.

A shorter excursion to include Loch Fell and Croft Head may be made from Craigbeck Farm, 1½ miles south-east from Moffat by following the route already described in the notes on these hills. From the top of Croft Head the line of the fence may be followed south-west down the ridge to rejoin the forestry road at a height of about 1250 ft. (381m.). This circuit covers 10½ miles (17kms.) and 4½ hours should be allowed.

Rights of Way. The following routes in the Ettrick district represent rights of way:

1. *Riskin Hope to Scabcleuch*
Riskinhope lies at the southern end of the Loch of the Lowes (M.R. 235190) and a track runs from here over the ridge to Scabcleuch on Ettrick Water (M.R. 247144). Distance 3½ miles (6kms.).

2. *Crosscleuch to Hopehouse*
Crosscleuch (M.R. 244204) lies slightly to the east of Tibbie Shiel's Inn at the foot of St Mary's Loch, and an unmetalled road begins here and runs south-east up the slopes of the hill. After 1½ miles the road alters direction to the north-east and a track begins at this point (M.R. 254190) and leads to Hopehouse on the Ettrick road (M.R. 295166). Distance 5 miles (8kms.).

3. *Whitehillbrae to Easter Essenside*
Whitehillbrae (M.R. 404245) lies about 1 mile east from Ettrickbridge End. Slightly further to the east is the starting point of a track which runs over Hutlerburn Hill to Essenside Loch and Easter Essenside (M.R. 454204). Distance 4½ miles (7kms.).

4. *Helmburn to Esdale Law*
Helmburn (M.R. 391244) is near Ettrickbridge End and an unmetalled road starts here and encircles Helmburn Hill. A track leaves this road and runs south-east to Tod Rig. The track continues to Whitslaid and crosses a stream to join a metalled road at Esdale Law (M.R. 440175). Distance 6 miles (10kms.).

5. *Helmburn to Redfordgreen*
Some 120 yards (110m.) west of the northern end of the Tod Rig–Esdale track, a second track begins and runs south by west to pass between the two Shaws Lochs. Continuing past Gildiesgreen it leads to Redfordgreen at M.R. 366163. Distance 7 miles (11kms.).

98. The Cheviot from Windygyle Hill. The fence marks the Union boundary and the cairns the Pennine Way.

99. The line of Dere Street near Crailinghall.

100. Bonnington Linn on the River Clyde.

101. Eildon Hills from 'Scotts View', Bemersyde.

102. Din Fell from the Billhope Burn.

103. The rocks of Traprain Law .

104 and 105. Salisbury Crags.

6. *Redfordgreen to Easter Deloraine*
An unmetalled road runs north-west from Redfordgreen (M.R. 366163) to Drycleuchlea and continues the line to the Deloraine Burn, which is followed to Easter Deloraine (M.R. 338209). There is a bridge over Ettrick Water at this point. Distance 5 miles (8kms.).

7. *Deephope to Buccleuch*
Deephope Farm (M.R. 278140) at the junction of the two glens, Tima and Ettrick, is the starting point for a track which runs east over the hills to Buccleuch on the Rankle Burn (M.R. 325143). Distance 3½ miles (6kms.).

8. *Meerlees to Buccleuch*
Meerlees Farm (M.R. 282118) lies 1½ miles south of Deephope and is also the starting point for a track running north-east to Buccleuch (325143). Distance 3½ miles (6kms.).

9. *Buccleuch to Muselee*
A longer and more complex route is the track from Buccleuch (M.R. 325143) which runs south-east to pass along Kingside Loch, over the Roxburgh boundary and through the northern arm of Craik Forest to Muselee on Borthwick Water (M.R. 398118). Distance 5½ miles (9kms.).

10. *Craigbeck to Wamphray Glen*
Craigbeck Farm (M.R. 106037) is on the east side of the unclassified road running from Moffat Water to Three Water Foot. A track runs from here along the line of the Cornal Burn to curve round Scaw'd Fell and descend to Wamphray Glen. Taking the terminal point at Laverhay (M.R. 140981) the distance is 8 miles (13kms.).

11. *Craigbeck to Garwaldwaterfoot*
This follows the same route as far as the point where the track turns south round Scaw'd Fell to follow the headwater of the Wamphray Burn. A faint track will be noted climbing the shoulder of Cowan Fell. This crosses the ridge at 1850 ft. (564m.), goes eastwards to cross a second ridge of Loch Fell and descend the burn in a south-easterly direction to Garwald Water. A more prominent track is then followed to the main road at Garwaldwaterfoot (M.R. 243004). Distance is 10½ miles (17kms.).

Additionally, the following pathways are recorded but not maintained as public rights of way:

Raeburnfoot to Borthwick Water

Raeburnfoot lies in Eskdale at the junction of the Rae Burn with the White Esk (M.R. 253992). The route follows the true right bank of the stream to Raeburnhead, but there is no track beyond this point. The line of the Roman road over Craik Muir to the north of Raeburnhead forms a more probable route, this road being marked on the 1-inch O.S. map.

This road was recognised as being of Roman origin only in 1945 through the work of Sir Ian Richmond, whose conclusions are quoted: 'The second point which emerges is the notable quality of the engineering of the original road. The impressive fact is not so much that a great roadway 20 feet wide has been driven for over six miles (10kms.) across wild moors and peat hags; it is that no roadway could have been here constructed at all without a penetrating appreciation of the local terrain, which imposes such formidable and peculiar conditions upon choice of materials and route.'

Raeburnfoot is the site of a Roman fort and at a point rather more than one mile upstream from here the road leaves the valley and climbs the moor on a steady north-east course to Craik Cross Hill 1481 ft. (451m.) (M.R. 303047), where there was a signal station. A steady descent then follows along the ridge until the modern road is joined at Craik on Borthwick Water (M.R. 348084). This distance is 9 miles (14kms.).

This section of Roman road is considered to be part of the route between Lockerbie and the major fort at Newstead (Trimontium).

Laverhay to Garwaldwaterfoot

From Laverhay on Wamphray Water (M.R. 140981) a track climbs the hill out of the glen to cross the ridge between Laverhay Height 1587 ft. (484m.) and Black Hill 1554 ft. (474m.) and descend to Dryfehead on Dryfe water. This valley is crossed, still holding the eastward line and the route crosses the next valley to reach Garwald Water. This is followed to Garwaldwaterfoot on the B709 road (M.R. 243004). The distance is 8 miles (13kms.).

Waterhead to Dryfehead

Waterhead lies on Dryfe Water at M.R. 188943 and this route follows the road northwestwards to Finniegill further up the valley. A track continues to Dryfehead at M.R. 170999. The distance is 4 miles (6kms.).

Bus routes. There is no public transport system in the upper reaches of the Ettrick valley. A service from Selkirk runs only as far as Ettrickbridge End, a distance of some six miles (10kms.), so that the only bus of direct assistance to the walker bound for Ettrick Water head is the Moffat–St Mary's Loch–Selkirk service.

Accommodation. The hotels at St Mary's Loch are well placed for reaching Herman Law, while the varied accommodation available at Moffat is even nearer.

There are Youth Hostels at Snoot near Roberton 5 miles (8kms.) west of Hawick and at Broadmeadows, four miles (6kms.) west of Selkirk on the road to St Mary's Loch.

Camping in the upper part of the Ettrick valley should present few difficulties.

BIBLIOGRAPHY

Scottish Mountaineering Club Journal
Vol. II *Bodesbeck Law*, Professor Veitch.
Proceedings of Society of Antiquaries of Scotland, Vol. 80, p. 103.

12

Broughton Heights

(1)	**Broughton Heights**	1872 ft. (571m.)	M.R. 123411
(2)	**Penvalla Hill**	1764 ft. (538m.)	M.R. 151396
(3)	**Clover Law**	1617 ft. (493m.)	M.R. 121389
(4)	**Trahenna Hill**	1792 ft. (546m.)	M.R. 136374
(5)	**Ladyurd Hill**	1724 ft. (525m.)	M.R. 150408

Maps: O.S. 1-inch, Seventh Series, sheets 62 and 69.
Bartholomew, ½-inch, sheet 41.

Broughton Heights is a compact area of not very high hills lying north-east of Broughton and only 1 mile east from the junction of the A72 and A701 roads. The whole area is little more than ten square miles (26 sq. kms.) in extent, yet it offers some admirable hill walking and what is possibly the finest viewpoint in Southern Scotland.

It may be thought that these hills are scarcely worth of inclusion in a guide, yet they have many qualities. They are accessible yet unfrequented; of modest height yet satisfying form and sufficiently detached from the main groups of higher hills to offer unexpected rewards on a day of good visibility.

Broughton Heights 1872 ft. (571m.) is accessible from either the A72 or the A701 road, lying as it does 1½ miles due east from the junction of these two roads north of Broughton. An approach from the A72 road is somewhat hampered by an extensive marsh lying to the south of Lochurd Farm and this should be avoided unless it is hard frozen. There are two alternatives, one being described below as a right of way and the other offering an approach walk over Trahenna Hill and the whole ridge. Take the unclassified road running east from Broughton village to the top of the ridge approaching Dreva. From this point (M.R. 128355) a way may be made up the ridge to the top of Trahenna, whence 3 miles of enjoyable ridge walking bring the top of Broughton Heights underfoot.

There is a triangulation pillar at this point and the hill has some claim to being the finest viewpoint in the Southern Uplands. A day of good visibility does not always offer equal atmospheric clarity through all points of the compass, but a good day on Broughton Heights will offer a memorable view. The northern shores of the Forth are readily seen, some thirty-five miles (56kms.) away, while to the south-west, through the Tinto–Culter Fell gap, the hills near Turnberry can be discerned, some sixty miles (97kms.) away. Most entrancing of all, perhaps, are the views into upper Tweedsdale.

Trahenna Hill 1792 ft. (546m.). The route to this hill, which lies 1½ miles east of Broughton village, has already been described.

Penvalla Hill 1764 ft. (538 m.). This hill lies 1½ miles north-east from Trahenna and may also be approached from the Dreva road at M.R. 128355. The southern ridge of Trahenna is crossed and a descent made to the Hopehead Burn and the lower slopes of the hill. An alternative approach is from the north, by Ladyurd Farm, off the A72 road on M.R. 150425. From here it is possible to walk over Ladyurd Hill to Penvalla and continue the round to Trahenna and Broughton Heights, returning to the starting point via Brown Dod and along the east side of the plantation above Ladyurd. This round covers ten miles (16kms.) and involves over 3000 ft. (914m.) of ascent and five hours should be allowed.

Ladyurd Hill 1724 ft. (525m.). This hill lies 1 mile to the north of Penvalla and may be readily ascended from Ladyurd Farm as already described.

Clover Law 1617 ft. (493m.) rises to the west of the ridge connecting Broughton Heights with Trahenna and lies nearer the A701 road than any other hill in the group. A walk of one mile from that direction will bring the top underfoot; the hill may, alternatively, be approached from Broughton Glen.

Right of Way. There is one right of way in the group, from *Broughton Place Farm to Stobo Hopehead.* From Broughton Place Farm (M.R. 114371) follow a faint track along the glen and over the ridge to Stobo Hopehead (M.R. 114397). There is no information as to the continuation as a right of way beyond this point. This route offers ready access to Clover Law and the northern end of the Trahenna ridge.

Bus routes. The information on public transport given in the chapter on the Culter Fells applies equally to this group, as do the notes on accommodation.

13

The Culter Hills

There are five hills of over 2000 ft. (610m.):

(1)	**Chapelgill Hill**	2282 ft. (696m.)	M.R. 068304
(2)	**Culter Fell**	2454 ft. (748m.)	M.R. 053291
(3)	**Hillshaw Head**	2141 ft. (653m.)	M.R. 048246
(4)	**Heatherstane Law**	2055 ft. (626m.)	M.R. 022272
(5)	**Gathersnow Hill**	2262 ft. (690m.)	M.R. 059257

and three subsidiary tops:

(6)	**Cardon Hill**	2218 ft. (676m.)	M.R. 066315
(7)	**Coomb Hill**	2096 ft. (639m.)	M.R. 069264
(8)	**Coomb Dod**	2082 ft. (635m.)	M.R. 047238

Maps: O.S. 1-inch, Seventh Series, sheet 68.
Bartholomew, ½-inch, sheets 40 and 41.

The Culter hills group about a point 6 miles east of the River Clyde at Roberton, and 6 miles (10kms.) south of Biggar. They form the highest part of a considerable stretch of hill country between the Clyde valley and the upper reaches of the Tweed.

Interest is concentrated on the continuous ridge running roughly north and south, which lies to the east of Culter reservoir, since only one hill of over 2000 ft. (610m.) lies off this general line. The slopes are steep in places but the ridges offer excellent walking and since the views are into almost unfrequented valleys a sense of isolation is quickly achieved.

The village of Coulter lies on the A702 road, 6 miles (10kms.) south-west from Biggar and 1 mile from the River Clyde. The spelling varies, but the pronunciation remains as 'Cooter'. From the village a minor road runs some 2 miles southwards to Birthwood Farm and cars should be left there. The right-hand branch of the road at this point goes to Cowgill reservoir and is of lesser interest than the left, which leads to Culter reservoir and forms the easiest point of access for Culter Fell.

Chapelgill Hill 2282 ft. (696m.). This hill lies 2¼ miles east from Birthwood and may be approached by walking a short distance up the road to Culter reservoir, then turning left up the slopes before crossing the Kings Beck. The level shoulder below Culter Fell shows Chapelgill Hill a short distance ahead. An approach via Holms Water, reached by a turning off the A701 road at Rachans Mill is even shorter, but in hill walking, the shorter approach is not necessarily the most satisfactory and there is much to be said for the approach up the ridge of Cardon Hill and Common Law, which stretches down to the Coulter–Broughton road at Kilbucho (M.R. 088350).

Cardon Hill 2218 ft. (676m.). This is a subsidiary top of Chapelgill Hill, ¾ mile north of the main top.

Culter Fell 2454 ft. (748m.). This is the highest point of the group and, although it falls below the 2500 ft. level, it overtops all the hills of the Moorfoot, Ettrick, Lowther and Lammermuir groups. Yet character in a hill rates higher than a figure in a guide book, and no one, seeing Culter Fell in the most favourable lighting conditions from the Biggar–Broughton road, could deny that character is there. Still less the walker who reaches the top late on a winter afternoon along the line of a fence heavy with fog crystals, for he will look over the seemingly endless ridges of the hills to the south and feel all the satisfaction and isolation which is the reward for gaining a higher mountain top.

There is a triangulation point on the summit and the Peebles–Lanarkshire boundary fence crosses the top and continues to the south over Coomb Dod.

The ascent of Culter Fell from Birthwood is straightforward. Kings Beck joins the main stream only a few yards along the road to Culter reservoir and the ridge on either side of this offers a satisfactory route. A slightly longer approach may be made from the end of the road along Holms Water on the east side of the group, but the most enjoyable of all is the route over Cardon Hill from Kilbucho. This may be completed by descending the north-west shoulder to the foot of Kings Beck and, keeping Culterallers Farm on the left, following the track along the true right bank of Culter Water until a descent can be made to Nisbet Farm. A way can then be made through the glen to Mitchelhill, Blindewing and Kilbucho.

Coomb Hill 2096 ft. (639m.) is a subsidiary top of Gathersnow Hill and forms part of the ridge running north-east from Coomb Dod to the angle of the River Tweed near Broughton. It may be ascended by that ridge or from Holms Water glen to the north or Kingledoors glen to the south.

Gathersnow Hill 2262 ft. (690m.). This hill lies two miles south-east from Culter Waterheads, at the foot of the reservoir and, for a walker enjoying the round of the horseshoe ridge encircling the reservoir, it forms the southern horizon for some time. It may be reached as a separate expedition, by an approach walk of 2½ miles up the Kingledoors glen or, alternatively, from the Holms Water glen, where there is a surfaced road as far as Glenkirk.

Hillshaw Head 2141 ft. (653m.). This hill lies only ¾ mile to the south-west from the top of Gathersnow, the boundary fence continuing over the summit. The hill, together with the outlying top to the south (Coomb Dod) may be made the object of a walk from Tweedsmuir by way of the ridge on the south side of Kingledoors glen. Make for the low point on the ridge between Upper Oliver Dod and Bank Head. From this point a traverse round the head of the glen may be made to finish at Coomb Hill and back to Tweedsmuir. Allow four hours for this round, road to road.

Coomb Dod 2082 ft. (635m.). This top lies ½ mile south of Hillshaw Head and access has been described with that hill.

Heatherstane Law 2055 ft. (626m.). This hill lies on the west side of Culter reservoir, 2½ miles south by west from Birthwood. It may be easily ascended from that point by taking the road to Culter Waterhead and the reservoir. Kings Beck, which descends from Culter Fell is passed on the left after a short distance and it is possible here to cross the main stream and gain the western bank. The left-hand side of the long plantation on the slopes of the hill may be followed to the ridge; gentle slopes then lead to the top of Ward Law and Heatherstane Law is reached after a further 1½ miles.

There is a right of way from east to west over this hill; the route is described under that heading later in the chapter.

There are grouse shooting interests on Culter Fell and most hill walkers are aware that reservoir keepers do not always share their views on the question of access. On a short winter day, however, an excellent round may be made by taking the route already described to Heatherstane Law and continuing along the ridge to Gathersnow Hill. A descent from here northward along the line of the fence makes a finish at Culter Fell, which is an excellent vantage point for a winter sunset. The newcomer to the area may be surprised to note that one may look over ridge after ridge of the Southern Uplands with not a house in sight, he may also be pleased to find the descent of the north-west ridge a simple matter even after dark. This would not be the case if the route was taken in the reverse way and it became necessary to cross the stream under these conditions.

The walk may be further extended by continuing north from Culter Fell to Cardon Hill and Scawdmans Hill. A finish may then be made down the west facing ridge, keeping Nisbet Burn on the left and returning to Birthwood along the eastern bank of the main stream.

Five hours should be allowed for this round, finishing on Culter Fell, with a further 1½ hours if the walk is extended to Scawdmans Hill.

The approach road from Coulter to Birthwood and the reservoir passes the western end of a subsidiary glen with Nisbet Farm lying at the entrance. This area deserves at least brief mention because of its remarkable richness in pre-historic remains. There are four areas of cultivation terraces, several forts and a crannog which was destroyed when the area was drained. The two most interesting forts are readily accessible and are to be found at map references 035322 and 043332 respectively.

Rights of Way. There are three routes in the district, which are known as rights of way:

Culterallers–Lamington. Culterallers Farm lies on the left a few yards before reaching Birthwood. Take the right-hand fork at this point and follow the road towards Cowgill reservoir. 1½ miles further on the road forks again and the right-hand road is taken to pass Cowgill Loch and joins the main A702 road at Lamington.

Culter Waterhead–Wandel. This is a longer route of somewhat greater interest. Take the left-hand fork at Birthwood and walk the 2 miles to Culter Waterhead at the foot of the reservoir. A way is then made to the top of Heatherstane Law, ¾ mile to the west and almost exactly

1000 ft. (305m.) higher. From this point the right of way follows the line of the Wandel Burn ahd the direct line would involve a somewhat pointless descent to Duncan Gill at the head of Cowgill upper reservoir. A more logical route is to follow the line of the parish boundary fence and take the right-hand branch at the junction of two fences a short distance south of the top of Heatherstane Law. The fence runs over Windgill Bank to Duncangill Head (M.R. 006256) where a descent may be made to the Wandel Burn. From Birnock (M.R. 974256) a track leads to Wandel on the A702 road. The distance from Birthwood to Wandel is rather more than 9 miles (14kms.) and four hours should be allowed for the walk.

Nisbet Farm to Mitchelhill. ½ mile along the road from Coulter to Birthwood a turn on the left leads to Nisbet Farm (M.R. 037329). There is a right of way from this point to Kilbucho Old Churchyard and Mitchelhill Farm. Shortly after leaving Nisbet the road forks; take the right-hand branch and continue the line along the subsidiary glen to the south of White Hill to Kilbucho Church and Mitchelhill (M.R. 068339). The Coulter–Broughton road is then within easy reach.

Bus routes. There is no public bus service between Glasgow and Coulter, but there is a frequent service to Biggar from Glasgow. The Edinburgh–Dumfries service from St Andrew's Square also serves the area. The road through Tweedsmuir in the upper Tweed valley is also served by the Edinburgh–Dumfries buses.

Accommodation. There is no accommodation available at Coulter, but Biggar, only 2½ miles away, offers an ample choice. Broughton, scarcely less convenient, also offers accommodation, while the Crook Inn, near Tweedsmuir is another possibility. The nearest Youth Hostels are Wanlockhead, some 14 miles to the south-west as the crow flies and Broadmeadows, near Selkirk, some 22 miles to the east.

14

The Cheviot Hills

There are six hills of 2000 ft. (610m.) and above:

(1)	**Windy Gyle**	2034 ft. (620m.)	M.R. 855152
(2)	**The Cheviot**	2676 ft. (816m.)	M.R. 909205
(3)	**Comb Fell**	2132 ft. (658m.)	M.R. 919187
(4)	**Hedgehope Hill**	2348 ft. (716m.)	M.R. 944197
(5)	**Bloodybush Edge**	2001 ft. (610m.)	M.R. 902144
(6)	**Cushat Law**	2020 ft. (616m.)	M.R. 928137

and one top:

(7)	**Auchope Cairn**	2382 ft. (726m.)	M.R. 891198

Maps: O.S. 1-inch, Seventh Series, sheets 70 and 71
Bartholomew, ½-inch, sheet 41

While it is clearly desirable that a Scottish guide should confine itself to Scottish ground, it is equally clear that no walker approaching the Cheviot hills from the north is likely to turn back at the border. A description of these hills is therefore included, but substantially confined to the approaches from the Scottish side.

Cheviot forms the culminating point of a continuous belt of high ground running east and north-east from the head of Teviot Dale, but the Cheviot hills as such are normally defined as commencing at the point where the A68 road crosses the border at Carter Bar. The Union boundary runs for some distance along the main ridge and of the seven hills and tops named above, only Windygyle and Auchope Cairn lie on the border, the other five being in England.

The section immediately to the east of the A68 road contains some comparatively unfrequented hills and, with access in the Kale Water district along narrow but well-surfaced roads, offers attractive walking country on grassy hills. South of the border it is impossible to ignore the restrictions imposed by the considerable areas of ground used for firing practice and under military control. The sight of a red flag flying in this area means that the walker must restrict his movements to the boundary of the range, but it may be possible to obtain day to day information as to the firing programme by telephoning Otterburn 241.

The hills tend to increase in height as one moves eastwards towards Cheviot with the ridge assuming the familiar characteristics of peat-covered ground with long heather and stretches of wet going. As might be expected, the increased traffic on the Pennine Way has reduced the track to a waterlogged trench on some stretches and this type of going inevitably becomes more strenuous and time-consuming.

Perhaps more than in most areas, the enjoyment of this walk depends to a large degree on the weather. This ridge running to Cheviot represents the southern limit of the drainage to the Tweed valley and to walk in either direction on a day of good visibility is to enjoy a superb prospect. Possibly an east to west direction is the more rewarding, for the eye then rests on the Eildon hills and Ruberslaw with all the seemingly limitless hills of Peebles and Selkirk for background.

The Northumberland National Park and the Border Forest Park both lie on the border. The Pennine Way crosses the Jedburgh–Newcastle road (A68) at Byrness, 1½ miles east of the dam at Catcleugh Reservoir and runs north to join the border near Coquet Head, a distance of 4 miles. It then passes to the south of the complex of Roman camps at Chew Green and regains the ridge a little to the east of Brownhart Law 1664 ft. (507m.). From this point the Way does not deviate from the ridge. At the angle of the fence where the direction alters from east to north-west, the highest point on the boundary is reached 2419 ft. (737m.) and the route diverts to Cairn Hill and the top of The Cheviot. The ridge is regained at Auchope Cairn and, keeping the Hen Hole and the College Burn on the right hand, the Way continues until the ridge narrows at Black Hag (M.R. 862236) and finally descends to the Halter Burn and Kirk Yetholm. The distance from Byrness to Kirk Yetholm is 26½ miles (43kms.).

There are references in 1173 to the River Tweed as the border and it is not until 1222 that any record appears of the position of the boundary being elsewhere than on the river. In that year a joint boundary commission met to define the border but covered only a small area. Further references may be found between 1542 and 1604, but the existing line seems to have been agreed only between 1604 and 1648.

Windy Gyle 2034 ft. (620m.). This hill lies on the national boundary, 4½ miles (7kms.) south-west from Cheviot top. It may be reached from the Bowmont Water valley which runs south then south-east from Yetholm. The metalled road finishes at Cocklawfoot and from this point there is a choice of routes. The track continues along the Kelsocleuch Burn, which is the right-hand branch of the stream and the line may be continued directly to the summit. The eastern ridge of this burn is Cock Law and a most pleasant approach may be made by the green drove road which takes this route from Cocklawfoot to cross the ridge 1 mile to the east of Windy Gyle. This route continues southward as a right of way. The third possibility is to follow the western ridge of the valley by the path beginning at Kelsocleuch Farm. On the ridge the route of the Pennine Way is by now sufficiently trodden as to be fairly obvious. The route is marked at intervals by turf cairns, each bearing a painted post and the marking 'P.W.'

The Cheviot 2676 ft. (816m.). There are three main routes of access to the highest summit of the group – from the west by Bowmont Water; from the north by the College Burn and from the east by the Harthope Burn. The Breamish valley also offers a possible route, but this is dealt with as a separate excursion.

The most fitting approach of all is by the route which seeks no valley for its shelter, but which strides the ridges like the auxiliaries of Rome. Such is the Pennine Way which goes from Kirk Yetholm by Burnhead on the Halter Burn to join the ridge at Black Hag (M.R. 864233), a little over 3 miles north of Auchope Cairn.

The approach from Bowmont Water may be made by the drove road up the ridge of Cock Law as described. The fence may then be followed to the highest point on the Union boundary at 2419 ft. (737m.), where the walker is ½ mile west of Cairn Hill, the southern edge of the Cheviot plateau. There is a very large ruined cairn at this point. The angle of the fence at the 2419 ft. point is marked by an old stile and Auchope Cairn 2382 ft. (726m.) lies less than ½ mile north-west from this point.

The top of Cheviot may prove somewhat disappointing, for the walker finds himself on a featureless plateau of considerable size, and if visibility is bad, the vague and amorphous character of the place, so typical of a peat moor, may even induce a sense of frustration when the actual summit point proves elusive. It is marked by a triangulation pillar on a concrete plinth and erosion of the peat has given the pillar a height of about seven feet.

An alternative route is by a track from Sourhope Farm along the ridge running east to Auchope Cairn. This enables a diversion to be made up the gorge of the Hen Hole, a diversion much to be recommended. The Hen Hole stream may be followed with all its diverting twists and tunnels through the peat of the summit plateau, where the discerning eye will note several possible bivouac sites.

The approach by the College Burn turns south from the Yetholm-Wooler road (B6351), the turning being marked 'Hethpool'. Rather less than 2 miles from this point the road is gated and bears a sign – 'Private road – no entry. Skiing prohibited.' The estate owners, however, have intimated that they have no objection to anyone walking through the estate to Cheviot provided that recognised roadways and footpaths are followed. Two miles beyond Hethpool the road divides, the left-hand route crossing the stream and following the left branch. When the extensive plantation at the foot of the ridge has been passed, the first tributary stream on the right leads to the plateau. This is the Bizzle or Bazzle Burn and the rocks on the right as one ascends contain a chimney some 80 ft. high, first climbed in 1899.

Cheviot may also be approached from the Wooler direction via the Harthope Burn to Langleeford. The metalled road ends at this point but there is ample parking space and the top is within 2½ miles.

Comb Fell 2132 ft. (658m.), lies 1½ miles south east from The Cheviot and the ridge joining the two forms the watershed of the Harthope Burn. Langleeford is 2½ miles away and is the easiest approach route.

Hedgehope Hill 2348 ft. (716m.). This hill forms the continuation of the ridge from Comb Fell, lying ¾ mile to the north-east. It is easily ascended from Langleeford.

Bloodybush Edge 2001 ft. (610m.). This hill lies rather less than 4 miles due south from The Cheviot and, with Cushat Law, forms the highest point on the stretch of moorland between the Alwin valley and the Breamish Burn.

Cushat Law 2020 ft. (616m.). This hill, like its neighbour Bloodybush Edge, may be ascended from the Breamish valley where Linhope lies 2½ miles away.

All the hills in the Cheviot group may be traversed in one strenuous expedition of about twelve hours. Start from the Breamish Burn and follow a route – Cushat Law; Bloodybush Edge; Windy Gyle; Auchope Cairn; The Cheviot; Comb Fell; Hedgehope Hill. The direct line from Bloodybush Edge to Windy Gyle involves a descent to 1150 ft. (351m.) at Uswayford and a corresponding ascent to regain the ridge. The remainder of the route involves high-level walking.

The hill walker must share his territory with other interests. Military activity in this area is of long standing, for the complex of Roman camps at Redesdale and at Chew Green near Coquet Head are of later date than the many Iron Age forts and settlements, which lie on the northern slopes, particularly round the head of Bowmont Water. Nor did this activity cease with the Roman withdrawal, for Sheet 70 of the 1-inch O.S. map shows no fewer than fourteen 'Danger Areas' in the Northumberland National Park.

One such area lies ½ mile south from the summit of Windy Gyle, but it is skirted by a right of way running from the long plantation on the Hepden Burn to the summit. It will be noted that the 1970 edition of Sheet 70 of the 1-inch O.S. map now indicates routes which are regarded as rights of way, but only on the English side of the border. It seems unlikely that this practical and useful feature will be extended to the northern side in the immediate future, for it has not proved possible to define any rights of way on the northern slopes of the Cheviot group. This is not to say that existing routes suitable for walkers should not be indicated, as the more often these routes are used the better.

Dere Street, the Roman road, is described as a long-distance walk in the chapter on 'Outlying Hills'.

The Street represents another footpath over the border. It commences in Coquet Dale at map reference 859115 and is marked as a pedestrian right of way along the ridge to Black Braes. Crossing the border at 1650 ft. (503m.) the route offers five miles (8kms.) of attractive ridge walking to Hownam in the upper part of Kale Water. Accommodation may be found here in an attractive and unfrequented area which has a great deal to offer the walker.

106. Craig Minnan from the south-west.

107. Loudoun Hill from the south.

108. The south face of Loudoun Hill.

109. Stayamrie.

110. Benbeoch.

111. The Slock.

Rock Climbing. There is some rock climbing to be found on Cheviot, this is described in the chapter of that heading.

Bus routes. There is a daily bus service between Kelso and Kirk Yetholm; there are also daily services between Edinburgh and Newcastle and Galashiels and Newcastle, both of which serve Kelso and Wooler. A further alternative is the service between Newcastle and Edinburgh via Otterburn, Catcleugh and Jedburgh.

Accommodation. There is an Hotel at Kirk Yetholm and a somewhat wider choice at Wooler. There are Youth Hostels at both of these places. Accommodation may also be obtained at Hownam on Kale Water.

As regards camping, it should not be difficult to find a site in either the Bowmont Water or Harthope valleys.

BIBLIOGRAPHY

The Cheviot, J.G.S. – S.M.C. Journal, Vol. I.
The Cheviot in 1726, Daniel Defoe – S.M.C. Journal, Vol. III.
Notes on the Cheviot Hills, A. Webster Peacock – S.M.C. Journal, Vol. XXII.
Additional Notes, John Dow – S.M.C. Journal, Vol. XXII.
Northumberland, National Park Guide No. 7 – H.M.S.O., 1969.

15

Outlying Hills

A number of hills in the Southern Uplands are in an isolated position and not readily associated with a particular group. Highest and most important are the Tinto hills in Lanarkshire; equally striking in their own way and of a quite different geological formation are Ruberslaw in Teviotdale, the Dirrington Laws near Duns, the triple peaks of the Eildons and the attractive eminences that add variety to the hill country between the Liddel and the upper reaches of the Teviot. Caldcleuch Head in Roxburgh is higher than any hill in either the Lammermuirs or the Pentlands and this distinction may be applied to three other hills in the same district. The relative neglect of these border hills arises from their isolation and the absence of an east-west line of communication, but in an age of growing pressures on these open spaces any tract of country which offers high-level walking over open ground is of increasing interest and importance.

The thoughtful walker who sees the restrictions imposed on the south side of the border by the extensive Ministry of Defence artillery ranges and the growing areas of conifer planting by the Forestry Commission on both sides, may well feel that the increasing volume of traffic and the extending road network are not the only pressures he has to face.

To look eastwards from Loch Fell in the Ettricks is to gaze over an area of afforestation, the extent of which cannot be appreciated when driving up the Esk valley. The change in the landscape is considerable but looking over the tree-clad lower hills from above produces an impression which is not unacceptable. There are a great number of access roads and these might be of interest to the walker since there is in general no objection to the use of Forestry Commission access roads by the pedestrian.

A somewhat different impression is given by the plantings in the Moffat Water valley, where the rectangular plantations and the straight lines of the access rides make an unfortunate visual impact when seen in conjunction with the curves of the corries and the rise and fall of a ridge against the skyline.

The Tinto Hills 2320 ft. (707m.) M.R. 953344. In heavily populated Lanarkshire on the south side of Glasgow, Tinto is almost as familiar a landmark as is Ben Lomond in the district to the north and its isolation and striking form give rise to almost the same degree of affection.

Tinto is actually the highest point of an east-west running ridge 5 miles in length. The 1970 reprint of the 1-inch O.S. map (sheet 68) shows the height as 2320 ft. but for many years the official height was 2335 ft. (712m.).

Lying close to the A73 road near Symington in upper Clydesdale, Tinto is readily ascended by leaving the main road on the western side at the crossroads and taking the Fallburn–Lochlyock road. A cattle-grid 400 yards from the main road marks the start of the most widely-used path to the summit, no more than 2 miles (3kms.) away.

A much more interesting approach, assuming that transport is available, is to start from the highest point of the road between Wiston and Douglas Water. Here, at a height of 1125 ft. (343m.) a fence marks the line of a parish boundary and leads over Howgate Hill, the western extremity of the Tinto ridge, to continue as a stone wall over Lochlyock Hill to the summit of Tinto itself. The prominent gap in the ridge, called Howgate Mouth, is crossed by this route and the rough track which passes through this gap is normally accessible to a car. It was through this gap, at a level slightly above that taken by the existing road, that the Roman road ran from the Clyde crossing at Roberton to the major fort at Castledykes near Carstairs.

A third and much steeper approach is from the south, where a track begins at a point a little to the west of Wiston Lodge and zigzags up the side of the steep and rather broken face on this side. It is this face which makes Tinto such an easily recognised landmark when seen from the east.

The red felsite rocks which inspire the name of the hill are very much in evidence in the enormous cairn on the summit. This is now ruined and the same fate has unfortunately overtaken the indicator, which for so long graced the summit. Not all visitors to Tinto it seems show the respect and affection which the hill deserves.

Cauldcleuch Head 2028 ft. (618m.) M.R. 458008. This hill lies in the county of Roxburgh, 3½ miles east by north from Mosspaul Inn on the A7 road (Langholm–Hawick). The 1-inch O.S. map (sheet 69) does not indicate the height beyond the inclusion of the 2000 ft. contour, but a triangulation pillar east of the top is shown as a height of 1996 ft. (608m.) and it is this height which is repeated on many maps. The point is of more than minor importance, since Cauldcleuch Head is the most easterly hill of 2000 ft. (610m.) or above, wholly on Scottish soil. Mount Keen, on the Aberdeen–Forfar boundary, is the most easterly Munro, but it lies some seven minutes of longitude further west.

The hill may be approached by taking the eastward turning off the main road, 2½ miles south of Mosspaul, the road being signposted 'Hermitage Castle 7½ miles'. This road climbs to a height of over 1100 ft. (335m.) before it descends to the Hermitage Water valley and follows the stream round the foot of the first of the two ridges which run north to the top of Cauldcleuch. Either ridge forms a satisfactory approach route, and a fence will be found running north and south over the plateau and joining a second fence at the summit. This runs down the south-east ridge and this route may be followed to Greatmoor Hill 1966 ft. (599m.) which lies 2 miles to the east.

The western side of Cauldleuch is equally rewarding, for only 1 mile to the north of the highest point of the road rises Tudhope Hill 1966 ft. (599m.) and this also can be conveniently included in a circuit of Cauldcleuch. Using the deserted house at Billhope (M.R. 445976) as a starting point, the circuit of Tudhope Hill and Cauldcleuch should not occupy more than three hours, road to road.

This by no means exhausts the possibilities of the district for on the west side of the A7 main road lies another hill approaching the 2000 ft. (610m.) mark. This is Wisp Hill 1953 ft. (595m.), which lies west of the Mosspaul Hotel at the road summit. The county boundary fence runs from the road to the top of Wisp Hill and the walker who has reached this point may well ponder on the fact that to follow that fence westwards would be to walk seventeen miles (27kms.) before the next road is reached and on a course which does not fall below 1150 ft. (351m.) and for the greater part lies on the 1400–1500 ft. level (457m.).

Ruberslaw 1392 ft. (424m.) M.R. 581155. 1-inch O.S. map, sheet 70, lies rather less than 5 miles (8kms.) due east from Hawick, and is an example of a hill of insignificant height but strong character. It is an isolated hill, volcanic in origin, which is still a prominent feature of the landscape when seen from the northern side of the Tweed valley. A 2 mile walk over moorland from the A6088 road will bring the minor crags of the summit underfoot and, from that viewpoint, the eye of faith will note that a ruined wall encircles the rocks at a slightly lower level. This represents the remains of an Iron Age fort and it is of especial interest in that some of the blocks have been identified as re-used Roman stones, presumably from a signal station of earlier date. A local rhyme runs:

'When Ruberslaw puts on his cap
and the Dunion on her hood,
Then a' the wives o' Teviotdale
Ken there will be a flood.'

The Dunion lies to the north-east of Ruberslaw and is some 300 ft. (91m.) lower. It seems to be rapidly disappearing into a quarry, which produces road metal, but whether its eventual elimination will lead to any permanent improvement in the local weather seems debatable.

The Eildon Hills 1385 ft. (422m.), 1-inch O.S. map, sheet 70, M.R. 550325. The triple peaks of the Eildon Hills at Melrose represent another example of an isolated group of hills so prominent and so well known that their low height is of secondary importance. Not only do they give their name to the major Roman fort of Trimontium, which was built at Newstead, near Melrose, but the northern hill contained a fortified town only matched in area by that on Traprain Law. There is evidence of the presence of not less than 300 houses in this enclosed area, but the site appears to have been evacuated shortly before the Roman occupation in A.D. 79, since a signal station was built on the remains of one of the houses.

Access to the Eildons presents few problems for the district is well served by footpaths. Nor are these likely to be unfrequented, as the district has considerable tourist attractions and represents in full measure one of the major characteristics of this part of Scotland – the mixture of farmland cultivated for centuries with rough hill country.

Dere Street, 1-inch O.S. map, sheets 62, 63, 70. 'Agricola's road into Scotland' may appear at first sight to bear little relationship to hill walking, but in view of the growing importance of long-distance walking routes and the increasing interest in defining and even initiating rights of way, it is thought that the subject is of sufficient interest to justify a detailed description. As a start can hardly be made at York in this guide, a compromise has been adopted by describing the course of the route from Bremenium (M.R. 833986) which was the fort ½ mile north of Rochester on the A68 road (England). Further complications arise in this portion of the Northumberland National Park since sections of the route lie in the danger area of the artillery ranges and can only be visited by permission in non-firing periods.

From Bremenium, the route descends to the Sills Burn then follows a metalled road for 3 miles (5kms.) to Featherwood, after which the stream is re-crossed and the road turns north again to the top of the hill. The line continues, marked by a wide belt of distinctive herbage. A steep descent by the Gammels Path leads to the headwaters of the Coquet and the complex of Roman camps at Chew Green on the border and at this point the Pennine Way comes in from the west and south.

The ridge is now followed with the headwaters of the Hindhope Burn on the left until Blackhall Hill is passed to the west of the summit and a well-defined line is followed past the practice seigeworks on Woden Law to descend to the ford over Kale Water at Tow Ford. A short stretch of metalled road follows to the junction at Pennymuir, where Dere Street continues the line and passes over the top of the next hill.

A delightful section of green lane follows to Whitton Edge, where the route follows the existing road to Shothead. Then comes a long section of green lane, straight run and well defined and crossing three minor roads in its course to North Eildon, clearly seen ahead. Some work has been done on these sections by Roxburgh County Council by the erection of signposts and clearance of obstructions, and that authority refers to the route as a right of way.

The crossing of Oxnam Water (M.R. 695214) may be easier by the bridge some distance downstream from the line of the road.

On arriving at Jedfoot it is extremely difficult to follow the line directly, since two river crossings are involved and the maze of paths and roads around Monteviot House. Dere Street, however, crosses the River Teviot just over ¾ mile above the junction with the River Jed.

At Howden the route becomes better defined, and, after a somewhat indefinite stretch at the road crossing near Harrietsfield, the definition improves until the main road is joined at Forest Lodge. It is then necessary to follow the existing road at Newstead, having covered 29½ miles (47kms.) from Brementium.

The second section of the road, from Newstead to Dalkeith, covers 27 miles (43kms.). Northward from Newstead the course is indefinite until M.R. 541384 is reached 2 miles north of Gattonside. Then an excellent line is followed over Kedslie Hill to Upper Blainslie, south of Lauder. Here the route is lost again until M.R. 506512 is reached at Midburn, but from here the route is traceable to the Roman camp near Kirktonhill and northward over the hill towards the Armet Water. This section is well preserved. From the Armet Water crossing the route runs past Soutra Aisle to join the A68 road, the line of which is followed to Fala. Then the line is traceable on the east side of the road to Pathhead and there is evidence to show that the unclassified road running so straight between that point and Dalkeith is Dere Street.

REFERENCES

Royal Commission on Ancient Monuments of Scotland. Roxburghshire, Vol. II.

Roman Roads in Britain, Vol. II – Ivan D. Margary.

The Bass Rock

The Bass Rock lies offshore from North Berwick and, since it is 1 mile in circumference and 313 ft. (95m.) high, it is a prominent feature. It represents the most accessible and best known gannet colony in Britain and the written record goes back to 1447. The castle on the Rock was held for the Crown during the English civil war and was the last place to surrender. In 1671 it became a State prison, one inmate being the Town Clerk of Glasgow!

In 1706 the Rock passed into the possession of Sir Hew Dalrymple and it has remained with the family to this day.

The gannets, or solan geese as they are sometimes called, have been subjected to a most detailed study. Dr J. B. Nelson and his wife lived through three seasons on the Rock from March to November and made an intensive study of some 250 nests from hides, much of the work being recorded on film under the title 'Gannet City'. Nelson's census of 1963, the latest available, gave 5200 breeding pairs, plus or minus 700, to allow for various errors in counting. The 1939 census gave 4374 occupied nests; thus, in common with many other colonies, it seems that the gannets of the Bass are on the increase still.

Landing by the general public is not permitted, but a system of permits has been developed so that keen ornithologists and historians may visit the Rock. The cost of a permit is £1 and this covers ten people. Permits may be obtained from Sir Hew Hamilton-Dalrymple, Leuchie, North Berwick or Mr Fred Marr, 24 Victoria Road, North Berwick. Mr Marr is the only boatman allowed to land.

BIBLIOGRAPHY

Tinto Hill, S.M.C. Journal, Vol. XX.
The Tinto Indicator, J. A. Parker – S.M.C. Journal, Vol. XXI.

112. Abseiling on the Tauchers.

113. Craigencallie.

114. Craigdews Gairy.

115. Kirkennan Crag.

116. Clifton Crags.

16

Rock Climbing

The extent and distribution of rock climbing areas in the Southern Uplands is much more limited than in the Highlands of Scotland. No comprehensive rock-climbing guide to the entire region has ever been published and some areas are seldom visited except perhaps by local climbers. It is hoped that the following brief and incomplete list will encourage climbers to take a fresh look at the region, and re-examine its potential.

What constitutes a worthwhile crag must remain a matter of opinion. Some small crags near to large centres of population assume more importance than they really deserve, while others two hours or more from the nearest road remain neglected. There is still scope for exploration in the region although no new crags of any great height will be uncovered.

Approximate National Grid numbers are given to help pinpoint the localities.

WEST RENFREWSHIRE AND NORTH AYRSHIRE

Maps: O.S. 1-inch, Seventh Series, sheet 59.

Girtley Hill, Auchenmaid Craigs, 1½ mls. (2½kms.) E. by N. of Largs. Short climbs and scrambles above Greeto Bridge. M.R. 226599. Also on west face of this hill. Access by track up hill from Flatt Farm on east side of Largs.

Gogo Gully, 2¾ mls. (4½kms.) east of Largs. A gorge known as the Black Linn on the Gogo Water. Very Difficult climb or harder. M.R. 245595.

The Three Sisters, Portencross, 6 mls. (9½kms.) S. by W. of Largs. Seacliffs, 200 ft. (60m.). Not recommended. M.R. 178502.

Craig Minnan, Glen Calder, 3¾ mls. (6kms.) N.W. by N. of Lochwinnoch. A fine crag with a variety of short routes. It stands on private land just outside the Muirshiel Estate Policies, which are open to the public. M.R. 322641.

EAST RENFREWSHIRE

Maps: O.S.,1-inch, Seventh Series, sheet 60.

Neilston Pad, 1 ml. (1½kms.) S.S.W. of Neilston. Outcrop on left of road from Neilston to Dunlop. Numerous short climbs. M.R. 475558.

EAST AYRSHIRE

Maps: O.S. 1-inch, Seventh Series, sheet 67.

Loudoun Hill, 2¾ mls. (4½kms.) E. by N. of Darvel. M.R. 609379. A very fine climbing ground – certainly the finest on the mainland of South-West Scotland. Access over fields, from the minor roads to the south-east and west. The climbs are on three sections of the south and east faces. None are easy. West end of south face – a low line of cliffs above a steep grassy slope. A large pinnacle known as the 'Pulpit Rock' stands out from the face beside some trees. There are short climbs on the cliffs and an exposed climb up the arete of the pinnacle of about 50 ft. (15m.).

South face – a fine crag with a wide variety of routes on it from difficult to very severe. Numerous variations are possible and these can be selected and linked to form a good route. Most of the hard climbing comes near the foot of the crag. The main feature of this face is an imposing looking flake jutting out at right angles to the crag, with an almost vertical crack on either side of it. The east crack is severe and the west crack about very difficult. The route up the flake can be started from either of the cracks, but normally from the west, and is very severe.

Farther east there is a 'long climb' of about 200 ft. (60m.) that is difficult, with variations at the start to hard severe. Between this and the flake there is a buttress with overhangs at its right-hand edge. In a corner of this to the right there is a small crack which gives an interesting variation to the 'long climb'.

East face – this has two main routes (1) a crack of about 100 ft. (30m.) – Hard Severe – starts near the bottom of the crag at the foot of an easy wall and goes straight up then bears to the right along the bottom of another wall. Descend slightly and climb the crack which has its crux at the last pitch. (2) the far east wall route 60 ft. (20m.) – a hard very difficult – goes straight up the wall on sloping ledges then traverses left on tiny holds. It then ascends to the right to a block belay beyond which there is easy climbing to the summit.

A large overhang at the base of the crags has a small tooth on its right. There are a number of variations around here (see also chapter 2).

Stayamrie, 5 mls. (8kms.) S. by E. of New Cumnock. A vertical wall of about 70 ft. (20m.) overlooking Glen Afton. M.R. 630055. Shorter and easier outcrops nearby. Access from Craigdarroch.
Benbeoch, $1\frac{3}{4}$ mls. ($2\frac{3}{4}$kms.) N.E. by N. of Dalmellington. Access from New Cumnock–Dalmellington road west of Clawfin on rough track to Benbain. A line of cliffs on south-east face averages about 60 ft. (18m.). The face is formed of hexagonal columns of slabby rock which is greasy when wet but quite enjoyable when dry. M.R. 496081 (See also chapter 4).
Glenmuck, 2 mls. (3kms.) S.E. by S. of Dalmellington. Short scrambles on east side of Dalmellington–Carsphairn road. This area looks unpromising from below but has some interesting moves. M.R. 500033.

WEST DUMFRIESSHIRE
Maps: O.S. 1-inch, Seventh Series, sheet 68.
Crichope Linn, 3 mls. ($4\frac{3}{4}$kms.) S.E. by E. of Carronbridge. A sandstone gorge where the Crichope Burn drops down from the moors. Access from the road between Newton and Closeburnmill – difficult because of vegetation. In places the gorge is only about 8 ft. wide and 80 ft. deep ($2\frac{1}{2}$m. and 25m.). A traverse is possible in dry conditions but parts must be swum. M.R. 911955.
Glenwhargen Craig, $4\frac{1}{2}$ mls. (7kms.) S. by W. of Sanquhar. M.R. 763031. A band of sound rock high on the hillside above the road where it crosses the Scaur Water. Good climbs and scrambles.

GALLOWAY
Maps: O.S. 1-inch, Seventh Series, sheets 73, 74, 79 and 80.
Buchan Hill, north side of Glen Trool. Scrambling. M.R. 422814.
Mullwharchar, S.W. of Loch Doon.

— the Slock M.R. 456895
— the Yellow Tomach M.R. 460885
— the Tauchers M.R. 455875

Granite outcrops broken by terraces. Scrambling and short climbs.

Dungeon Hill, S.E. of Mullwharchar

The Cooran Buttress, 350 ft. (110m.). Very Difficult. M.R. 462849. The climb is on the face overlooking the Cooran Lane and starts at the lowest point of the buttress where steep smooth slabs are broken by a chimney (cairn). The chimney is climbed until it narrows. Move left to a detached block and up to a ledge, 30 ft. (10m.). A wall with large holds finishes at a heather ledge near the summit.

First ascent – J. W. Simpson and Miss J. Ratcliffe. 1955.

Craignaw, N.E. of Loch Trool. Scrambling on granite, mainly on the east and north faces of the hill. Snibe Hill to the south-west has several short climbs. M.R. 462835 and M.R. 466815.

Milldown, Kells Range, M.R. 513841. The steep slopes above Loch Dungeon offer some scrambling but the rock is very unreliable.

Craiglee, E. of Loch Trool, M.R. 465805 and elsewhere. Scrambling on granite outcrops.

Cairngarroch, above Craigencallie west of Clatteringshaws Loch. M.R. 501781. Granite cliffs with short climbs.

Craigdews Gairy, 7 mls. (11kms.) N.E. of Newton Stewart. Outcrop on north side of Newton Stewart–New Galloway road. M.R. 499722.

Cairnsmore of Fleet, E. of Newton Stewart. Scrambling on granite along the east and south faces of the hill. M.R. 505665 and M.R. 515645.

Clints of Dromore, 6 mls. (9½kms.) N.W. of Gatehouse of Fleet. Granite cliffs offering a number of short routes of all grades. M.R. 546641.

Screel Hill, 4½ mls. (7kms.) S.S.E. of Castle Douglas. Good scrambling. M.R. 787551.

Kirkennan Crag (the Lion's Head), 2 mls. (3½kms.) S.S.W. of Dalbeattie. A superb buttress standing boldly above the road surrounded by trees. Several climbs on granite. M.R. 822579.

Clifton Crags, 5½ mls. (8¾kms.) E.S.E. of Dalbeattie. A low line of cliffs offering numerous short climbs. Access through farmyard at Upper Clifton. Ask permission. M.R. 909572.

SEA CLIFFS. Numerous cliffs fringe the shores of Galloway. The most spectacular and best for climbing are those at the *Mull of Galloway*, M.R. 155304, where there are routes of over 200 ft. (60m.).

Meikle Ross, M.R. 650434, has cliffs of about 170 ft. (50m.).

Burrow Head, M.R. 457341, has possibilities but is inferior to the last two areas.

The following areas also have sizable cliffs but are not recommended:

Port o' Warren	M.R. 877534.
Rascarrel Bay	M.R. 813483 (O.S. 1-inch, Seventh Series, sheet 81)
Port Mary	M.R. 749449 (O.S. 1-inch, Seventh Series, sheet 81)

Few opportunities arise in the eastern half of the Southern Uplands for serious rock climbing, but a number of routes have been made.

Traprain Law, 1-inch O.S. map, sheet 63. With 68 recorded routes and variations, this crag is the most important in the area and is featured in the rock climbing guide published by Graham Tiso of 44 Rodney Street, Edinburgh, under the title *Creag Dubh and the Eastern Outcrops*. The following details are taken from the guide and represent the preliminary description.

The hill lies 3 miles east of Haddington and 1 mile south of A1. All the climbs face south so that the rock dries quickly and often offers acceptable conditions in mid-winter.

There are two main cliffs – Overhang Wall and Lammer Wall and several other less important crags. The rock is trachyte, a microcrystalline igneous rock. It is generally sound and clean and small holds abound on slabs lying at between 50 degrees and 70 degrees. The climbs are up to 200 ft. (61m.) and range through every grade of difficulty.

Traprain Law, M.R. 582747, can be reached easily from Edinburgh either by private or public transport. Buses leave St Andrew's Square at ten minutes past the hour. By getting off the bus at Overhailes, three miles beyond Haddington, it is possible to walk to the crag in 25 minutes. Follow the side road past two farms, cross the river Tyne by a footbridge and follow a path to another road. Go right, past another farm then left up a track, eventually crossing fields past a small outcrop of rock, to the north-west corner of Traprain. Walk round to the cliffs on the south face. By car one can get within 200 yards of the crag by a back road, turning off the A1 before Haddington and going through the town.

Traprain Law contains other interests for the visitor in addition to the rock climbing, for it is considered to have been an occupied site for 1000 years, from about the middle of the first Millenium B.C. At one time it was the capital town of the Votadini, extending over some 40 acres and supporting numerous industries including metal working. It represented a free British town in Roman times, while the long and continuous occupation and its degree of sophistication when compared to the bucolic settlements all round about make it by far the most important place in the late pre-history of Scotland. The Traprain Treasure was found in 1919 and represents the largest treasure-trove ever found in Scotland. It is now in the Museum of National Antiquities in Edinburgh.

The steady advance of the working face of the quarry operated by the East Lothian County Council as a source of road metal forms a depressing picture on so valuable a site.

Cheviot. The best rock climbing on Cheviot lies on the northern slopes of **Auchope Cairn** on the headwaters of the College Burn. The crags are on the English side of the Border, but so very close that exclusion for that reason would be pointless. Access to the College valley has already been described in the chapter on Cheviot and the crags lie on both sides of the stream where it turns east for the final section, running up to the Cheviot plateau. The north-facing crag on the left bank is crossed with grass ledges and the gully in the centre is the only natural line. The buttress on the opposite or right bank has a cave at two-thirds height and this lends its name to – *Cannon Hole Direct*, 120 ft. Severe. The right-hand edge of the buttress offers a second route – *Black Adam's Corner* (Difficult). To the left of the Direct route there is a wide rake on which a number of lines either start or finish, with a tendency for the harder climbs to fall in the lower section.

Further up the slopes and somewhat to the west is another crag of about 100 ft. with a number of routes –

Platform and Chimney (Moderate) is an easy and attractive route up the centre.

Zig-zag (Difficult) has its hardest move at ground level, but the next route – *College Groves* (Severe) has the crux in the exposed shallow groove some distance above the initial overhang. The left hand end of the crag has some hard routes, among which is – *Long John* (Severe).

There is a crag on the left hand side of the Bizzle Burn where it runs north from the plateau of **Cheviot** to Dunsdale. The deep rift in this crag is *Bizzle Chimney* (Very Difficult), first climbed in 1899.

Fast Castle Head

Fast Castle Head, 1-inch O.S. map, sheet 63, is a stretch of sea cliff at M.R. 860711. It lies east of the A1107 road, which branches from A1 just south from Cockburnspath. The side road to Dowlaw is followed to a line of cottages from where a track leads to the ruins of Fast Castle.

To reach the foot of the climbs an abseil can be made down the gully from the bridge, or the steep grassy slope to the south can be descended.

The following routes were made in July, 1965, by Gordon Davison and Jack Binns, to whom the authors are indebted for the following notes:

Abseil Gully, 200 ft. Difficult.

Climb the wall to the right of the chimney for 30 ft. Continue up the right-angled groove, using many bridging moves, all the way to the bridge at the top.

The East Arête, 150 ft. Severe.

1. 100 ft. Climb the slab and arête at the east end of the crag for 60 ft., then tend left to a ledge and loose blocks. A poor spike belay and good stance can be found under the overhanging arête.

2. 50 ft. Go left on to the arête and continue for 15 ft. traversing to the left of two cracks in the steep wall. Climb this to a stance and belay.

Urinal Wall, 180 ft. Very Severe.

1. 130 ft. Start at the very foot of the deidre just to the right of the huge main mass of slabs. Climb the wall and groove for 130 ft. to a ledge and piton belay.

2. 50 ft. Continue up the corner for 30 ft. then left on to loose blocks on the arête and so to the top.

Atlanta, 150 ft. Very Severe.

This is a continuously interesting route. Starts 15 ft. right of the East Arête at the foot of a holdless looking corner.

1. 100 ft. Climb directly up the left corner of the wall, using friction

holds for the right foot and small holds in the corner for the left foot. Piton protection can be arranged in the crack. At the overhang a thread belay can be arranged in the crack on a jammed block. Now go right for 5 ft. and continue up the wall tending back left on dubious holds. Spike belay and good stance below the arête.

2. 50 ft. Continue straight up the crack and wall for 20 ft. then go left on to the arête and climb the right-hand of the twin cracks in the steep wall above.

Vertigo, 180 ft. Very Severe.

This route follows the largest and most obvious line of weakness up the slabs. Towards the middle of the slab mass two cracks can be seen cutting through the folds about 20 ft. up. The right hand and larger of the two marks the route.

1. 45 ft. Climb the slabs to the foot of the crack. Here a piton can be inserted low down in the crack for protection. Climb the crack and continue to a small ledge for a stance and piton belay.

2. 130 ft. Continue directly up the crag over three small overhangs, separated by a slab, climbing to the top. No difficulty is encountered on this pitch. And the climbing is delightful.

A rather broken and scrappy route exists up the rock just to the left of Abseil Gully. It is about very difficult standard, but because of the loose nature of the rock is not worthy of description.

The following two routes were completed by Gordon Davison and Peter Lockey in September 1966:

Castle Wall, 150 ft. Very Severe.

This route runs up the solid face which is separated from the slab mass by a cave and a 40 ft. water strip at high tide. The foot of the route is reached by abseiling from the outermost tip of land beyond the castle ruins. On the first ascent a Tyrolian was arranged between the two sections of crag over the water strip as an emergency escape route.

The climb has only one pitch. Climb the crack in the middle of the face then traverse left towards the groove. Finish with an upward traverse to the right.

Gannet Groove, 220 ft. Very Severe.

Perhaps the hardest climb on the crag. The route follows the obvious crack up the bands on the east face of the crag. As soon as the route is started one is over the sea.

1. 50 ft. Step from the pinnacle at the left-hand corner into the

groove. Move slightly downwards and to the right. Across the wall then up to a pointed stance in the groove. Here the crux is found. Jammed wedges can be placed in the back of the groove for protection. Climb the groove with the right leg hanging over the wall and the left jammed in the groove. After about 15 ft. the groove ends and the wall is climbed for 10 ft. Continue up another groove for about 6 ft. to a stance and piton belay (in place).

2. 75 ft. Continue up the groove and round the overhang at the top to a large stance and excellent block belay.

3. 115 ft. Traverse round corner on the left and continue up a small gangway for 30 ft. The rock now becomes a little loose. Traverse right back on to sound rock and then straight up to the top.

It would be idle to pretend that *Salisbury Crags* on Arthur's Seat, Edinburgh have not been thoroughly explored by Edinburgh climbers; so large an area of climbable rock within a city boundary could hardly be ignored and the records of both the S.M.C. and the E.U.M.C. bear ample witness to the fact. Yet it must be made abundantly clear that climbing on these crags is held to be illegal and that by the publication of routes no claims are being made.

Nevertheless, the records of these climbs are of historical interest and for this reason alone the 'Shorter Guide to Arthur's Seat' merits reproduction, being based on an earlier publication of the Edinburgh University Mountaineering Club. Whether the authors of this guide bore charmed lives in their persistent disregard of the embargo on climbing, or whether they were habitual early risers is best left to the reader's imagination. Authority has been known to turn a blind eye on occasion. In any event the details add interest to an otherwise idle stroll through the Park and enable the sympathetic eye to follow the routes.

This Shorter Guide to Arthur's Seat consists of some fifty climbs chosen from those contained in 'Arthur's Seat, Edinburgh' (by Messrs J. G. Parish, C. G. M. Slesser and D. R. Haworth), the comprehensive survey of this area. We make no claim to have collected only the cream of the climbs; for what is sweet cream to the expert is sour indeed to the novice. Rather have we listed routes from the chief climbing grounds in the King's Park. Because of this, all the climbs of higher standard than Severe have been given near to the Little Quarry, where extrication of those in difficulties can most easily be managed. Routes on unsound rock have been excluded, and mention made of any local insecurities.

The classification has been left in the original form, being Easy, Moderate, Difficult, Very Difficult, Severe, Hard Severe and Very Severe. The standard footwear at the time was nailed boots and modern equipment would tend to reduce these gradings.

Topographically, a few points should be found sufficient. The Cat Nick is the obvious cleft midway along the Salisbury Crags; Hunter's Bog is the marshy depression behind the Crags and containing a rifle range; the Gutted Haddie is the long stone shoot from the summit of Arthur's Seat to the upper end of the Bog. The upper, Dunsapie and the lower, Duddingston Roads are best reached from the West Gate, from which the Hause is seen as the great gap in the south end of Salisbury Crags.

INDEX

The following scheme has been adopted for the convenience of beginners. The first thirty-two routes would provide a good introduction to rock climbing technique.

Section I: SALISBURY CRAGS

The North Climbs. These lie to the left of Cat Nick.

1. *Pic Robbieson.* Moderate; 35 ft. Mentioned by H. Raeburn, 1897. This is an isolated pinnacle of rock some 20 ft. high, resembling the Inaccessible Pinnacle in Skye, situated some 100 yards up the Radical Road opposite Holyrood Palace. The traverse from the lower end to the upper is sensational but the rock is good and excellent holds abound.

2. *Cat Nick Arête.* Moderate; 100 ft. Mentioned by H. Raeburn, 1897. The last of the North Climbs, running up the left edge of Cat Nick Gully itself. A fine route on sound rock except for the avoidable initial sandstone wall. Pitches (i) 15 ft. A broken sandstone wall is ascended to a ledge, also attainable from the Gully. (ii) 10 ft. Mount overhang and traverse into gully on right to reach small ledge. Belay. (iii) 25 ft. Follow the arête above to small stance and traverse to right by striding across a branch of Cat Nick Gully to ledge on the subsidiary arête. (iv) 40 ft. From top of subsidiary arête ascend corner on right to reach groove leading to grassy ledge on left directly above top of subsidiary gully. Easy slabs continue to crest, with belay on left at top.

3. *Cat Nick Gully.* Easy; 100 ft. The polished rocks testify to the age of this route, which affords in good conditions the finest snow climb in the Park. In 1947, the cornice was some 6 ft. thick, with an overhang of 10 ft. and lasted for many weeks, despite much tunnelling.

There are several other North Climbs, but they are broken up and rotten, and any material dislodged may not stop until it has reached the motor road beneath the scree slope.

THE SOUTH CLIMBS. These lie to the right of Cat Nick, and include routes in the Great Quarry, Western Buttress, Little Quarry, Eastern Buttress, Middle Quarry and Pinnacle Quarry, in that order.

4. *Cat Nick Buttress.* Very Difficult; 100 ft. H. Raeburn and W. Inglis Clark, 11.7.1900. Ascends fairly sound rock immediately to the right of the Gully and provides an interesting problem. Pitches: (i) Easy ledges for 20 ft., then climb chimney in right wall to top of prominent projecting block. Belay (30 ft.). (ii) 25 ft. Cross slabs on left up to a right-angle corner, the crux. Step across to sloping ledge on upper side, using fingerhold on edge at head-level. Stance at foot of shallow chimney. (iii) 35 ft. Follow chimney to belay at top.

Many Severe and Very Severe climbs may be found in the Great Quarry, but the rock is treacherous in parts and as an introductory route only one can be recommended.

5. *Great Buttress Original Route*. Difficult; 140 ft. Morrison, Newbigging and Briquet, 25.7.1902. A fine, very exposed climb on righthand buttress of the Great Quarry; the rock needs care on the easier sections. Pitches: (i) 40 ft. Runs up left-hand edge of buttress for 15 ft.; follow terrace diagonally upwards to right. Belay above ledge with care, obvious belay being loose. (ii) 60 ft. Follow ledge round vertical nose across face of buttress into Great Quarry. At end of ledge ascend 10 ft. corner (crux) on small holds. Follow another ledge to left, then over mantelshelf to staircase. Flake belay on right. (iii) 40 ft. Follow staircase to upper recess and escape to top.

WESTERN BUTTRESS ROUTES. Western Buttress is the left-hand buttress of Little Quarry. A broad, level ledge, the Platform, runs across the lower part, and a broken ledge, the Terrace, runs the length of the face just below the top. There are several interesting climbs here of greater difficulty.

6. *Hewit's Groove*. Hard Severe; 40 ft. J. R. Hewit and W. Nisbet, 4.9.33. At left-hand side of buttress some yards to left of end of Platform is a prominent red slab, with groove on left running to large ledge at 40 ft., whence scrambling leads to the top. Groove negotiated by balance, with feet on sloping ledge on left.

7. *Horne's Slab*. Very Severe; 40 ft. A. Horne. Slab lies to right of Hewit's Groove (6). From centre of slab use layback hold near top to lever body to sloping ledge on right. Then traverse left into groove, up left-hand crack to top of split block and ledge.

8. *Wall Route*. Severe; 80 ft. Hewit and Nisbet, 2.10.37. On good rock but for easy upper part. From left end of Platform, follow groove 10 ft., traverse upwards to right over steep slab to ledge round corner at the top. Move back left, swing out to left on vertical face, using level hold, and by pull-up gain upper ledge; climb direct to Terrace.

9. *Slab and Wedge Route*. Very Difficult; 70 ft. Pleasant route on good rock, but finish needs care. Starts up slab a little to right of the top of the right-angled chimney near right end of platform. Above slab traverse left and up to ledge and on to Wedge, then mount steep wall diagonally to right, finishing directly to top.

Between (8) and (9) lie many easy routes, but care is needed for the friable upper ledges.

LITTLE QUARRY ROUTES. The most important centre on the Crags. Much of left wall rendered unsafe by rockfall, but rest of quarry excellent. Only a selection of the routes can be described.

10. *Doubledecker*. Severe; 80 ft. D. H. Haworth and J. G. Parish, 22.1.47. Close to left limit of rockfall on sound rock. Starts 20 ft. right of end of Platform, up white slab in rockfall to red groove above; two pull-ups, latter to left of blast-hole, gain ledge. Easier climbing slightly to left leads to final wall.

11. *Harrison's Climb*. Severe; 60 ft. A. Harrison. Ascend to small shelf above shallow cave to right of rockfall over slabs on left. Surmount mantelshelf, move right and swing to grassy ledge; easy ledges provide exposed finish.

12. *Archie's Slab*. Very Severe; 60 ft. A. Hendry. Slab immediately to right of grassy ledge in (11) above. Start 20 ft. right of (11); at 15 ft. traverse left leads awkwardly to right lower corner of slab; from here to good handhold in centre of slab, whence continue up to upper right corner.

13. *Wicked Lady*. Hard Severe; 40 ft. D. H. Haworth, 15.5.56. About 20 ft. right of (12.) above, is sloping slab beneath overhang, appearing from below to be a stomach traverse. Easy climb for 10 ft., then take traverse right standing, projecting nose (Wicked Lady) forcing body outwards; use undercut, then flat holds on top of overhang; stance at upper end; continue slightly left to top. So named because 'She tries to cause your downfall just as you're getting round her!' Beware!

14. *Original Route*. Moderate; 32 ft. In left hand corner of Little Quarry. Traverse easy slab with blast-hole in centre and overhang above, to left on to platform; then traverse right above slab on ledge beneath overhang. Ascend to top of overhang up to left to another platform, then vertical groove to top.

15. *Layback or Blasthole*. Difficult; 32 ft. The direct start of Original Route. Ascend slab and use right edge of both slab and overhang for layback, pressing up with left hand on ledge below. Then as above.

16. *Long Stride*. Moderate; 30 ft. Starts up corner 15 ft. right of Original Route; ascend 10 ft., then long stride left to ledge with spike; spike used as foothold to ascend vertical groove to upper ledge, and so to top. Or (Difficult) carry on up corner; exit on left to ledge.

17. *White Slab.* Very Difficult; 27 ft. Steep white-flecked slab to left of previous climb. Runs up centre of slab to two consecutive ledges. From uppermost reach to horizontal crack and pull up. Small holds to top on right of overhang. Avoid rock on left of route.

18. *The Splits.* Severe; 35 ft. Goes up corner on left of Lift, 28 ft. right of White Slab. From hold in corner stride to notch in wall on right, and raise body to small ledge. Easy ledges lead up to recess; traverse out on smooth groove on left, using nose on right above, and pull up to platform and so to top.

19. *The Lift.* Moderate; 35 ft. The usual means of descent. Follow obvious break in rear wall of quarry, 50 ft. from Western (left) corner. Goes up right-angle chimney for 10 ft. to ledge on right; then on up over ledges to steep finish, using bridging method.

20. *Initial Route.* Hard Severe; 35 ft. J. R. Hewit, 5.7.36. Follows layback route 8 ft. to right of the Lift (19) until horizontal crack half way up the face is reached. Upper section of layback is insecure. Then ascend obliquely to right to small projection, using fingerholds in small crack above; from here the top is reached more easily, but balance throughout is delicate.

21. *Red Slab.* Very Difficult; 37 ft. Red Slab 25 ft. right of the Lift (19). Goes by groove to lower left corner of slab, then up left edge on small holds. From top of slab traverse left and obliquely upwards to right on easiest line.

22. *Hyphen Route.* Very Severe; 38 ft. A. Hendry, 14.5.44. Connects start of previous climb with finish of subsequent one. Starts up small crack just right of Red Slab route and continues up centre of Red Slab mainly on finger holds; delicate traverse right leads to overhang; ascend groove on left, with blasthole, to top of overhang; easier, but severe, finish above.

23. *Black Slab.* Severe; 37 ft. 20 ft. right of Red Slab (21) a black mantelshelf overhang appears halfway up the cliff, the shelf beneath it being reached by an arête finishing at its right-hand end. From top of overhang an upward traverse to left leads to good ledge; finish is a pull-up to platform above.

24. *Notch Climb.* Severe; 38 ft. Technically one of the best boot climbs on the Crags. The easier upper rocks need care. Route runs up smooth V notch 25 ft. right of the previous climb. At top traverse obliquely up and right to arête, which is ascended to easy reach of top.

25. *Rib and Mantelshelf*. Hard Severe; 38 ft. D. H. Haworth and A. Dick, 12.5.46. This fine unusual route follows rib to left of Sentry Box Route (26) to mantelshelf on left about 10 ft. from finish, which is climbed facing right. Overhang above mantelshelf avoided and climb finished direct.

26. *Sentry Box*. Severe; 40 ft. J. R. Hewit and J. Donaldson, 4.8.35. 16 ft. below the top and some 40 ft. right of the Notch Route (24) is a recess resembling a sentry box. This is reached from the groove on the left, with a delicate traverse across top of steep slab on right into the Box. Exit to right along horizontal cracks to ledge at top.

27. *Black Chimney*. Severe; 45 ft. Goes up dark right-hand corner of the Little Quarry. Climb direct till groove reached; enter this from left on balance holds to jug-handle further in. Pull-up to foothold on right. Exit via ledge on left and then left of large projection, much used for abseiling.

EASTERN BUTTRESS ROUTES. Eastern Buttress lies to the right of Little Quarry. There are several routes, none above Very Difficult, but the rock generally requires care, and near the top is flaky and friable. The following are the best –

28. *Black Chimney Buttress*. Difficult; 65 ft. Route lies up left edge of Eastern Buttress and on wall overhanging Little Quarry. Starts 5 ft. right of edge; pull up to ledge at 10 ft. Traverse left and ascend wall above on small holds and to block and good stance. Traverse up to right for 5 ft. past awkward overhang, then up to left along exposed fault overlooking Little Quarry for 25 ft. to groove on right and summit rocks; large flaky holds.

29. *Hackenback*. Very Difficult; 70 ft. D. H. Haworth and J. G. Parrish, 13.10.46. Ascends rib about 15 ft. left of middle of south (right) buttress face, and on left of vertical groove at 20 ft. Opposite top of groove rock rotten, and traverse made to right to platform. Friable wall above leads to top.

MIDDLE QUARRY ROUTES: Middle Quarry is the next bay to the right of Eastern Buttress. Of the few good climbs so far made here, we include one suitable for beginners.

30. *Centre Slab*. Difficult; 40 ft. Goes up rocks to left of whitish fault. After easy overhang at foot, ascend red slab obliquely to right until white rock is reached and fault followed to belays.

Further easy slab practice may be had to the right.

PINNACLE QUARRY ROUTES: Pinnacle Quarry is the deep quarry near the right end of the Crags. On the left and rear walls are many short climbs; the Pinnacle is on the right and offers several others.

31. *Pinnacle Face Route.* Very Difficult; 60 ft. D. H. Haworth and P. R. Myerscough, 23.4.46. Start below centre of Pinnacle face, and ascend to ledge at 10 ft.; traverse up to right on sloping holds until pull-up is made on to large projection. After short ascent traverse left under overhang to good ledge and finish directly.

32. *Pinnacle Chimney.* Difficult; 30 ft. Interesting route up right side of Pinnacle between it and main line of crags. Awkward overhang and slab with small holds.

Section II: HAGGIS KNOWE

This small crag lies to the left of the path from the North (Holyrood) Gate to the Hause, just as it enters the depression of Hunter's Bog. To the South a fault separates it from Long Row. It contains several routes up to 25 ft., which have not been described.

There is also a crag overlooking the Chapel ruins, but this is unsuitable for climbing. A cliff in the same line of rocks to the south has not been explored.

Section III: LONG ROW

Continuing up Hunter's Bog by the path a line of cliffs will be seen on the left, resembling Salisbury Crags in miniature. Although over 30 ft. high at the north end, it rapidly diminishes in height and contains technical problems rather than definite routes. Nevertheless the cracked and rugged formation offers many intriguing climbs, of which only a few can be given.

33. *Fallen Column Climb.* Severe; 35 ft. Mentioned by H. Raeburn, 1897. From the north end of the crags the fallen 20 ft. column is a conspicuous feature, leaning against the cliff face. The route goes up the outside and the wall above, on small holds.

34. *Waverley Crack.* Difficult; 30 ft. J. G. Parish and D. G. Duff, 16.6.46. First crack in wall to right of fallen column. Pull up and mantelshelf movement on to ledge, finishing direct.

35. *Stomach Layback.* Very Difficult; 25 ft. J. S. Berkeley, 1946. Next crack to right of previous climb; has obvious overhang in middle; stride to right across slab below overhang, and a pull-up into rest of crack on right of overhang; continue to top.

36. *Editor's Crack.* Difficult; 25 ft. G. J. Dutton, C. M. Slesser, Miss Bainton, 19.1.47. Lies to right of easy slabs directly above disused hut; ugly unclimbed crack 3 ft. right of start.

Section IV: THE DASSIES

The Dassies are three small crags below Long Row and nearer Hunter's Bog Range. The central Dassie offers the best routes.
37. *Central Crack.* Very Difficult. Lies in middle of central Dassie with holdless slab on right and overhang on left.

Section V: *Raven's Crag.* This is the prominent black crag facing north at upper end of Hunter's Bog and lying to right of the Gutted Haddie. It is some 140 ft. high and though many long climbs of severity have been made, the unsoundness of the rock precludes their mention here.

Section VI: LION'S HEAD. A number of easy climbs have been made on these crags directly below the summit of Arthur's Seat on the N.W. side. These routes have the advantage of loftiness and widespread views. Typical are the following:

38. *Red Chimney.* Difficult; 60 ft. A convenient approach to the upper crags by perhaps the largest chimney in the Park. Lies in slabby rock just right of the Dassies; easy escape to right near top.

39. *Nose Chimney.* Difficult; 30 ft. Prominent chimney in centre of vertical portion of upper crags; ample holds, fairly reliable rock.

On May Day Buttress:

40. *Early Morning Exercise:* Difficult; 30 ft.

41. *Limber Up.* Difficult; 35 ft. Two grooves 10 and 30 ft. respectively left of previous route. Good holds.

On May Day Ribs. Numerous ribs to right of Nose Chimney. First and second offer good climbs, and also

42. *Hanging Over Gladys.* Very Difficult; 30 ft. Starts with overhang above amatory inscription, surmounted by layback pull with left fingers in crack.

Section VII: HAWORTH'S CRAG

This crag lies above the Dunsapie Road opposite the summit of Samson's Ribs between Raven's Crag and Red Craig.

43. *Wee Chockstone Crack Route.* Severe; 30 ft. D. H. Haworth, 22.2.47. Follows prominent crack at extreme left of crag; good rock and probably finest crack in the Park. Small shrubs at foot. Crux at 10 ft. needs the small chockstone.

Section VIII: RED CRAIG.

The buttress stretching nearly 100 yards above Dunsapie Road to right of Haworth's Crag. Is of a pinkish colour, with sloping terraces.

44. *Pentland Slab.* Moderate; 80 ft. Steep prominent slab on extreme left. Route follows foot of overhanging wall to right for a third of the height, then follows bulge of rock to left for 20 ft., zigzags over bulge and then parallel to wall and 15 ft. from it for remaining 30 ft.

45. *Crescent Climb* and *Vibrating Pinnacle.* Difficult; 100 ft. D. H. Haworth and J. G. Parish, 8.3.47.

Above and to right of overhanging wall of previous climb is a terrace; climb starts at lower end and ascends groove topped by bush, to reach wide terrace. Descend terrace for 10 ft., go up wall to arête; follow to recess beneath tree. Traverse and descend to right for 30 ft. to reach Pinnacle; traverse this left to right.

46. *Red Buttress Route.* Severe. A. Graham. Fine climb up right-hand buttress of Red Craig, up big steps to right of prominent (ivycleft) chimney, with exposure.

Section IX: DUNSAPIE BUTTRESS

Promising but undescribed crag over lonely Dunsapie Loch.

Section X: SAMSON'S RIBS

Gigantic basalt columns above Duddingston Road, from West Gate. Very Severe long route recently forced, but as yet ungardened.

Arthur's Seat is of very considerable geological interest. Professor G. P. Black in his book 'Arthur's Seat', makes the following succinct description:

'Clearly there must be an optimum stage in the dissection of an extinct volcano when all the parts have been exposed, but when each part is sufficiently preserved to permit of a detailed study of the eruptions from the first to the last. Arthur's Seat owes its pre-eminent place among extinct volcanoes to the fortunate chance that it happens to be in this optimum stage of dissection at the present time. In consequence, it is among the best known ancient volcanoes in the world today, a natural textbook visited by countless geologists from all corners of the globe.'

The Railway Wa's, Currie

Dougal Haston's introduction to this area in the rock climbing guide *Eastern Outcrops* begins:

'This could be called "climbing with a difference". The Currie Wa's were man-made for the purpose of holding up railway embankments, but built by craftsmen who must have been intuitive climbers. While the first function is now secondary as the line is closed, they can still flourish in full splendour as the best finger-training grounds around Edinburgh.'

The Wa's are reached by taking the Balerno via Slateford bus from St Andrew's Square to Riccarton Hotel (Currie Toll). Take the first road on the left after the bus stop and descend the hill until a bridge over the railway is reached. The climbs run from this point west to Balerno.

BIBLIOGRAPHY

Arthur's Seat as a Scrambling Centre, 'Auld Reekie' – *S.M.C. Journal*, Vol. IV.

The Cat Nick in Winter, W. Inglis Clark – *S.M.C. Journal.*, Vol. IV.
Arthur's Seat and the Salisbury Crags, Harold Raeburn – *S.M.C. Journal*, Vol. IV.
Some Climbs on the Salisbury Crags, W. Inglis Clark – *S.M.C. Journal*, Vol. VI.
Salisbury Crags, Eastern Buttress, Great Quarry, W. A. Morrison – *S.M.C. Journal*, Vol. VII.
Arthur's Seat – *S.M.C. Journal*, Vol. X.
Salisbury Crags, Edinburgh – *S.M.C. Journal*, Vol. XI.
Benbeoch, E. C. Thomson – *S.M.C. Journal*, Vol. XIX.
The exploration of the historic cave at Fastcastle, W. Douglas – *S.M.C. Journal*, Vol. XV.
Fastcastle, Ian M. Campbell – *S.M.C. Journal*, Vol. XX.
Loudoun Hill, an Ayrshire Sub-Munro, Douglas Scott – *S.M.C. Journal*, Vol. XX.
The Crags Near Largs, G. C. Curtis & G. H. Townend – *S.M.C. Journal*, Vol. XXIII.
Edinburgh Castle Rock – The Closet Climb, Robin Smith & A. Frazer – *S.M.C. Journal*, Vol. XXVI.
Rock Climbs in Galloway, A. G. Waldie – *S.M.C. Journal*, Vol. XXVI.
Notes – Grey Mare's Tail, Winter ascent – *S.M.C. Journal*, Vol. XXVIII.
'*Arthurs' Seat*', *a History of Edinburgh's Volcano*, G. P. Black.
'*Roman and Native in North Britain*', I. A. Richmond.
Through Crichope Linn, W. A. Carruthers – *The Scots Magazine*, March, 1960.
Creag Dubh and the Eastern Outcrops, Graham Tiso – 44 Rodney Street, Edinburgh.
A Short Guide to Fastcastle Head, G. L. Davison – 34 Dean Street, Newcastle upon Tyne.

General Amendment

The change from counties to regions

The major reorganisation which has already taken place in England will not be completed in Scotland until after this amended edition has been passed to the printers. It is not anticipated that the individual hill-walker will be much concerned since he has little interest in county boundaries as such. He is concerned, however, with those boundaries which are defined by wire fences or stone dykes and which run along hill routes likely to be followed; examples are described on pp 164-165. The maintenance of these dykes and fences is the responsibility of the landowner, not the county/regional authority so that no great change need be envisaged when the reorganisation has been completed.

Metrication and maps

1. Ordnance Survey

It is now possible to give more information concerning the changes in the one inch to one mile (1/63,360) referred to on p. 19. A new series, in the scale 1/50,000, will be issued, commencing in 1976. These sheets will be based on a re-survey starting from a new base line and some changes will occur in the quoted heights of mountains in a few cases, as compared with the old sheets. Sheet numbers for Scotland will be numbered 1 to 85 and all heights will be shown in metres, although the intervals between contour lines will be retained at 50ft. The slight increase in the scale of the new series should be to the walker's advantage.

Sheet numbers of the new series for the Western Area will be:

Title	Area covered
63 Firth of Clyde	Bute and West Renfrewshire
70 Ayr and Kilmarnock	Kilmarnock; Ayr; Cumnock
71 Lanark and Upper Nithsdale	Cumnock; Crawford; Sanquhar
76 Girvan	Maybole and Girvan to River Cree
77 New Galloway and Glen Trool	Loch Doon and New Galloway
78 Nithsdale and Lowther Hills	Nith; Moffat; Dumfries
82 Stranraer and Glen Luce	Glen Luce
83 Kirkcudbright	Wigtown; Kirkcudbright
84 Dumfries	New Galloway; Dumfries; Dalbeattie
85 Carlisle and Solway Firth	Annan; Gretna

For the Eastern Area:

Title	Area covered
66 Edinburgh	Midlothian
67 Duns and Dunbar	East Lothian
72 Upper Clyde Valley	Biggar
73 Galashiels and Ettrick Forest	Penicuik; Galashiels; Peebles; Selkirk
74 Kelso	Duns; Kelso; Jedburgh
79 Hawick and Eskdale	Hawick; Eskdale
80 The Cheviot Hills	Jedburgh to North Tyne

2. Bartholomew

p. 18 The reference to the six mile to the inch map should be deleted as this series has been withdrawn.

p. 19 The reference to half inch maps is similarly out of date. A new series of national maps was issued in March 1975 on a scale of 1/100,000. The sheet numbers of these maps will correspond with the previous 1/126,720 series; the references in each chapter heading to sheet numbers will therefore be unchanged. Heights in these maps will be shown in metres and contours will be colour shaded at either 50m. or 100m. intervals according to altitude. The increase in scale will make these maps of greater interest to the hill-walker, although each sheet will be larger than at present.

WESTERN HILLS

1. West Renfrewshire and North Ayrshire

This area now forms part of the districts of Inverclyde, Renfrew, and Cunninghame in the Strathclyde Region.

The Clyde - Muirshiel Regional Park (formerly Renfrewshire Regional Park) now has a visitor centre to the south west of Loch Thom. This is at the Cornalees Bridge on the moorland road between Greenock and Inverkip. A 2½ mile (4 km.) trail leads from the centre along Shielhill Glen and follows for a short way two interesting aqueducts designed by Robert Thom in 1827. The Kelly Cut carried water from the Kelly Reservoir near Skelmorlie to the compensation reservoir north of Cornalees. From here, the Greenock Cut carried water round Dunrod Hill by a channel cut in the side of the hill to Greenock. This provided drinking water and power for the town's mills and eased a chronic shortage.

A Roman signal station has been discovered on Hillside Hill (near Cornalees) and is thought to lie on a route from the River Clyde to Largs.

Two cross country footpaths are planned from Muirshiel Country Park: to the Rottenburn Bridge on the moor road from Greenock to Largs; and to Ladymuir on the Kilmacolm to Lochwinnoch road.

Transport

Fairlie pier is now closed. Shipping services are operated by Caledonian Macbrayne Ltd.

Bibliography

The Climber & Rambler - August 1974. The Spout of Garnock, John Barr.

2. Eaglesham to Sanquhar

A Roman road from the direction of Loudoun Hill has been traced across the S. W. shoulder of Cairnsaigh Hill, the West Burn M.R. 611352, Avon Water, and the shoulder of Greystone Hill M. R. 620342 to Slouch Moss. Beyond here it is thought to head across the shoulder of Bankend Rig and the west and south flanks of Bibblon Hill in the direction of Muirkirk. The route is then thought to lie partly beneath the Muirkirk - Sanquhar road as far as the March Burn M. R. 724208 where it assumes an E. N. E. direction heading for Tinto Hill.

The site of the former Kaimes Colliery at Muirkirk has now been landscaped.

Bibliography. Discovery and Excavation in Scotland, 1971, 1972.

3. The Lowther Hills

Queensberry may be approached from the south by a longish route through the Forest of Ae from Ae village to Branrigg. The southern slopes of Wee Queensberry have some steep ravines and outcrops.

Bibliography

Scots Magazine, May 1972. Tales of the Enterkin, Robert Kinloch.

4. New Cumnock to Carsphairn

The road from Afton Reservoir dam to the Montraw Burn now exists.

Transport

Buses run from Penpont to Thornhill, and Moniaive to Dumfries now. There is no service between Dalmellington and New Cumnock.

5. Galloway Hills

The Glentrool Forest Park has been renamed the Galloway Forest Park.

The Forestry Commission propose to reduce eventually the number of red deer in the area to around 500, as was the population in the 1950s. The Galloway Deer and Natural History Museum M.R. 552763 on the A712 at Clatteringshaws Loch depicts the history of the red deer in Galloway as well as exhibits on roe deer, wild goats, archaeology, geology and botany. Admission is free.

Campers can be accommodated at Talnotry now provided they have their own chemical closets. Facilities are limited to water standpipes, a shop and a chemical disposal point. Twelve furnished holiday houses in Glentrool village are available to let all year on a weekly basis or for weekends in winter from the Forestry Commission.

The Black Laggan bothy M.R. 469777 is a ruin. The White Laggan M.R. 467775 and Shiel of Castlemaddy M.R. 539901 have been renovated by the Mountain Bothies Association. Both belong to the Forestry Commission but are open for visitors.

Craigmalloch Lodge M.R. 482946 on Loch Doon and Craigenrae M.R. 353893 near Rowantree Toll are outdoor centres run by Ayr County Council.

The Awful Hand

The route to the Merrick has been clearly waymarked from Glentrool. A direct line is marked with posts from Culsharg to Benyellary, joining the dyke on the upper slopes of that hill.

Bennan Hill, on the route between Benyellary and the Fell of Eschonchan, has some interesting pot holed rocks due to exfoliation M.R. 405825.

Goat Fell and Caisteal Abhail in Arran are the only Scottish hills higher than the Merrick south of Ben Lomond and the Highlands (page 87).

The forest road from the south-west corner of Loch Doon by the Carrick and Whitespout Lanes continues north and west of Loch Riecawr and west of Loch Slochy. The north end of the Awful Hand is easily reached from here. A branch of this road runs N. W. from Loch Riecawr to Ballochbeatties and the Straiton-Newton Stewart road. A branch over the Whitespout Lane east of Loch Riecawr leads south-west by a more direct route towards Shalloch on Minnoch but stops farther from the hill. A shorter branch to the east, south of the Whitespout Lane, runs parallel to the Eglin Lane. The locked gate on the road from Loch Doon to Loch Riecawr is now 1 km. nearer the latter.

The Dungeon Range

Access to this range from Loch Doon is now easier by the forest road east of the Gala Lane than from that west of the Eglin Lane.

The Kells Range

Access to this range has become harder from the Forrest Estate on the east. This is due to the growth of the forests and walkers being less welcome now due to inconsiderate fools causing damage. The southern half of the range, as far as Corserine, may be reached from the road end at Craigencallie (west of Clatteringshaws Loch). The forest road from here leads to the bridge over the River Dee and the road north of Clatteringshaws Loch to Backhill of Bush. This can be left at a junction at the Curnelloch Burn and the road taken past Backhill of Garrary, which gives access to the western slopes of Meikle Millyea (partly forested). A forest road starts well up on the western slopes of Millfire and leads down to Backhill of Bush and a long but straight forward walk out to Craigencallie or Clatteringshaws Loch.

The Minnigaff Hills

Larg Hill is now part of the Galloway Forest Park and much of it has been forested. The old pack horse bridge across the Minnoch west of the hill M.R. 373759 is well worth a visit. The routes to and from it have now disappeared leaving it in mysterious isolation. The forestry road from Craigencallie (west of Clatteringshaws Loch) to Loch Dee gives good access to these hills and the White Laggan bothy.

Stretches of the Old Edinburgh Road between Minnigaff and New Galloway are now under forest.

The Solway Hills

Cairnsmore of Fleet may be reached from the south-east from the former railway halt at Gatehouse of Fleet. Alternatively, the road may be taken under the Big Water of Fleet Viaduct to Loch Grannoch and a circuit made over Craigronald, Meikle Mulltaggart and Cairnsmore of Fleet's two summits.

This railway line was closed in 1965 and the rails lifted. Some of the land has been sold off but it is still possible to walk 63 miles (101 km.) of the route from the outskirts of Dumfries to Dunragit near Stranraer. Viaducts over the Rivers Urr, Cree and Bladnoch have been dismantled. The Urr can usually be forded but the Bladnoch and Cree necessitate $\frac{1}{2}$ mile (1 km.) and 6 mile (10 km.) detours respectively (unless 3 miles (5 km.) of the line is bypassed beyond the Cree). At least three days should be allowed for the walk. Crossmichael and Newton Stewart are the most convenient overnight stages. The middle stretch of the line between New Galloway and Newton Stewart is the finest and passes through an area remote from public roads.

Bibliography

Highways and Byways in Galloway and Carrick, Rev. C.H.Dick - MacMillan & Co. Republished E. P. Publishing Ltd., 1972.

Galloway Forest Park Guide, Forestry Commission.

Scots Magazine -

January 1972 The Call of the Back Bush, K. M. Andrew.

February 1974 Across the Silver Flowe, Tom Weir.

May, June, July 1975 The Galloway Railway, K. M. Andrew.

EASTERN HILLS

Rights of Way

While it is hardly hill country, mention might be made of the proposal to establish a right of way from Glasgow to Lanark along the River Clyde, mainly on the east bank, a distance of 30 miles (48 km.). This is under consideration, but at the time of writing a route has been established from New Lanark going upstream on the east bank past Corra Linn and the gorge to the bridge at Bonington and downstream to Corehouse Nature Reserve.

p. 125 Medwinhead is now Medwynhead.

p. 141 The Old Herring Road

The construction of the Whiteadder Reservoir has introduced a complication into this route and the description should be amended so that the second sentence reads, "Continue south-west to cross the road bridge over the northern arm of Whiteadder Reservoir, then follow the track to Penshiel and Kilpallet (M. R. 629606)."

p. 142 Oxton to Stow

"This line is followed until it turns south at map reference 480519." This should be amended as the cart road continues to M. R. 477507 and ends there. There is no through route to Inchkeith which is now uninhabited. From M. R. 485501 the old track to the Stow-Lauder road (B. 6362) is clear in parts only.

p. 177 Deephope to Buccleuch

Meerlees to Buccleuch

It has been reported that both these routes have been blocked by plantations. Consultations with the landowners have indicated that the northern of these two routes, i. e. Deephope to Buccleuch, may be kept open but not necessarily on the line of the right of way.

Buccleuch to Muselee

The route through the northern arm of Craik Forest is complicated by the fact that the forest roads do not offer a clear west-east route and it is hoped that it will be possible to have guide posts erected to define the way more clearly.

p. 178 Laverhay to Garwaldwaterfoot

This route has now been blocked by new forestry planting.

Clyde Valley

One notable change in the Clyde valley is the creation of Strathclyde Park. This lies to the east of the M. 74 motorway between Hamilton and Motherwell and is, of itself, of little interest to the hill-walker. Since the creation of a new loch of over 200 acres (81 hectares) is involved, however, the change should not go unremarked for the loch will have a length of over 2100m. The park will also offer caravan sites.

Bibliography: General

The Scottish Lochs, Vol 2, Tom Weir, Constable, 1972

Scottish Hill Tracks, D. G. Moir. (In preparation)

INDEX

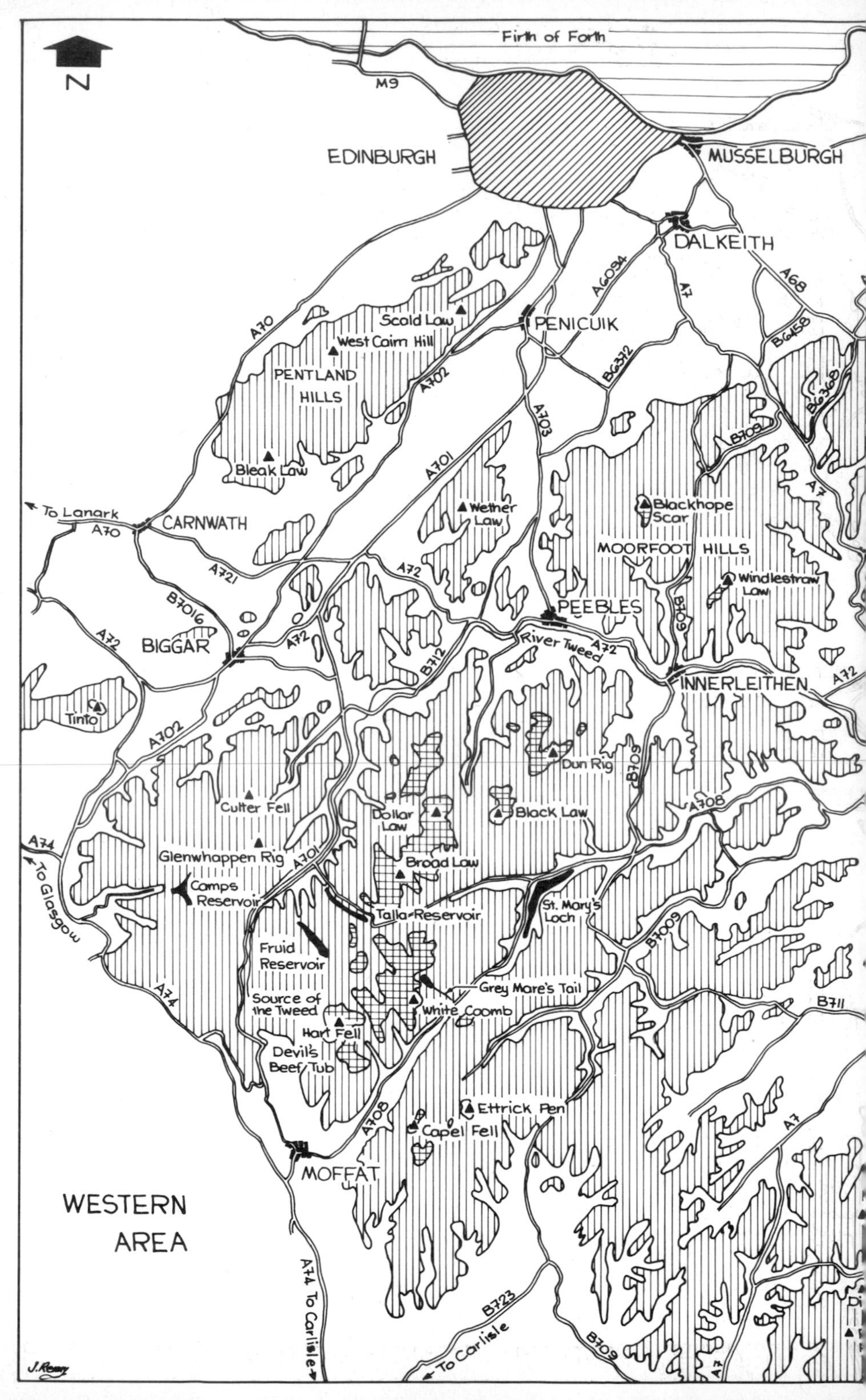
N
Firth of Forth
M9
EDINBURGH
MUSSELBURGH
DALKEITH
A6094
A7
A68
B6458
PENICUIK
B6372
Scald Law
West Cairn Hill
PENTLAND HILLS
A70
A702
A703
Bleak Law
A701
To Lanark
CARNWATH
Wether Law
Blackhope Scar
MOORFOOT HILLS
Windlestraw Law
B709
A721
B7016
A72
BIGGAR
PEEBLES
River Tweed
INNERLEITHEN
B712
Tinto
Dun Rig
Culter Fell
Dollar Law
Black Law
A708
A74
To Glasgow
Glenwhappen Rig
Broad Law
Camps Reservoir
Talla Reservoir
St. Mary's Loch
B7009
Fruid Reservoir
Grey Mare's Tail
Source of the Tweed
White Coomb
B711
Hart Fell
Devil's Beef Tub
Ettrick Pen
Capel Fell
MOFFAT
WESTERN AREA
A74 To Carlisle
B723
To Carlisle